OVID'S ME

Continuum *Reader's Guides*

Continuum's *Reader's Guides* are clear, concise and accessible introductions to classic works. Each book explores the major themes, historical and philosophical context and key passages of a major classical text, guiding the reader toward a thorough understanding of often demanding material. Ideal for undergraduate students, the guides provide an essential resource for anyone who needs to get to grips with a classical text.

Reader's Guides available from Continuum

Aristotle's *Nicomachean Ethics* – Christopher Warne
Aristotle's *Politics* – Judith A. Swanson and C. David Corbin
Plato's *Republic* – Luke Purshouse
Plato's *Symposium* – Thomas L. Cooksey

OVID'S *METAMORPHOSES*

A Reader's Guide

GENEVIEVE LIVELEY

continuum

Continuum International Publishing Group

The Tower Building	80 Maiden Lane
11 York Road	Suite 704
London SE1 7NX	New York, NY 10038

www.continuumbooks.com

British Library Cataloguing-in-Publication Data
A catalogue record for this book is available from the British Library.

ISBN: HB: 978-1-4411-2519-4
PB: 978-1-4411-0084-9

Library of Congress Cataloging-in-Publication Data
Liveley, Genevieve.
Ovid's Metamorphoses : a reader's guide / Genevieve Liveley.
p. cm. – (Reader's guides)
Includes bibliographical references and index.
ISBN 978-1-4411-0084-9 (pbk.) – ISBN 978-1-4411-2519-4 (hardback)
1. Ovid, 43 B.C.–17 or 18 A.D. Metamorphoses. 2. Fables,
Latin–History and criticism. 3. Mythology, Classical, in literature.
4. Metamorphosis in literature. I. Title. II. Series.

PA6519.M9L58 2011
873'.01–dc22

2010028033

Typeset by Newgen Imaging Systems Pvt Ltd, Chennai, India
Printed and bound in India by Replika Press Pvt Ltd

CONTENTS

ACKNOWLEDGEMENTS

Thanks to Greta Hawes, Duncan Kennedy, and Patricia Salzman-Mitchell for generously reading and commenting upon early drafts of the manuscript, to the students in my Ovid classes (particularly Antonia Jeans, Jon Kirwan, Polly Whitton) for sharing my enthusiasm for the *Metamorphoses*, and to Richard Huxtable for everything else.

I have metamorphosed some characters and ideas from the following works: *Ovid – Love Songs* (2005); 'Tiresias-Teresa: A Man-made-woman in Ovid's *Metamorphoses* 316–38' (2003) *Helios* 30.2. 147–162; 'Cleopatra's Nose, Naso, and the Science of Chaos,' (2002) *Greece and Rome* 49: 27–43.

I am grateful for permission to reproduce copyright material from David Raeburn's Penguin translation of *Ovid: Metamorphoses*, translation copyright David Raeburn, 2004. Reproduced by permission of Penguin Books, Ltd. All other translations, unless otherwise identified, are my own.

Bristol
April 2010

A NOTE ON TRANSLATIONS

Throughout this *Reader's Guide*, I have used David Raeburn's Penguin translation of the *Metamorphoses*. Occasionally, where a more literal translation of the original Latin helps to illustrate a reading of the poem, I have added my own. Here, I have relied on William S. Anderson's edition of the text of books 1–10, and J. P. Goold's text of books 11–15. All line-numbering follows that of the Latin text for ease of reference.

In addition to Raeburn's verse translation, readers of Ovid in English have the choice of numerous alternatives. The Harvard University Press Loeb Library offers a useful prose translation by Frank Justus Miller set alongside the Latin text and Melville's fine blank verse translation also offers a fair and faithful rendering of the Latin. Arthur Golding's 1567 translation is well worth a read (although the 'Mary had a little lamb' rhythm of his four-teener couplets can make Ovid's epic seem even longer than it really is), as is George Sandys' witty 1626 rendering, and Samuel Garth's sparkling 1717 collection, where Dryden, Addison and Gay all turn their hands to translating the *Metamorphoses*.

Indeed, readers looking for 'poetry' in modern translations of Ovid's poem should try the versions produced by other poets. David Slavitt's beautifully idiosyncratic 1994 translation – or rather, 'adaptation' – of the *Metamorphoses* perfectly captures the playfulness and humour of the original, while Ted Hughes' 1997 *Tales from Ovid* ingeniously transforms Ovid and his epic for a modern audience. Christopher Martin's excellent *Ovid in English* offers a comprehensive collection of translations and adaptations of the *Metamorphoses* from Chaucer to Hughes and is also well worth reading. Full details of this work and all other translations cited here can be found in the bibliography.

CHAPTER 1

CONTEXTS

There are fifteen books on changing forms,
  Poems only just now saved from my funeral pyre.
Tell people that the face of my own fortunes
  Can be reckoned among those Metamorphoses.
                                    Ovid, Tristia. *1.1.117–120*

As Ovid himself tells us, his own life story reads much like one of the tales of transformation narrated in his book of *Metamorphoses*. Born on March 20th 43 BC, a year after the assassination of Julius Caesar, Publius Ovidius Naso grew up in the small mountain town of Sulmo (Sulmona), part of a wealthy Roman family. His family intended him to follow a suitable career in the courts or the senate, sending him with his older brother to Rome to further his education – just as a young Octavian was about to receive the official title of 'Augustus' and Rome was about to enter its own new phase of radical transformation under his rule as 'Princeps' or 'First Citizen'. After studying law and rhetoric with one of Rome's most illustrious tutors, Arellius Fuscus, Ovid embarked on a short-lived political career, serving briefly on the 'Committee of Three', before stepping down from this first rung on the *cursus honorem* or political ladder and turning to poetry. In an autobiographical poem written towards the end of his life (*Tristia* 4.10.19–26), he tells us that:

> For me, even as a boy, divine poetry was a pleasure
>   And the Muse kept drawing me to her private work.
> Often my father said, 'Why do you bother with such profitless pursuits?
>   Even Homer himself left no money.'

I was influenced by his words and, abandoning poetry
   completely,
I kept trying to write words free of verse.
But a song would come with its own rhyme
   And whatever I tried to write became poetry.

Most of that poetry would be written in elegiac couplets – a long
line or *hexameter* made up of six feet, followed by a short line
or *pentameter* of five feet. Elegy is one of the oldest forms of
classical poetry, used by the ancient Greeks to sing tales of myth
and war, of politics and pederasty, of loss and love. But for the
Roman elegiac poets Horace, Tibullus, and Propertius – and
their successor, Ovid – elegy was primarily associated with the
subject of love and it is this theme that provides a common
thread throughout Ovid's poetry.[1]

Ovid's literary career probably began in his late teens and
continued for over forty years, during which period he produced
an extensive body of work – an ever changing and mutating
poetic *corpus*. It is possible that the first poems of the elegiac
Amores (*Love Songs*), a sparkling collection of poems offering
an original and witty reworking of the traditions of Latin
love elegy, were begun as early as 25 BC – when Ovid was only
eighteen – and first published around 20 BC, with a second
edition (the version that we have today) reissued around 10 BC.
In the meantime Ovid produced the first volume of the *Heroides*
(*Heroines' Letters*), another highly innovative and imaginative
collection of elegiac writing, in the form of a set of poetic letters
or verse epistles from the heroines of classical myth and poetry
to their absent lovers. It is likely that the first two books of his
next work, the didactic *Ars Amatoria* (*Arts of Love*), giving
lessons in the techniques of seduction and sex, also appeared at
this time – a period of prolific poetic activity that was to quickly
establish Naso (as Ovid was known to his contemporaries) as
Rome's greatest living poet. Published shortly afterwards, his
Medicamina Faciei Femineae (*Cosmetics for Women*) – of which
only a fragment remains – was followed by the third book of the
Ars Amatoria, addressed this time to a female audience, along
with Ovid's antidote for unhappy lovers, the *Remedia Amoris*
(*Cures for Love*). In each phase of his new literary career, and
in each of these innovative elegiac works, Ovid effectively

transformed the world of elegy, playfully metamorphosing every character and characteristic of the elegiac tradition into a new shape – a feature of his approach to poetry that would reappear (along with distinct echoes of the *Amores, Heroides,* and *Ars Amatoria*) in his next literary phase and in his most important piece of work, the epic *Metamorphoses.*

Although the *Metamorphoses* is the only one of Ovid's extant poems to be written in dactylic hexameter verse (the characteristic metre of epic), it is possible to trace distinct evidence of continuity across the changing phases of his poetic *corpus* – and the influence of his earlier elegiac works upon the epic *Metamorphoses* should not be underestimated.[2] Despite the change in genre and metre, repeated allusions to his earlier elegiac works remind the readers of this poem that the poet himself is one of the first of its characters to be transformed, as Ovid the *tenerorum lusor amorum* or 'playful poet of tender love' (as he describes himself in *Tristia* 4.10.1) is metamorphosed into Ovid the playful *epic* poet. What is more, work upon the epic fifteen book *Metamorphoses* appears to have been carried out concurrently with work on the elegiac *Fasti* (*Calendar*), a poem based on the Roman calendar, and there is a notable degree of overlap and mutual influence between the two, with several characters and episodes appearing in both poems.[3] In particular, both works seem to share a common preoccupation with Augustus and his regime – a controversial and ironic topic given the poet's subsequent fate.

In AD 8, while on holiday on the island of Elba, with the *Metamorphoses* and *Fasti* unfinished, Ovid's life was transformed once more. He received the sudden news that Augustus had ordered his banishment from Rome. Ovid was to spend an unspecified period – which turned out to be the rest of his life – in Tomis, a cold and austere outpost on the western shore of the Black Sea, on the edge of the Roman Empire and the civilized world. For an urbane, cultured, and emphatically *Roman* poet, whose work had been inspired by the people and politics of Rome, Roman lifestyles and Roman literature, to be banished from the capital itself was a harsh sentence, but to be sent to an inhospitable settlement of armed barbarians who spoke no Latin was a particularly cruel form of punishment. In Tomis (modern Constanta in Romania) he continued to write for a further ten years until his death in AD 17 at the age of sixty, revising the *Fasti* – possibly the *Metamorphoses* too – and producing the elegiac *Tristia* (*Sorrows*) and *Epistulae ex Ponto* (*Letters from the Black Sea*). Technically and officially, Ovid was punished not with *exsilium* (exile) but with *relegatio* (banishment) – an ostensibly more lenient penalty that did not involve the seizure of the poet's financial assets, but did entail the public banning of his works. Ovid had been effectively silenced.[4]

In *Tristia* (2.207–12), Ovid explains the background to this punishment, but does not provide us with any particulars behind the '*carmen et error*' that seems to have so offended Augustus:

> Though two crimes, a poem and a mistake, have destroyed me,
>   On the cause of the one deed, I have to remain silent.
> For I am not worthy of reopening your wounds, Caesar.
>   It is more than enough that you have been pained once.
> The other charge remains: I am accused of becoming by a
>   shameful poem
>   A teacher of obscene adultery.

The offensive poem (*carmen*) was probably his *Ars Amatoria*, but Ovid gives us very few clues as to the nature of his mistake (*error*), hinting only that he saw inadvertently something which he should not have (*Tristia* 2.103f). The reasons behind the poet's banishment by the emperor Augustus remain a mystery. If it was really the publication of the *Ars Amatoria* that so offended Augustus, as Ovid suggests, then it seems strange that the emperor should wait almost nine years after the poem's publication in 1 BC to punish its author. Certainly, the *Ars Amatoria* is no Roman *Kama Sutra*; its poetry is provocative rather than pornographic. Augustus' real motive, Ovid implies, was some other unknown offence – often presumed to be a scandal related to the emperor's granddaughter Julia, who was banished from Rome at around the same time as Ovid. But we will never know whether Ovid was ever really caught up in any serious affair concerning Julia, or whether Augustus was simply offended by the challenge to his personal credibility as champion of old-fashioned morality and decency that Ovid posed. What is clear is that Ovid regarded his punishment as akin to the tragic

transformations described in his own *Metamorphoses*, identify-
ing himself with the victims of wrathful gods – most obviously,
with the tragic figure of Actaeon who stumbles upon the
goddess Diana bathing and who, in punishment for this *error*,
is transformed into a stag and ripped to pieces by his own
hunting hounds (3.155–255). Writing from his exile in Tomis,
Ovid explicitly evokes the story of Actaeon as a parallel to his
own (*Tristia* 2.76–83):

> Why did I see anything? Why did I make my eyes criminals?
>   Why was a wrong, unwittingly, made known to me?
> Actaeon, unaware, saw Diana naked:
>   Still he became prey to his own hounds.
> Even bad luck must be atoned for among the powers that be,
>   To an offended god bad luck is no excuse.
> On that day when my unfortunate error misled me,
>   My poor, innocent house was destroyed.

The poems of the *Tristia* turn again and again to reflect characters,
motifs and images familiar from the *Metamorphoses*. So, in the
opening poem of the collection (*Tristia* 1.1.71–4, 79–82), Ovid
identifies himself with Phaethon who, like the poet, is represented
in the *Metamorphoses* as the unfortunate and innocent victim
of a thunderbolt 'unjustly launched' (2.377f) by a punitive deity.
This motif, in which Augustus is aligned with thunderbolt-
wielding Jupiter, is repeated again and again in the *Tristia*, each
repetition reinforcing the idea that Ovid's own fate mirrors the
tragic transformations described in his *Metamorphoses*. Indeed,
so strongly is this impression stamped in the *Tristia* that it is
tempting to see in the text of the *Metamorphoses* itself signs of
revision and rewriting by Ovid while in exile.[5]
   Ovid certainly claims that the *Metamorphoses* remained
unfinished at the time of his banishment; he even asserts that he
had tried to burn the manuscript before leaving Rome. But,
he confesses with tongue in cheek, other copies were already in
circulation, so the poem survived (*Tristia* 1.7.13–34). He even
goes so far as to write a short preface for the allegedly unfinished
text already circulating privately in Rome, protesting that he
would have liked to have corrected its defects, if only he had
been allowed. However, while it is likely that Ovid did indeed

take both the *Fasti* and the *Metamorphoses* into exile with him, the book burning story is too close to the legend of Virgil's deathbed instructions that his own unfinished *Aeneid* be burned to deserve too much credit. We can only speculate whether or not the text of the *Metamorphoses* that we possess today was revised by Ovid in exile, and whether or not the features that seem to foreshadow his fate were added or enhanced during that revision.

In either case, Augustus' influence can clearly be felt throughout the fifteen books of the *Metamorphoses*. Unlike his poetic predecessors, who had experienced at first hand the bloody breakdown of Rome's democratic government and its chaotic transition from Republic to *de facto* monarchy under Augustus, Ovid entered adult life at a point of relative order and stability in Rome's troubled history. Unlike Virgil, who had lost his family's estate to pay off war veterans, or Horace, who had actually fought against Octavian during the civil war, or Propertius, who lost his brother to the conflict, Ovid had no personal experience of the civil strife that had dominated life for the generation before him, and knew no other political authority before the Augustan regime. Critics have tended to see this important difference as offering an explanation for the comparative irreverence and playful disrespect for all things political – and particularly Augustan – that Ovid displays throughout his poetry. But while it is certainly significant that Ovid lived and wrote under the social and political calm afforded by the Augustan peace, the unbroken continuity of this *pax* would and could not have been taken for granted by any of Rome's citizens (including its *princeps*) at the time. The threat that chaos might return to devastate the order of the Augustan cosmos remained. And this threat is articulated both in Augustus' experimental efforts after his victory in civil war to also 'win the peace' by stamping his authority on every facet of Roman life, and in Ovid's own experimental *Metamorphoses*.

CHAPTER 2

OVERVIEW OF THEMES

*Changes of shape, new forms, are the theme which my spirit
    impels me
now to recite. Inspire me, O gods (it is you who have even
transformed my art), and spin me a thread from the world's
    beginning
down to my own lifetime, in one continuous poem.*

*In nova fert animus mutatas dicere formas
corpora; di, coeptis (nam vos mutastis et illa)
adspirate meis primaque ab origine mundi
ad mea perpetuum deducite tempora carmen.*

Ovid, Metamorphoses *1.1–4*

So many themes are interwoven through the tapestry of Ovid's
Metamorphoses that a detailed overview might run to the same
length as the epic itself. Across its fifteen books the poem exam-
ines (among many, *many*, other motifs) war and peace, birth and
death, love and loss, gender and sexuality, anger and desire, creation
and destruction, poetry and politics, art and nature, violence and
vegetarianism, morality and monstrosity – changing many of its
human characters into animal, vegetable, and mineral form along
the way. In the short prologue to his epic, however, Ovid himself
outlines for us the shape and scope of his poem, providing his
own brief overview of its most central themes. An appreciation
of the nuances of this prologue is key, then, to appreciating and
understanding the rest of the poem and each of the 250 or so
stories of transformation that it narrates.[1]

CHANGES OF SHAPE, NEW FORMS ARE THE THEME . . .

Transformations, changes of shape, new forms: this, Ovid tells
us, is the mercurial subject of his new poem, which he himself

calls '*mutata*' or *Metamorphoses* (*Tristia* 1.1.119). His epic opens with the Latin words '*in nova*', a clear statement from the outset that here we are about to enter into something entirely new and original – both for Ovid and for the classical world (although such a claim is itself hardly novel). Originality, novelty, innovation, and new things (*nova*), then, are the watchwords for this new epic undertaking, significantly described by Ovid in his prologue as a *coeptis* – that is, *a work in progress*, a project as unfixed and uncertain as its metamorphic theme.[2]

Ovid's own metamorphosis from elegiac love poet to Augustan epic poet is both the first innovation and the first transformation that we witness in this poem. In fact, that transformation visibly takes place within and across the opening lines of his prologue – its effects enhanced by the syntax of the original Latin, in which the reader or listener must wait for the end of a complete sentence to fully grasp its meaning. So, Ovid begins with the half line phrase: *in nova fert animus . . .* (literally '*my spirit impels me to new things*'). And we understand that this will be a new project for the poet famous for his elegiac love poetry. But as the second half of the hexameter line reveals the specific nature of this new project we discover that the Latin *nova* is not a substantive adjective but a qualifier for the Latin *corpora* (*mutatas dicere formas / corpora . . .* – literally '*my spirit impels me to speak of forms changed into new bodies*'). This is a radical departure from the erotic and elegiac subjects for which Ovid had become famous as he sets out now to transform and translate Greek stories of metamorphosis into Latin. But the end of the second line reveals the poet's first change of form: the second line is the same length as the first. This is not elegiac verse (comprising a couplet of one long hexameter line followed by a short pentameter line): this is epic. Ovid, the *tenerorum lusor amorum* or 'playful poet of tender love' has been transformed and the elegiac poem we were anticipating has metamorphosed before our eyes.[3]

But Ovid's claim to speak of *forms changed into new bodies* (rather than bodies changed to new forms) hints that, although both he and his familiar form of poetry may have changed physically (his elegiac couplets have mutated into epic verse) and so look and sound differently, this transformation has changed only the external shape of his poetry and the essential elegiac character of his *corpus* remains unaltered. It should not surprise the readers who knew the old elegiac Ovid, then, that love and sex, and the relationships between men and women, will still form the focus of so many of the stories that make up his elegiacally epic *Metamorphoses*. Traces of his former playful elegiac self – particularly the insights into *amor* and the psychology of passion that he explored in his *Amores* and *Heroides* – will be clearly visible in this new outwardly epic form.

In this 'continuity through change', Ovid achieves his second change of form: the character of his own poetry may not have significantly altered, he suggests, but the character and form of epic itself will be radically transformed here. Initially shaped by Homer's *Iliad* and *Odyssey*, and then given its Roman form by Virgil's *Aeneid*, the traditional epic genre had been characterized by a number of formal features, essentially comprising a long hexameter narrative focused upon a single hero who, with divine aid and interference, battled against enemies and adversity. With the exception of its length and its meter, Ovid's epic is nothing like this. Even when he is dealing directly with Homeric or Virgilian material in books 12–14, he playfully subverts the conventions of epic, giving a comic, erotic or elegiac twist to familiar epic narratives – all the while suggesting that these 'essentially' comic, erotic and elegiac characteristics were always already there in the originals.

O GODS (IT IS YOU WHO HAVE EVEN TRANSFORMED MY ART) . . .

It is the gods who are given the credit (or perhaps, the blame) for inspiring Ovid's personal metamorphosis from elegiac to epic poet and thus his *Metamorphoses* – offering us a sneak preview of Ovid's general attitude towards and treatment of the gods in his poem. Ovid's gods outwardly look like the familiar epic gods of Homer and Virgil – the anthropomorphic, omnipotent and interfering 'divine machinery' that we expect to find in epic – but their behaviour in the world of the *Metamorphoses* reveals a darker side to the Olympians.[4] Here the gods lack the moral authority given them by Virgil in the *Aeneid*, behaving towards mortals – and each other – with callous and casual self-interest. The gods are directly responsible for inflicting numerous metamorphoses upon their mortal victims, sometimes in answer to a prayer or in reward for a good deed, occasionally as a punishment, but most often through anger, jealousy, or lust. The story of Callisto (2.401–530) offers an extreme example of this divine cruelty: first Jupiter, disguised as the virgin huntress Diana, rapes her; then Diana, discovering Callisto's pregnancy, angrily banishes her from her band of virgin followers; and Juno, learning that Callisto has given birth to a baby boy, jealously transforms her into a bear. But Callisto's suffering does not end there: a selfish Jupiter then transforms Callisto and her grown-up son into stars to prevent an unwitting matricide; and a petulant Juno further sees to it that the constellation of Callisto the Great Bear can never wash away the pollution of her 'crime' by setting into the ocean.

In episodes such as these, we witness the unremitting and unjust cruelty of the gods, as Ovid details the potential for great harm that comes with great power. But Ovid also shows us a lighter side to his gods, frequently representing them as comedic figures of fun – particularly when their divine majesty is robbed of dignity by *amor* and sex. So, the same Jupiter who treats Callisto so cruelly is shown disguised as a prancing bull, giving slobbery cow-kisses to Europa (2.833–75); Juno is repeatedly presented as the ill-tempered 'hen-pecking' wife of a philandering husband (1.607f, 2.476–85, 2.530, 3.256–315, 3.316–38, 4.416–562); and both Diana and her bad temper are comically exposed when the nymphs who attempt to protect her modesty and her nudity from Actaeon's eyes, prove to be too short to cover-up more than the lower half of her naked body (3.178–255). Indeed, the shifting tone that Ovid adopts in the representation of his gods – now serious, now humorous – is characteristic of the way in which he treats all of his subjects in the world of the *Metamorphoses*, where the tone and mood of the poem are constantly changing and where *pathos* is readily transformed into *bathos*, tragedy into comedy.

FROM THE WORLD'S BEGINNING DOWN TO MY OWN LIFETIME . . .

The scope of Ovid's poem is unlike anything ever attempted in the epic genre before: rather than following a single hero through a series of adventures, he promises to tell the history of the world from its first creation (*primaque ab origine mundi*) right up to the present day (*ad mea tempora*) – or, at least, from creation right up until the death and apotheosis of Julius Caesar in 44 BC and Augustus' accession to power. This chronology appears to lend the poem an obvious narrative framework – a timeline along which Ovid can string his tales of transformation in order of occurrence, from pre-history through to the Augustan Age. But in practice this timeline offers only a rough guide to the sequence of events as they are narrated in the poem, and there are numerous flashbacks (*analepses*), flashforwards (*prolepses*), and chronological slippages, allowing – even encouraging – each one of the 250 individual stories narrated in the *Metamorphoses* to be read as an independent unit.[5]

A more significant aspect of Ovid's claim to bring his material 'up to date', perhaps, is the way in which he provocatively draws parallels between mythic and modern characters and events. Early in book 1 he sketches such a parallel between the gods of Olympus and the Roman Senate, establishing an unambiguous correspondence between Jupiter and Augustus in a direct address to the Emperor himself (1.199–205). The effect of such 'anachronism' is deliberately unsettling for Ovid's readers, as Jupiter's behaviour in the *Metamorphoses* (his sexual behaviour and violent authoritarianism, in particular) reflects an especially unflattering light upon his Augustan counterpart.[6] Indeed, critical opinion diverges widely upon whether or not Ovid and his epic are to be read as 'anti' or 'pro' Augustus, and upon the extent to which the mythical world of Ovid's *Metamorphoses* caricatures or comments upon life in the contemporary world of Augustus' Rome. We can only speculate upon the nature of Ovid's 'Augustanism', given the contradictory character of his treatment both of Augustan motifs and of Augustus himself who is sometimes the subject of (ironic?) praise and at others the object of (ironic?) blame. It is frequently difficult to distinguish satire from sincerity, compliment from criticism, and perhaps too easy to suggest that such political ambiguity and ideological changeability is exactly what we should expect from a protean poem such as the *Metamorphoses*.[7] Yet, it is worth bearing in mind that the *Metamorphoses* does not straightforwardly relate to the Age of Augustus but to *Ovid's* own distinctly personal vision and version of that Age: the poem, after all, leads us into '*my* own lifetime' (*mea tempora*).[8]

ONE CONTINUOUS POEM . . .

Throughout most of its life the *Metamorphoses* has been viewed as something akin to an anthology or encyclopaedia of myths, a more or less random collection of discrete stories to be read and enjoyed individually. But Ovid's prologue actually promises that his epic will be arranged as one long 'continuous poem' – a *carmen perpetuum* – with a unifying thread connecting all of his myths of transformation. This promise reveals much about the poem – both about its structure and organization and about the literary influences shaping its form. When Ovid tells his readers that he intends to 'spin . . . a thread (*deducite*) . . . in one continuous poem', he evokes two competing literary traditions: he suggests that his poem will be at once a lengthy unified epic like those of his predecessors in the genre, Homer and Virgil, and one that is also 'finely spun', in accordance with the sort of refined literary aesthetic defined by the Greek poet Callimachus in his *Aetia* or *Causes* (Fr. 1.3) and more usually associated with the elegiac writing of the Roman love poets.[9] The *Metamorphoses*, it seems, will incorporate characteristics of both genres and both traditions in an entirely new narrative form – an elegiac epic, a Callimachean *carmen perpetuum*.[10]

We have already seen that chronology offers a superficial appearance of continuity and unity to the poem, as Ovid begins with the creation of the cosmos out of chaos and then progresses up until his own day and the dawn of the Augustan Age. It is also obvious that metamorphosis provides a unifying theme for the poem: all of Ovid's stories involve transformation in some way, even if – as in the tale of Phaethon where metamorphosis seems only an afterthought, or in the tale of Icarus where it is unclear what kind of metamorphosis has actually taken place – transformation is sometimes only incidental to the narrative. Indeed, the full range of Ovid's 'metamorphoses' includes not only mythological transformations but changes of mind, of name, of tradition, of meaning. It seems that Ovid's theme of transformation, and of 'continuity through change', provides him with an organizational scheme that is itself subject to change and mutation in the course of the poem.

In this respect, any attempt to map a rigidly fixed organizational structure or framework onto the *Metamorphoses* is liable to fail – although this has not deterred numerous efforts to do so.

In the 1960s, Brooks Otis' influential analysis of the poem divided the text into four principal sections based on the common themes of 'Divine Amor' (1.5–2.875), 'Vengeance' (3.1–6.400), 'Amatory Pathos' (6.401–11.795), and 'Troy and Rome' (12.1–15.870) – inexplicably locating the stories of chaos, creation, flood and fire as part of a section on 'Divine Amor', and squeezing Ovid's stories into an uncomfortable straitjacket.[11] Otis' contemporary Walter Ludwig identified 'Time' as the unifying principle for his own structural analysis of the poem, dividing the narrative into chronologically ordered sections located in prehistory (1.5–1.451), mythical time (1.452–11.193), and historical time (11.194–15.870) – revealing a somewhat uneven structure in which 11 of the poem's 15 books are contained in just one section.[12]

A more useful map of Ovid's shape-shifting poem divides the *Metamorphoses* broadly into thirds, each section containing roughly five books – the map of the poem that is followed in this Reader's Guide.[13] This organizational pattern follows the chronological ordering of the poem that Ovid promises his readers, moving through the Ages of gods, of heroes, and finally of men, to reach a climactic conclusion in the Age of Augustus – who is (of course) both man, hero *and* god. What is more, this tripartite arrangement coincidentally echoes Ovid's own description of the *Metamorphoses* in the *Tristia* (1.1.117–120) as comprising three times five books. But it is important to remember that, in a poem concerned with continuity alongside transformation and change, structural divisions and thematic distinctions are easily blurred.

Ovid's *carmen perpetuum* achieves its (illusion of) unity and continuity across its fifteen books and its 250 myths using a variety of ingenious techniques, including the frequent employment of internal narrators and audiences – where characters within a story being told by Ovid become storytellers themselves.[14] Perhaps most visibly, his telling of a myth often continues across the 'break' between one book and the next: so, the tale of Phaethon entering the palace of the Sun leads the reader across the threshold between books 1 and 2; disguised as a bull, Jupiter carries both the reader and the abducted Europa across the gulf between books 2 and 3; and the narrative of the river-god Achelous flows smoothly between books 8 and 9. In the case of Europa, Ovid even signals a direct correlation between the narrated events of the story that he is interrupting and the physical event of their reading. So, the bull's horns or *cornua* to which Europa holds on as she is carried away to sea may also refer to the horn book-rods – also known as *cornua* – around which books were rolled in antiquity and which the reader would hold in her own hands as she read.[15] In other book divisions, Ovid bridges the narrative and physical breaks imposed by a book's ending and beginning by following the adventures of a key character – such as Orpheus, Perseus, or Aeneas – across the divide, thereby producing an appearance of unbroken continuity that allows the narrative to metamorphose easily from one story into another.

The poem's transitional links between its individual stories are even more ingenious, as Ovid varies a range of stock techniques to move on (more or less) seamlessly from one tale to the next. The bridging techniques he employs in book 1 establish a pattern that he subsequently adapts for the rest of the poem and are worth looking at in some detail. Here, Ovid segues from the story of Daphne's metamorphosis into a tree into the story of Io's metamorphosis into a cow almost as a cinematographer might move between scenes, using a single long tracking shot (1.566–85): he tracks up and away from the final image of Daphne as a laurel tree, waving her newly-formed branches, to offer us an aerial shot of the trees that cover the ravine of Tempe; moving down from the spray that a waterfall throws up into the treetops, he takes us into the depths of the ravine and follows the river until it flows into a rocky cave where the river god Peneus himself lives; without breaking his shot, he then moves in to focus more closely upon Peneus (father of Daphne) surrounded by the gods of all the local rivers who have come to console and congratulate him on his daughter's strange fate; only the river god Inachus, father of Io, Ovid tells us, is not there – he is at home mourning the loss of his own daughter Io; and only at this point does Ovid finally cut his long tracking narrative to tell us what has happened to Io in a flashback sequence.

Here then, we see several of Ovid's most creative transitional devices used to great effect: (1) the cinematic segue and (2) the flashback connected by (3) the notable absence (or absent presence) of a character. A further linking device used in this story is

(4) the inset narrative, an intricate feature of the epyllion or mini-epic, of the type for which Callimachus and his followers were renowned. For, set within the tale of Io is a second story: Mercury puts Io's watchful guard Argus to sleep (for good) by becoming an internal story-teller within Ovid's main narrative and relating the tale of Syrinx and Pan. What is more, the story of Syrinx's attempted rape and transformation into a marsh reed, followed by her appropriation by the god Pan to form his emblematic 'pan-pipes', mirrors the story of Daphne and Apollo, and so continues (5) the thematic connection between the 'gods in love' – or 'gods in lust' – that unifies this section of the poem. Finally, in Ovid's transitional link from the end of Io's story to the beginning of the next, we witness another characteristic device, as he (6) subtly shifts his focus from a minor character, Epaphus (the son of Io), to an impulsive young friend named Phaethon – and so to the start of an entirely new story and a new twist in the fine-spun thread of Ovid's *carmen perpetuum*.

This *Reader's Guide* will follow the intricate twists and turns of this unbroken thread through all fifteen books of Ovid's 'continuous poem', commenting upon each episode in turn. Influenced by Ovid's own emphasis upon storytelling (in both proem and poem) no less than by recent narratological studies of the *Metamorphoses*, particular emphasis will be placed upon the narrative structure of the poem and the ingenious ways in which Ovid spins his tales of transformation. As we will see.

CHAPTER 3

TEXTUAL READINGS

3.1 BOOKS ONE TO FIVE

Book One

Creation (1.5–88)

Having told us in his prologue that his epic will cover the history of the world from its first creation (*ab origine mundi*), Ovid actually begins his poem a moment *before* that, with the anarchic aboriginal chaos in and from which the universe was formed – and to which the world of the *Metamorphoses* constantly threatens to revert. Ovid's primordial chaos thus sets the stage for the tales of transformation to follow, and (with echoes of Callimachus' *Aetia*) offers us a kind of aetiology or explanation for the inherent instability and mutability of both the cosmos and Ovid's poem. Ovid's chaos (like his poem) represents a state of continuous change in which nothing retains its own shape (1.17 – *nulli sua forma manebat*): its constituent elements – earth, water and air – exist in a constant condition of dynamic flux where its primary forces of earth, air, fire, and water exist in a perpetual state of violent opposition (1.5–20).

According to Ovid, the cosmos – that is, the universe conceived as a harmoniously ordered whole – is formed from chaos by the intervention of an unnamed primordial god of whom we never hear anything again (1.21). In this, the first 'proper' metamorphosis described by the poem, god (or, possibly nature – Ovid offers us both options) imposes order and stability upon the primordial chaos by brokering a 'peace agreement' between its warring factions, imposing limits and boundaries upon its conflicting elements, separating and relocating earth, water and air (1.32f) and dividing the newly formed earth into zones reflecting those of the sky (1.45–8). But the new order imposed upon the primordial chaos by this god – the first of many creative artists in the poem[1] – is not absolute, and confusion and conflict continue to exist. Order is imposed upon the waters as they are separated into seas and springs, pools, lakes and rivers (1.36–42). But, as in their former chaotic state, the waters do not entirely maintain their distinction from the soft earth (1.40) or from each other, as springs become rivers and as rivers flow into the sea (1.42). The air is similarly turbulent, with the continuing conflict between the winds threatening to tear apart the newly formed world (1.58–60). Moreover, as the description of the new cosmos illustrates, earth, water and air continue to merge together and to take on each other's characteristics: fog and rain soak into the earth and fill the 'liquid' air (1.65–8). The newly formed universe appears to be stable and ordered but, in essence, the cosmos is simply ordered chaos and, as such, retains the chaotic potential of its former state.

This characterization of the world as a 'chaosmos' would have held particular significance for Ovid's contemporaries. After years of conflict, culminating in the chaos and bloody fratricide of civil war, Augustus had only relatively recently restored Rome and its warring citizens to order and harmony, establishing peace and a new Augustan 'cosmos'. Ovid's description of a fratricidal conflict between the winds threatening to tear apart the new world order (1.58–60) adds a political subtext to his Creation story. Here, Ovid reminds his readers that the new Augustan peace in itself is inherently fragile and that the world might return to chaos and conflict at any time. In fact, Ovid's account of the creation of humankind illustrates just how easily this can happen (1.78–83). Moving swiftly over the orderly allocation of gods, fish, beasts, and birds to their respective zones (1.72–5), he tells us how the cosmos still lacked a nobler creature to rule over them all (1.77). And so, man was born, with no allocated zone of the cosmos in which to restrict himself, and with the potential to assert his domination and order over every other creature. The potential nature of the relationship between man and the gods is left ambiguous here (as it will be throughout the poem), but there is one clue as to the intended bond. Ovid distinguishes man from the other animals as 'holier' (*sanctius* – 1.76), suggesting that a key role to be played by man on earth is the worship of the gods in heaven: man is the only animal who literally and figuratively 'looks up to' the gods. Moreover, it is this tripartite hierarchy – god, man, beast – which will be transgressed in and by the stories of metamorphosis to come.

Ovid gives us a mixture of philosophy and mythology in his account of the origins of man: either we were made from 'divine seed' in the gods' image – in accordance with Stoic accounts of creation – or, as Greek myth relates, we were made out of mud by Prometheus (the second of many artists and artisans to feature in the poem).[2] In this second version, man is formed from a mixture of the very elements – earth, air and water – that until very recently composed the primordial chaos, and which even in the newly ordered cosmos still display chaotic patterns of behaviour. So, the first mortal is fashioned out of the new earth only recently drawn from the air and still retaining some elements of its related sky (1.80f). The chaotic elements which were separated to form the cosmos are now mixed again to form mankind. Man not only populates the newly transformed earth, but embodies the new chaos, it seems. Little wonder, then, that such mortal creatures will go on to defy the rules of order imposed upon them by both gods and society, to transgress physical, social, and moral boundaries, and so bring chaos and transformation back into the world.[3]

Four Ages (1.89–150)

The creation of man, like the creation of cosmos out of chaos, presents us with another false new beginning: the human race turns out to be so degenerate that after a few generations – styled by Ovid (varying Hesiod's *Works and Days*) as four ages of gold, silver, bronze and iron – Jupiter decides to destroy everyone and start afresh. In keeping with Ovid's theme of continuity through change, the description of the first golden age shares a number of common features with that of the primordial state of chaos from which it emerges, and is likewise defined in terms of absence. Amidst the chaos there was no sun, no moon, no earth, nor ocean; nothing identifiable as distinct from anything else. Now, in the golden age, there is no law, no fear of punishment or penalty, no judges or defendants, no ships, no cities, no trumpets or horns and no helmets or swords – all because there is no war (1.91–100).

Ovid then moves chronologically through the ages of silver, bronze and iron, but quickly seems to grow bored with this self-imposed narrative timeline, devoting twenty four lines to his description of the golden age, twelve to the silver, and less than three to the bronze age, as he moves swiftly on to the age that most interests him, the one most like his own. The fourth and final age of iron brings with it crime, greed, violence, and war. Inviting direct contrast to the utopian peace of the golden age, gold itself is now debased and is even more harmful than iron (1.141), as men fight each other for it. For, as Ovid had already observed of his own Augustan age in his *Ars Amatoria* (2.277), 'Now is truly a golden age; with gold you can buy honour, with gold you can buy love.' His description of the iron age in the *Metamorphoses* is no less cynical or politically charged: here he effectively represents a world returned to chaos, a world of civil war, where men defy all rules of order, and transgress every physical, social, and moral limit. Transgressing the physical boundaries that had been respected by previous ages, men now have ships that take them across the water to new lands, they delve down into the depths of the earth to mine iron and gold and, although the careful surveyor marks out property boundaries upon the land, such borders are drawn up only to be disputed and breached (1.132–40). Social and moral order is similarly violated as hosts murder their guests, and fathers their sons; brothers fight; husbands and wives plot each other's deaths; wicked stepmothers and cold-blooded sons contrive the murder of their own family members; and the gods, no longer revered by mortals, abandon the earth and its bloody chaos (1.144–50).

The Giants (1.151–62)

Even heaven is not immune from this disorder, and Ovid next describes how the giants piled up mountains in order to climb up and assault heaven itself, attempting to transgress perhaps the ultimate boundary – that between heaven and earth. Ovid does not narrate this assault in any detail: he does not need to. This battle between the gods and giants would have been over-familiar to Ovid's Roman audience as an allegory for the recent civil war, with Jupiter's inevitable victory and restoration of order here, seen as an obvious (and unequivocally positive) parallel for Augustus'. But the sub-genre of gigantomachy with its reputation as the dullest of dull epic, was unpopular among Augustan poets aspiring to a sophisticated Callimachean aesthetic: Ovid even jokes in his *Amores* (2.11–20) that, once upon a time, he had started to write a gigantomachy but had stopped when he realized that it just wasn't 'sexy' enough and that this was not the sort of poetry that would ever get a girl into bed with him.

After the non-event of the gigantomachy (seemingly introduced to break-up the narrative monotony of the four ages), Ovid briefly mentions a second race of human beings which sprang up from the blood-drenched soil: a race born of blood (1.162), obsessed with violence and slaughter. And although this race of (vampire-like) men is clearly supposed to be distinct both from the giants and the people of the iron age, Ovid's emphasis upon their blood-lust and the blood-soaked earth from which they spring (1.157f) instantly recalls the violence and the blood-stained earth of the iron age (1.149), providing an easy transition back to this era and the bloody tale of Lycaon, the epitome of his age.

Lycaon (1.163–252)

The story of Lycaon ostensibly offers us a dramatic case-study exemplifying the vicious blood-lust and impiety that was characteristic of humanity in the iron age. But it also serves as a dramatic model typifying the characteristics of human metamorphosis upon which Ovid will go on to base all such transformations in his poem and so bears particular significance as both a moral and narrative *exemplum*.[4]

The story begins with a council of the gods – a typical feature of traditional epic – in which the gods discuss their particular concerns for a hero or his people, and consider how best to help. Here Ovid transforms the convention and has Jupiter summon a council meeting in order to discuss the particular case of Lycaon and to consider how best to exterminate the entire human race. The fact that, as part of his transformation of this epic *topos*, Ovid represents the council as a meeting of the Roman senate, with Jupiter as Augustus, adds a provocative political dimension to the entire episode. So, with playful, even satirical anachronism, he explicitly assimilates the homes of the gods on Mount Olympus to Augustus' marble residences on Rome's Palatine Hill (1.176), he describes the lesser gods as *plebs* (1.173), and ranks the major deities as the equivalents of Roman aristocrats or *clari* (1.174) who even worship their own household gods or *penates* (1.174). He does apologize for the boldness of his analogy but then goes on to compare Lycaon's impiety to that of the band of senators who carried out Caesar's murder, drawing attention to his analogy with an apostrophe addressed to Augustus himself: 'And just as your people's loyal devotion is welcome to you, / Augustus, so was his subjects' to Jove' (1.204f). But whether the tone of this apostrophe is intended to be read as sarcastic, satirical or serious, it is impossible to tell.

The story of Lycaon is then narrated in flashback by Jupiter himself (as a biased internal narrator), as he recalls for the assembled gods, Lycaon's crime and punishment. This aspect of the narration, and the fact that Jupiter is using the story of Lycaon's depravity to justify to the gods his planned annihilation of all mankind, is crucial in shaping the tone of the story that follows. Reports have reached Jupiter concerning the infamy of the iron age, so he heads down to earth from Olympus to see for himself, first disguising his godliness by putting on human form (*deus humana . . . sub imagine* – 1.213) – his easy metamorphosis from god to human here, described as if he merely slips on the guise of humanity like a cloak or fancy-dress costume (a common description of divine transformation in the poem).[5] Up and down the land Jupiter finds further evidence of mankind's depravity, but when he singles-out the Arcadian king Lycaon as a test case, he finds himself the object of a parallel test as Lycaon launches a dangerous experiment to see whether Jupiter really is a god: Jupiter tells how Lycaon first planned to feed him a meal of human flesh and then to kill him. As if the attempted murder and impious challenge to the authority of the king of the gods himself were not enough to condemn him, Lycaon further compounds his crime by violating the laws of hospitality – twice: in failing to show due respect to Jupiter as his disguised guest, *and* in slaughtering a hostage in order to prepare a cannibal feast. As Ovid had already warned us about the iron age, the ordered rules of custom, society and morality have completely broken down, and here no guest is safe from his host – even a god in disguise.

Indeed, Lycaon's kingdom is represented by Jupiter as a realm of violence and chaos where the most fundamental of boundaries are tested and transgressed; not only do mortals consort with gods (albeit unwittingly) here, but men behave like animals, blurring the categorical distinctions between them. In this light, Jupiter's throwing off of his human disguise to reveal his own divine status, his destruction of Lycaon's lawless palace, and the flight of Lycaon out into the wilds of the countryside, represent a restoration of order, the regrouping of characters into their proper places. And when Lycaon, always already the 'wolf-man' in both name and nature (*lykos* means 'wolf' in Greek), literally becomes a wolf, he too is unequivocally reassigned to his rightful sphere. As Andrew Feldherr observes: 'Just as the creation of the world involved the separation of the lighter elements from water and earth, so here this wild beast who had somehow been grouped among men has finally been returned to his rightful category.'[6]

As the first human metamorphosis of its kind, Lycaon's transformation is worth examining in detail (1.232–9):

> Frightened out of his wits, Lycaon fled to the country
> where all was quiet. He tried to speak, but his voice broke into
> an echoing howl. His ravening soul infected his jaws;
> his murderous longings were turned on the cattle; he still was
> possessed
> by bloodlust. His garments were changed to a shaggy coat
> and his arms
> into legs. He was now transformed to a wolf. But he kept some
> signs
> of his former self: the grizzled hair and the wild expression,
> the blazing eyes and the bestial image remained unaltered.

In the quiet of the countryside the drama of a wolf howling in the night is amplified, while the horror of this moment is further intensified by the realization that this sound is being produced by a man. In the poem's subsequent stories of human metamorphosis the emphasis upon this key psychological moment, when a victim first realizes the physical effects of transformation upon his or her power of speech, will become a standard feature. So too will the startling accent upon continuity through change that is highlighted here and recurs variously in all of Ovid's 'metamorphoses'. Here, Ovid describes how Lycaon's jaws begin to slaver with familiar lust for blood (1.233–4), literally 'his mouth gathers savagery from itself with his usual bloodlust'. Lycaon's transformation, it seems, turns the inside out, matching the essential violence and savagery of the man's inner character with his new external form. His clothes may have become fur, his arms legs, but crucially he retains some traces of his former (inhumane) human self even as a wolf (1.237), in the same grey hair, blazing eyes, and wild look. Ovid has turned metaphor into metamorphosis. The man, who already looked *like* a wolf, was named 'Wolf', and who, Ovid and Jupiter warned us at the start of the story, was famed for his savagery (1.198), has become what he always was in essence: a wolf. As Ovid promised in his prologue, the same form has been changed into a new body.

When the story is over, the 'senate' of gods initially responds with sycophantic support for Jupiter's plan to destroy mankind: Jupiter has elicited precisely the effect he had intended for his propagandist narrative, with the council reacting as an ideal audience to his 'dodgy dossier' of evidence against mankind. But quickly, the gods express their own self-interested concern that if Jupiter destroys the entire human race or turns them all into wild animals like Lycaon, there will be no mortals left on earth to worship them. So, Jupiter promises them that he will create yet another, better, race of men – just as soon as he has destroyed this one.

The Flood (1.253–312)

At first, Jupiter toys with the idea of destroying the world with a cosmic conflagration, sending down his thunderbolts to set the earth on fire. But he reconsiders when he realizes the damage that might also be done to the heavens in such an inferno. He also 'remembers' the Stoic theory (popular in Augustan Rome) that the entire universe would one day be destroyed by fire, so he changes his mind and opts for a flood instead. Once again, chaos returns to the earth as Jupiter marshals the wind and rain to fill the sky with clouds of water. Neptune aids him by releasing the seas and rivers from their ordered courses, until the rioting waters cover all signs of human civilization, and there is no longer any distinction between sea and land (1.291f). The careful ordering and separation of the universe that had marked its creation (1.5–20) is swiftly undone and the earth transformed into sea.

With what appears to be cruel detachment, Ovid goes on dispassionately to describe the impact of the flood upon earth's human and animal inhabitants in a series of strange vignettes: a man sails over the submerged roof of his farmhouse; another catches fish in a tree; dolphins swim through the woods; wolves, lions and tigers swim together in the flood; and an exhausted bird with nowhere to land drops into the sea (1.293–308). Meanwhile, water nymphs or Nereids gaze in wonder at this strange new under-water world, as do we – until Ovid reminds us that most of these creatures drowned and the rest starved to death. The emotional detachment of his description of the flood, it seems, is deliberately engineered to reflect that of the gods who have themselves cruelly orchestrated and observed the destruction of all life on earth.

Deucalion and Pyrrha (1.313–415)
After this bleak ending, the next story opens with something of a surprise. Amidst the otherwise universal devastation of the flood, two survivors and two peaks of land suddenly emerge, as Deucalion and Pyrrha are safely washed up in their boat on the peaks of Mount Parnassus. This couple alone have been saved from the thousands of others because of their simple innocence, goodness and piety. Here Deucalion and Pyrrha introduce an element of humanity into the poem, both literally and figuratively, as they weep for the loss of the human race and the emptiness of the silent, desolate earth that emerges as the floodwaters recede. In this they offer a far more humane response to the flood than that previously exhibited by either the gods or the Nereids, and Deucalion's fear that either he or his beloved wife Pyrrha might yet be left totally alone, as the last soul on earth, is genuinely poignant. Ovid, however, rarely allows pathos to dominate the tone of an episode for too long, and when Deucalion starts to lament that he lacks the skills of his father Prometheus – he who made man out of clay in Ovid's first creation story (1.78–88) – we begin to notice the comic subtext to this situation. The syntax of the Latin (and its alliterative repetition of *p*) playfully draws our attention to the fact that when Deucalion complains, 'I wish I could use my father

Prometheus' skill to create / mankind once again' (*o utinam possim populos reparare paternis / artibus* – 1.363f), the most obvious way in which Deucalion might set about repopulating the world would be to become a *father* himself.

Exposed as sexually naive innocents, then, it is unsurprising that Deucalion and Pyrrha should be utterly baffled by the oracular response they receive when (having dutifully cleansed and prostrated themselves before a flood-slimed altar) they pray to the gods for advice. The goddess Themis tells them to throw the bones of their great mother (*magnae . . . parentis*) over their shoulders (1.381–3). Pious Pyrrha is adamant that she will not desecrate the bones of her mother, even if directed to do so by the gods, and the couple struggle with the puzzle for some time. Until, at last, Deucalion reveals himself worthy of the epic name *Promethides* ('son of Prometheus') and solves the riddle, deciding that their 'great mother' is the earth itself and her 'bones' are the stones around them. Following the directions of the oracle, the couple do precisely as they have been told, and the stones they throw behind them are slowly metamorphosed into human form (like statues chiselled from rough stone), as yet another race of men is born from the earth – our own hardy ancestors.[7]

Python (1.416–51)

The story of Deucalion and Pyrrha accounts for the human repopulation of the earth after the flood, but the earth is still lacking animal life. This, with a quasi-scientific explanation reminiscent of Lucretius' *De Rerum Natura* (*On the Nature of Things*), Ovid attributes to spontaneous regeneration from the 'seeds of things,' (*semina rerum* – 1.419) buried in the fertile earth after the flood. With echoes of the primordial chaos from which the cosmos itself was first generated, the mixture of moisture from the floodwater and heat from the sun produces a state which is naturally suited to the creation of new things. Thus, a new era of metamorphosis is born as innumerable species of creatures emerge from the ooze, some familiar from the old antediluvian days, others novel and strange. Among these new monsters is the Python, a terrible snake-like creature, which terrorizes the newly-formed race of men until Apollo steps in with his bow and kills it with a thousand arrows, instituting the

'Pythian' games in honour of his triumph. At these games, the victors would receive a garland of oak-leaves – just like Apollo himself used to wear in his hair – for, at this time the laurel-tree did not yet exist (1.450). And so we slide unexpectedly from the myths of prehistory straight into the story of how the nymph Daphne became Apollo's laurel.

Apollo and Daphne (1.452–567)

The story of Apollo and Daphne signals a major shift in both tone and theme for the *Metamorphoses*, marked by Apollo's own abrupt transformation from monster-slaying epic hero to frustrated elegiac lover. For, as the god of poetry, Apollo's transformation here indicates that the poem itself is about to undergo a significant metamorphosis. Indeed, the story opens with the introductory formula, 'Apollo's first love was Daphne' (***primus** amor Phoebi Daphne* – 1.452), implying that, although Daphne may be the first, she will not be the last, confirming that we are now about to embark upon a series of elegiac love stories concerning the amorous (mis)adventures of the gods – for which Daphne's attempted rape will provide the narrative template.[8]

Echoing his own self-styled metamorphosis as a poet, sup-posedly forced by Cupid to give up epic and to write love elegy instead (*Amores* 1.1), Ovid directly attributes the cause of Apollo's transformation to the interference of Cupid and, in an inspired metapoetic competition sets Cupid and elegy against Apollo and epic. Still bragging about his recent conquest of the Python, Apollo mocks Cupid and his bow, belittling the god of love as a 'mischievous boy' playing with 'grown-up weapons' (1.456).[9] Cupid responds to this insult with all the dynamism of an epic hero, flying swiftly up to the peak of Parnassus and shooting two arrows: one, made of gold, into Apollo, instantly inflaming him with *amor*, and a second, made of iron, into the unsuspecting Daphne, causing her to flee from the very idea of *amor* and, of course, from Apollo.[10] With evident irony, Apollo, the virile hero of martial epic, is penetrated and un-manned by Cupid the playful love-god of erotic elegy.

The painful paradox of Daphne's role in this situation is high-lighted in Ovid's apostrophe to the girl: *votoque tuo tua forma repugnat* (1.489), literally 'your form/beauty fights against your desire', where the juxtaposition of the Latin *tuo/tua* perfectly conveys her inner conflict – but also darkly hints that part of Daphne herself is actively complicit in her own attempted rape.[11] Indeed, the emphasis here upon Daphne's beauty or *forma* actively mitigating against her own wishes adds a disturbing tone to this tale: it is as if Daphne's beauty makes her 'fair game' for Apollo – a trope that will reappear in Ovid's other rape stories. Ovid, however, playfully revels in the comedy of this situation: Apollo sees Daphne with her long hair flowing loose and wonders what it would look like put up (that is, he immediately desires to change her); he admires her fingers, hands, wrists, her arms and bare shoulders and he imagines how much more beautiful the rest of her must be (that is, he immediately imagines her breasts); and fearing that she may scratch her bare legs as he chases her through rough scrub, he begs her to slow down, promising that if she does, he himself will run more slowly too! The uneven syntax of the Latin further adds to the comedy of this chase scene, ingeniously reproducing the effect of Apollo's breathless panting speech as he tries to run and talk at the same time, puffing '*nympha, precor, Penei, mane!*' (1.504).

Apollo tries in vain to persuade Daphne to stop running, boasting about his godly attributes, but eventually gives up any attempt at persuasion and puts all of his energy into the chase. Here too Ovid changes to a more serious tone and introduces an epic-style simile, likening Apollo to a hound and Daphne to a fleeing hare, only inches away from the dog's muzzle as it closes in behind her (1.533–9). This striking simile prepares us for the inevitable end of the chase, as Daphne's strength and speed fade and Apollo gains ground. Praying to her father, the river-god Peneus, in desperation she pleads: 'If rivers have power over nature / mar the beauty which made me admired too well, by changing / my form' (1.546f). Metamorphosis comes swiftly and almost before she has finished praying her transformation into a laurel tree has begun, her feet turning into roots, her arms into branches and her hair into leaves (1.548–52). Ovid's Latin conveys subtle effects here that an English translation cannot capture: the suddenness of Daphne's transformation is caught neatly by the description of her swift feet, abruptly changed into sluggish roots (*pes modo tam velox pigris radicibus haeret* – 1.551), where the juxtaposition of *velox* (swift) and *pigris* (sluggish) conveys the very moment of metamorphosis. What is more, Ovid's Latin description of the transformation of Daphne into laurel here inscribes the intriguing possibility of an extra-textual parallel metamorphosis: that of Daphne into a character in Ovid's own *Metamorphoses*. The layer of bark or *liber* (*libro* – 1.549) that encases her body could also be taken to refer to the book or *liber* in which she is now bound in her new form. Like Apollo, with whom Ovid identified at the beginning of this tale, the poet also gets his hands on the girl in the end.

At the level of the narrative, the beautiful nymph has now become a beautiful tree, her external form but not her essential *forma* (beauty) has been changed. This effect of continuity through change is further enhanced by Apollo's response to finding the object of his desire suddenly transformed into a tree: even in this new form, Ovid tells us, Apollo still loved and desired her, feeling her breast encased in bark, embracing her branches as if they were still arms, and planting kisses upon the wood of the trunk, which shrinks back from his touch (1.553–6). Apollo's attempts to possess Daphne physically – that is, to rape her – have been thwarted, but he is still determined to have her as his own, declaring that her evergreen leaves will henceforth be his, that in the future they will wreathe the heads of victorious Romans at their triumphs, and hang on the door of Augustus himself.[12] Having made his possession of Daphne complete – even up to Ovid's own Augustan age, (recall Ovid's prologue at 1.4) – Apollo falls silent and the newly formed laurel sways her head/tree top in the breeze (1.566f). Apollo chooses to interpret this as a sign of Daphne's consent, but Ovid leaves room for other interpretations of this, and of the story as a whole. For Daphne only 'seems' (1.567) to nod her assent, and the verb which Ovid chooses to describe this action (*agitasse* – 1.567) carries with it connotations of agitation, of upset and distress. Perhaps Daphne refuses her consent to this final act of (mis)appropriation, just as she refused her consent to Apollo's initial attempts to physically possess her. It is left up to the reader to decide.

Io (1.568–746)[13]

The Io story, narrated in flashback, offers a stylistic variation upon the type of rape narrative in which Apollo and Daphne have just featured. In fact, Jupiter's (successful) rape of Io can be viewed as a transformation or *variatio* of the narrative template that we have just encountered in Apollo's (unsuccessful) rape of Daphne. Comically, but with an underlying hint of menace (the mixed tone of the entire episode), Jupiter addresses Io as 'a virgin worthy of Jove' (1.589) and cheesily declares that she is destined to make someone a happy husband (literally, 'happy in bed' – 1.590): sleazy Jupiter clearly has himself in mind. With the same unsubtle mix of humour and veiled sexual threat, he then suggests that Io protect herself from the heat of the midday sun by seeking the shade of the forest where he – a god – will protect her from any wild beasts: the time and place will become a *topos* for future rapes and dangerous encounters in the poem. But for now neither we nor Io are fooled by Jupiter's affected concern for her well-being and, mindful of Daphne's recent encounter with Apollo, it is no surprise to find Io running away. But here similarities with the encounter between Apollo and Daphne end: Io is certainly fast, but Jupiter is the king of the gods and he succeeds where Apollo failed. Without giving chase, Jupiter simply and swiftly covers the earth with a cloud to cover his crime, stops the girl and rapes her: the syntax of the Latin, where the verbs follow each other in quick succession, emphasizes the rapidity of these events (*occuluit tenuitque fugam rapuitque pudorem* – 1.600) and Io's vulnerability against the force of Jupiter's desire.

But Io's troubles are far from over. With the dark blend of humour and pathos that pervades each element of this story, Ovid wittily relates Juno's suspicions of her husband's new infidelity: seeing a suspicious cloud covering Arcadia she mutters 'Either I'm wrong or I'm wronged' (1.607f). Significantly, Juno views herself (rather than the victim of Jupiter's rape) as the injured party here – a typical response that will once again become a familiar feature of such rape stories in the *Metamorphoses*.[14] There follows a ridiculous encounter between Juno and Jupiter, who are both fully aware of the other's deception but nevertheless try to outwit each other, with no thought for the suffering thereby inflicted upon the hapless mortal caught-up in their squabble. Thus, in an attempt to cover-up his adultery, Jupiter transforms Io into a beautiful white heifer: Ovid gives us no details of the metamorphosis itself, offering only the detail that, even as a cow, Io was still beautiful (*formosa* – 1.612). Undeceived by the transformation, Juno asks Jupiter to give her the cow as a present. Swayed on one side by shame/guilt and on the other by love/lust, Jupiter's battle with his conscience is represented as an absurd moral dilemma, the irony under-scored by Ovid's use of the same term (*pudor*) to describe both Io's virginity and Jupiter's shame at its violation: Jupiter gives no thought to the sufferings of Io here.

This ludicrous ethical conflict is finally resolved by Jupiter giving the cow to Juno, who is, after all, both his wife *and* his sister, as Ovid wryly observes (1.620). Still jealous of her rival, Juno sets the hundred-eyes of Argus to guard over the bovine Io and it is here that Ovid explores the misery and the comedy of Io's dual identity as both cow and girl more fully. As the details of her transformation were not narrated in any detail, Ovid's account of Io's life imprisoned inside the body of a cow offers him the opportunity to exploit the psychological impact and the comic potential of the metamorphosis. So, she is forced to wear a halter around her neck, to eat grass and leaves, to sleep on the ground, and to drink water from a muddy stream (1.631–4). In a gesture that will become a familiar feature of human to animal metamorphosis in the poem, she tries to stretch out her arms in supplication but finds that she has no arms to stretch;[15] she tries to speak, but is frightened by the mooing sound that she finds herself making; she looks at herself reflected in the waters of her own father's clear stream and is horrified by the horned creature she sees looking back at her, and in terror she tries to run away from herself (1.635–41).

Ovid goes on to describe Io's tragicomic reunion with her father Inachus, whom she follows and offers herself as a pet. She eats the grass he holds out for her, giving cow kisses to his outstretched palm, and unable to speak, scratches out her name and her story in the dirt (1.649f), for Io's blessedly short name means 'woe' and 'alas' in Greek. Thus, tracing IO in the dirt simultaneously reveals both her true identity and the sad fate that has befallen her. As if reading and translating (or perhaps transforming) her 'IO' from Greek into Latin, Inachus responds to his daughter with the Latin equivalent of 'woe' and 'alas' (*me miserum* – 1.651, 653), before launching upon an extended lament for his *own* sad loss: it would have been easier for him if

Io had never been found; he had high hopes for her marriage and a future dynasty; and, since he is an immortal river god, he cannot even hope to end his sorrows in death (1.651–63). Although he is Io's own father, this immortal shows little compassion for mortal suffering, and it almost comes as a relief when Argus finally leads Io away and Inachus' orgy of self-pity is brought to an end.

Finally, Jupiter can bear Io's torment no more and orders Mercury to kill Argus. Disguised as a shepherd, Mercury lulls Argus to sleep with his pastoral pipe music and begins to tell Argus the story of how the reed pipe came to be invented (1.687f).[16] And so, in the guise of a pastoral interlude, with one of the easy metamorphoses of genre achieved by Ovid throughout the poem, we hear the aetiology of the Pan-pipe, and the story-within-a-story of Pan and Syrinx.

Syrinx and Pan (1.689–712)

The story of Syrinx and Pan represents a clever metamorphosis of the Daphne and Apollo story, a transformation in which the names have been changed but the essential narrative remains the same: god sees beautiful girl, starts to woo her, she flees (leaving him in mid-speech), he gives chase, she prays for rescue in the form of metamorphosis, she is transformed, he takes possession of her in her new body (1.698–712).

In spite of its brevity, this short story works hard for Ovid. As an inset narrative, told by an internal narrator, it presents a novel opportunity to link one story to another as part of Ovid's *carmen perpetuum*. As an internal narrative in which its audience does not pay attention to the whole story (a bored Argus falls asleep at the start and is then murdered by Mercury), and whose narrator stops at a crucial point (Mercury stops telling the story as soon as he has sent his victim to sleep and Ovid takes over) it offers valuable insights into Ovid's own story-telling technique. Indeed, numerous internal narrators and audiences appear throughout the *Metamorphoses* and the motif of a narratee who fails to pay attention and is duly punished recurs regularly.[17] So, Argus is beheaded and his eyes transformed into the tail of the peacock; the raven is turned black for ignoring the crow's cautionary tale in book 2; and Pentheus tragically disregards the stories about Bacchus in book 3. We would be wise to pay close attention to all of the stories in Ovid's long *carmen perpetuum*, it seems.

In this light, it is significant that it is a story about attempted rape that fatally sends Argus to sleep here. As Sarah Brown has observed, 'Argus' boredom is a grim reminder that male violence against women is an everyday occurrence, not worth staying awake for'.[18] Indeed, this is an issue that continues to trouble readers and critics of the *Metamorphoses*: how should we respond to Ovid's representation of rape and violence against women in this poem? Some readers see the poet and his text as sympathetic to women, others as sexist, and even misogynistic. Some maintain that Ovid's literary objectification of women is akin to pornography, others that Ovid possessed 'an intuitive understanding of female psychology'.[19] What is particularly interesting about the story of Syrinx and Pan, however, is that it is Ovid's *internal* narrator and audience who bore and are bored by this familiar tale of sexual violence; and, if it is indeed the case that this story reminds us of the ubiquity of rape and sexual violence in Greek and Roman poetry, it is Ovid, as external narrator, who draws this to our notice.

If we pay close attention to the conclusion of this story, we may also notice that it is the victim who gets the last word here. As Pan sighs in disappointment at his failure to catch (and to rape) Syrinx, his breath blows upon the reeds which resound with something 'like a complaint' (1.708). Yet the narrative is distinctly ambivalent about *whose* complaint this is. We may assume that, given Pan's disappointed sigh, the sound that emerges from the reeds is his. But at the same time we may also hear in this sound a complaint from the nymph-turned-reed for her ill treatment at the hands of the god – an elegiac complaint on the behalf of all women so ill-treated in the world of Ovid's *Metamorphoses* – and in the world outside.

Phaethon (1.747–79)
Returning briefly to the story of Io, Ovid describes her reverse metamorphosis from cow into girl, an innovation that encourages him to linger on the details that were passed-over in the narrative of her first transformation (1.738–46). Ovid then allows Io to lead us into his next story: *now*, he tells us (bringing the tale into his own time), Io is known as Isis, mother to a son

named Epaphus, and her son once had a friend named Phaethon, child of the Sun (1.747–51). The two boys, alike in age and temper, quarrel with each other about their illegitimate parentage, prompting Phaethon to run to his mother Clymene for proof of his divine origin.

So, the story of Phaethon and his search for origins begins just as book 1 of the *Metamorphoses* ends. And, as if explicitly returning us to the start of the poem, Clymene's final words to her son echo those spoken by Ovid in his prologue: 'If your spirit impels you (*si modo fert animus*), be off on your way and question the sun god' (1.775). Phaethon's search for his father's rising place (and thus the place where he himself comes from) recalls then the programmatic 'rising place' (1.779) of both Ovid and of his poem as we set off into the next book, like Phaethon, already looking forward to what we may find there.

Discussion points and questions
1. How far does Ovid achieve his aim to spin a *carmen per-petuum* in book 1 of the *Metamorphoses*?
2. What does book 1 tell us about narratology or story-telling in the *Metamorphoses*?
3. What do the stories in book 1 reveal about Ovid's attitudes towards Augustus?
4. What do the stories in book 1 reveal about Ovid's attitudes towards women?

Book Two

Phaethon (2.1–400)[20]

Continued across books 1 and 2, the story of Phaethon is the longest single episode in the poem, taking us on an intricate narrative journey through time and space. We left Phaethon hurrying impetuously to find his father at the end of book 1 but as he reaches the Palace of the Sun, Ovid effectively stops the boy – and the poem's reader – in his tracks. He opens book 2 with an epic ecphrasis or extended description of the Palace of the Sun, focusing aptly enough upon the closed doors of the entrance that will eventually lead us and Phaethon into the Palace and into book 2.[21] The elaborately decorated doors, whose workmanship is even more wonderful than the silver material from which they are made (2.5), depict the ordered cosmos. In a direct allusion to the opening of Ovid's own *opus* (literary work) and his poetic description there of the ordering of primordial chaos into its constituent parts, here we are shown a visual representation of the ordered cosmos, the waters encircling the earth, and the sky overhanging the land, each zone with its proper complement of gods, nymphs, men and beasts, and with the twelve signs of the zodiac arranged above them (2.5–18).[22]

As he enters these magnificent doors, Phaethon crosses an important symbolic boundary and, as the carvings on the doors themselves remind us, when mortals transgress such boundaries in the *Metamorphoses* chaos often follows. That Phaethon is out of place and out of his depth here is quickly made clear. The otherness of the Sun-god's divinity strikes both Phaethon and Ovid's reader as soon as he crosses the threshold of the Palace: surrounded by the Seasons and by allegorical figures of time, the Sun is so bright that Phaethon cannot look at him directly (2.23–32). Nevertheless, Ovid repeatedly emphasizes the father-son relationship between Phaethon and Phoebus (a cult name that applies to Sol or Helios as well as to Apollo), repeatedly drawing attention to the Sun's role as *pater* and *genitor*, and finally revealing the family trait of foolhardy recklessness that will bring tragedy to both father and son. For Sol, embracing his son and acknowledging his paternity, impulsively swears a binding oath to give Phaethon whatever he asks for – immediately regretting his rash promise when Phaethon asks to drive his father's chariot in its daily circuit around the earth.[23]

All that the father can do is to anoint his son's face with a powerful sun-block (*sacro medicamine* – 2.122) to protect him from the heat of the sun and to give the boy detailed directions on how to follow the 'middle way', driving neither too high or too low (the same advice that Daedalus will later give to his son Icarus in book 8) before Phaethon sets off in the Sun's chariot – with predictably chaotic and tragic consequences. But as Phaethon loses control of the horses, and the chariot of the sun runs out of control, Ovid takes up the poetological reins (2.167f) and he drives the narrative through a series of ingenious metamorphoses. He transforms the constellations of the Bears, the Serpent, Bootes the Waggoner, and Scorpio into real creatures which either terrify Phaethon or are themselves terrified as the Sun's chariot runs out of control into unknown celestial territory. Indeed, in a playful anachronism, Phaethon scorches the constellation of the Bears – although they will not be created until the next story in the poem (2.401–530). As the sun scorches the earth, its meadows, trees, crops and cities are turned into ash; the people of Ethiopia become black-skinned as the sun darkens their faces; Libya becomes a desert as her waters dry up; and a mini-epic catalogue lists the fountains and rivers that boil and dry up, in a universal destruction to parallel that of the Flood.

The gods of the sea and of the underworld panic as the earth burns, until Tellus, the scorched Earth personified, pleads with Jupiter for aid, appealing to his self-interests by pointing out that the safety of heaven itself is compromised by this cosmic conflagration – as Jupiter himself had foreseen in book 1 (1.255–8). With a well-aimed thunderbolt, Jupiter knocks Phaethon out of the chariot and to his death. Phaethon falls, blazing like a star or a comet through the sky (2.321) and we expect his transformation into an actual star or comet to follow – for metaphor to become metamorphosis. But Phaethon falls dead to the earth: there is no physical metamorphosis in this, the longest single episode in the whole of the *Metamorphoses*.

Instead, tagged-on to the end of the story almost as an afterthought, Ovid offers us two incidental transformations that occur as an indirect result of Phaethon's death. First he tells how Phaethon's mother and sisters – the Heliades – collect his scattered body-parts and lament, weeping over his grave for four long months. Then one day the eldest sister feels her feet grow cold and stiff, another finds herself literally rooted to the spot, and a third finds her hair has turned into foliage. With a reprise of Daphne's metamorphosis into laurel, the Heliades find themselves turning into poplar trees, the bark slowly closing around them. With a touch of dark humour, Ovid describes their mother desperately trying to rip the creeping tree-bark away from their bodies only to find that she is tearing the flesh from them: they have become trees (2.358–63). Yet still their weeping continues, the tears of the Heliades hardening into the beads of amber that will one day be worn by Roman brides: a fine example of continuity through change. Then, with a final tendentious link, Ovid adds that a fellow mourner and witness of the miraculous transformation of the Heliades went weeping along the banks of the river where Phaethon's body fell until his voice became shrill, his hair became plumage, a web joined his fingers, and Cycnus became a strange new bird – a swan (2.377). And with a nice aetiological twist, Ovid adds that the newly formed swan, fearing the sky and the fiery thunderbolt that had destroyed Phaethon, preferred not to fly but to spend his time in the water (2.377–80). Ovid's tale of 'changes of shape, new forms' is back on track.

Callisto (2.401–530)

As omnipotent Jupiter checks and repairs the state of the earth after the great fire, returning life and order after disorder and destruction, he spies a beautiful nymph – and so returns the poem to one of its familiar themes, interrupted by the long interlude of Phaethon's fiery drama. How Callisto, daughter of Lycaon, survived the flood that followed her father's meta-morphosis in book 1 is not clear, although it has been suggested that Phaethon's misadventure with the chariot of the Sun disrupted the fabric of time itself and that the timeline of Ovid's narrative has therefore been reset somehow to a period before the flood.[24] Certainly we seem to have returned again to the type of rape narrative (or divine *amor*) that dominated book 1 of the poem: Jupiter is inflamed with desire at the very first sight of this unnamed nymph (2.410); she is a modest virgin and a hunter, devoted to the service of Diana (2.411–416); the sun is high in the sky when the girl seeks the shade of the (aptly) virgin forest (2.417–21); and, though apparently mindful of his recent trouble over Io, Jupiter decides that sex with this girl is worth the risk.

But here the familiar pattern changes and Ovid introduces a new variation on the rape motif, as Jupiter first metamorpl.oses into Diana, 'putting on' her identity and her gender as easily as putting on her dress (*induitur faciem cultumque Dianae* – 2.425). Callisto hails this false Diana as 'greater than Jove' (2.429), to the great amusement of the disguised god, who unexpectedly begins to kiss her on the lips.[25] There follows one of the most empathetic and psychologically perceptive accounts of the trau-matic aftermath of rape in any work of literature, ancient or modern – made all the more remarkable by its inclusion in a poem by a male poet notorious for his characteristically light-hearted treatment of violence against women. Ovid describes how the girl fought uselessly against the 'omnipotent' god, observing that if only Juno had seen her struggles, she would have been more sympathetic (2.435). But Callisto is denied sympathy from everyone but Ovid in this awful story.[26]

Immediately after the rape, Jupiter disappears, leaving Callisto traumatized, hating the very woods that had witnessed her awful experience, and in her distress almost forgetting her quiver and bow as she heads out of the forest (2.438f). When she sees Diana and her band of virgins she initially flees in terror, afraid that it may again be Jupiter in disguise, and when she does rejoin the group she is silent and ashamed, entirely unlike her former confident self. But her ordeal is far from over and her next abuser will indeed be Diana. For, when nine months have passed and Callisto's pregnant belly testifies to her lost virginity, Diana expels her former favourite from the troupe without hesitation or hearing. And when Callisto gives birth to a baby boy, Juno's jealous wrath is inflamed and she enters the narrative to add to the girl's torment, her anger directed wholly against the victim rather than the perpetrator of the rape.

Having already been cruelly abused by Jupiter and Diana, Callisto is now made to suffer at the hands of a third god as Juno determines to take away the beauty that had made the girl attractive to Jove in the first place: in Juno's view the rape was entirely Callisto's own fault for being so pretty.[27] Ovid's description of Callisto's subsequent metamorphosis highlights Juno's vicious cruelty towards the girl as she grabs her by the hair and throws her to the ground before deforming her smooth skin and beautiful features into those of an ugly, growling bear (2.476–85).[28] Yet, just as he had previously captured the psychological ordeal of Callisto's plight as a victim of rape, Ovid now imaginatively captures the parallel emotional trauma of her transformation – portrayed emphatically as a *deformation* – into a terrifying wild animal. Disgusted and terrified by her own body, a body that she no longer recognizes as her own, the old Callisto is trapped inside this new form, her mind just as it was before the metamorphosis (2.485). So, she hides from the other wild animals, forgetting that she herself is one, she is terrified by the sight of bears, again forgetting that she herself is one, and she trembles at the sight of wolves, even though her own father Lycaon now runs with the pack (2.489–95).

However, Callisto's multiple metamorphoses – virgin to mother, favourite to outcast, human to animal, hunter to hunted – are not over yet. Her story takes a final cruel turn when her grown-up and unknown son is on the verge of killing her before Jupiter reappears and turns them both into stars (2.507). Jealous Juno, her anger not yet assuaged, interprets this as another personal insult, persuading the gods of the sea to refuse 'that harlot' (as she still calls Callisto) to ever set into their waters (2.530). The cruelty and anger of the gods once aroused, it seems, know no bounds – as the banished Ovid himself would one day experience at first hand.

The Raven and the Crow (2.531–632)

The shift from Callisto's story into the next is not the most adroit transition in the poem, although the arch wit of the following highly convoluted narrative suggests that this effect may be deliberate on the poet's part: the ensuing tales could be read as an Ovidian master-class in how *not* to tell stories. Juno's punishment of her 'rival' now complete, she travels back to Olympus in her gaudy peacock-drawn chariot whose feathers, Ovid reminds us with a glance back to 1.715f, have only recently been decorated with Argus' eyes. This minor detail recalls for Ovid a series of other bird-related stories of transformation which he then proceeds to narrate, one story set within another, like a set of misshapen Russian dolls.

He begins with the story of the raven, which had experienced a similar change to its plumage around the same time as the peacock got its eyes. So, Ovid narrates in flashback the 'just-so story' of how the raven – once as white as a dove or (with glaring anachronism) a Capitoline goose – was turned from white to 'the opposite of white' (2.541), for informing Apollo of his lover Coronis' illicit sexual activities. As the tell-tale raven sets out to inform on Coronis, a gossiping crow becomes an internal narrator and tells him a short morality tale about her own bad experience of being a stool pigeon, followed by the story of her own metamorphosis (a version of the already familiar rape narratives from book 1), and the even shorter tale of Nyctimene who has sex with her father and turns into an owl (2.590–95). The raven ignores the crow's stories – with predictably tragic consequences. Hearing of Coronis' betrayal, Apollo kills his unfaithful lover in a jealous rage, repents his rashness but is unable to heal her, gives her an elaborate funeral (snatching his unborn child from the pyre just in the nick of time), and then punishes the raven who had brought him the bad news (2.596–632).

The effect of so many stories, albeit echoing motifs with which we are already familiar (the transformation of a bird's plumage, the attempted rape avoided by metamorphosis, the impetuous god who brings death to a loved-one) is disorientating. There is an obvious bird-theme (with an underlying erotic sub-theme) tying the stories together into a semblance of unity, but what these tales also share is a common caveat about the dangers of careless talk, and the restrictions set upon freedom of speech by those in authority. Whether or not Ovid did later edit his poem while in exile, this section of the *Metamorphoses* certainly offers a suggestive commentary upon the hazards of seeing and saying that which one should not.

Ocyrhoe (2.633–75)

This same highly-charged motif is repeated in the next story. The infant that Apollo rescues from Coronis' funeral pyre is the unnamed baby Aesculapius, like his father a healer, who Apollo now sends to be fostered with the centaur Chiron. The narrative follows Aesculapius into Chiron's home, where we meet his daughter Ocyrhoe and learn of her metamorphosis into a mare. Ocyrhoe is a gifted seer who foretells the future of both Aesculapius and her father before the Fates forbid her to speak further, curtailing her powers and transforming her (appropriately, given her father's identity) into a horse. Ovid's description of Ocyrhoe's metamorphosis typically focuses upon her loss of human speech as she is transformed alike in both voice and appearance, stressing continuity through change as her fingernails become hooves and her flowing hair a horse's mane. However, this description is lent particular poignancy by the background of Ovid's own story of 'metamorphosis' and punishment by the Fates (or rather, their agent Augustus).

Indeed, Ocyrhoe's final words might have been spoken by Ovid himself (2.659f). Ovid describes her words of complaint as *querellae* (2.665), a term explicitly associated with elegy. He notes that she has more stories to tell, but that her freedom of speech is being blocked. And he has her declare that her prophetic arts or *artes* were not worth the divine wrath that they inspired against her (*non fuerant artes tanti, quae numinis iram / contraxere mihi* – 2.659f). Just like Ovid, whose own *Arts* (in the form of the elegiac *Ars Amatoria*) brought down the divine wrath of Augustus upon his head, Ocyrhoe has been punished for saying – and seeing – too much.

Battus (2.676–707)

With an elegant transition – Chiron weeps for his lost daughter and calls upon Apollo for help, but Apollo is busy elsewhere – we move on to a new story, and a new twist on the same freedom of speech theme. Apollo cannot help Chiron or Ocyrhoe because Ovid has temporarily transformed him into a typical pastoral lover, dressed in a shepherd's cloak, playing the pan pipes, neglecting his herd, and thinking only of his new love (2.676–85). Meanwhile, the wily Mercury steals the herd from under Apollo's distracted nose, and an old man named Battus witnesses the crime.[29] When Mercury tries to buy the old man's silence about what he has seen, Battus promises that 'This stone will inform on you sooner than I' (2.696). But when he is tricked by Mercury into betraying his secret, the god twists the old man's own words against him and turns him into a stone, silencing him forever.

Aglauros (2.708–832)

An elaboration of this same motif continues into the next story, where the narrative picks up a loose thread previously dropped by the crow: the story of the daughters of Cecrops – Herse and Aglauros. Flying over Athens, Mercury sees the beautiful Herse and is inflamed with desire for her (2.708–36). Without delay or disguise he heads straight for her bedroom, but is spied by her sister Aglauros, who demands a hefty bribe as the price of her silence – envious of her sister's luck. In turn the goddess Minerva, spying from above, seems to be envious of Aglauros' profiteering, allowing Ovid to embark upon an elaborate allegorical description of the House of Envy (2.760–86) – the first of several such allegorical ecphrases in the poem in which Ovid metamorphoses an abstract concept (such as envy, rumour, hunger, or sleep) into a visually striking personification.[30]

At Minerva's behest, Envy duly infects Aglauros with an all-consuming jealousy for her sister's potential happiness with Mercury. The girl then stations herself outside Herse's bedroom door to obstruct both that happiness and the god when he returns, adopting a position familiar from the world of Roman love elegy, where third parties regularly attempt to shut out the elegiac lover. But when she stubbornly refuses to move, Mercury responds just as he had to Battus, twisting the girl's own words against her and turning her into a stone statue. Ovid's account of the metamorphosis broadly follows the typical pattern of transformation seen throughout the poem, with an emphasis upon Aglauros' inability to speak (2.829f) and upon continuity through change, as the darkness in her heart stains the inanimate stone statue to black (2.832). However, in keeping with the motif of infection and poison that colours this episode – particularly in Ovid's description of Envy herself – the process of this transformation is described in novel terms that evoke the idea of a malignant disease slowly spreading through Aglauros' body (2.828). The potent image of metamorphosis as an incurable cancer bears particular significance here, for Ovid's account of Aglauros' transformation into a statue is also necessarily an account of her death. The gruesome detail of her slowly suffocating as the stone chokes her breath, and the chilling suggestion that her mind was still conscious as this dreadful change took place, reveals both Ovid's talent and taste for horror.

Europa (2.833–75)

After the horrific tale of Aglauros, the tone of the poem lightens as we again follow Mercury (who has provided a suitably mercurial bond between the previous two narratives) into the final story of book 2 and the well-known tale of Europa: so well-known, in fact, that Ovid does not need to name her here. Reprising his role as cattle-man, Mercury follows Jove's instructions to drive a herd of Tyrian cattle down to the sea shore where the young princess Europa and her friends like to play (2.833–45). The scene is duly set for another rape narrative, but Ovid quickly makes it clear that this episode represents a more light-hearted view of the gods and their amorous misadventures than we have previously seen. Contrasting majesty (*maiestas*) and love (*amor*), Ovid reminds us that love can make a fool out of anyone – including the king of the gods, who now disguises himself as a bull in order to make his move on Europa (2.846–51). Like the other effortless metamorphoses of the gods in the poem, Jupiter 'puts on' the form of a bull (*induitur faciem tauri* – 2.850) as easily if it were a pantomime cow costume.[31] Love (or lust) has made a monkey – or rather, a bull – out of Jupiter as he moos with the other cattle and shows off his new bovine physique. Indeed, as Ovid exploits vocabulary that might elsewhere be applied to an elegiac lover, the obvious sexual overtones to this description are unequivocally funny: Jupiter flaunts his muscles, his 'dewlaps', and his little horns (*cornua parva* – 2.855) – this last detail fatally undermining the image of sexual prowess that Jupiter seems keen to promote. For, part of the humour here derives from the popular use of *cornum* in ancient Rome as synonym for 'penis'.

Unaware of the beast's true identity and charmed by its apparent tameness, Europa pets the bull, decorating its horns with flowers, sitting on its back, and allowing it to kiss her hands (2.858–69). But Ovid reminds us that within this horned animal is a horny god, a lover (*amans* – 2.862) who can barely contain his desire, a would-be abductor and rapist who, little by little, carrying Europa upon his back, is now edging closer and closer to the water's edge. Just as imperceptibly, Ovid himself has taken us closer and closer to the end of the book, and now – like Europa, holding on to Jupiter's *cornum* (2.874) – the reader finds herself being carried into the unknown, looking back at what she leaves behind, while physically holding on to the *cornua* or book ends at the close of book 2 of the *Metamorphoses*.

Discussion points and questions
1. How effective is the transition between books 1 and 2? Does Ovid maintain the continuity of his *carmen perpetuum*?
2. How do the stories in book 2 revisit and rework the stories in book 1?
3. Is it legitimate to say that the theme of metamorphosis is only incidental in the story of Phaethon?

4. What do the stories in book 2 reveal about Ovid's attitudes towards the gods?
5. What evidence is there in book 2 to suggest that Ovid revised the poem after his banishment by Augustus?

Book Three

Cadmus (3.1–137)[32]

As we arrive at book 3 and the shores of Crete, we expect Ovid to continue the story of Europa. Certainly the opening words of the book, 'And now the god . . .' – *Iamque deus* (3.1), suggest as much. But as quickly as Jupiter 'confesses' his true identity to Europa, rapes her, and leaves her, Ovid too leaves Europa behind, and reveals his true intentions, turning his attention towards Europa's brother Cadmus, the legendary founder of Thebes.[33] As a bridging character to link the two stories, Ovid briefly introduces the father of Europa and Cadmus, Agenor, who, like the fathers of Daphne and Io, is ignorant of what has happened to his daughter and so sends his son to look for her, threatening the boy with exile if he does not find her. Agenor is a wholly unsympathetic character. His concern for his daughter makes him behave cruelly towards his son, making him – in Ovid's eyes – both pious and sinful in the same act (*pius et sceleratus* – 3.5). Indeed, it is a favourite Ovidian paradox that piety and devotion can sometimes be wrong.[34]

Having searched unsuccessfully for Europa across the whole world, Cadmus becomes an exile, unfairly banished from his home by Agenor's unreasonable anger. In Ovid's narrative, he also becomes an epic hero in the style of Virgil's Aeneas, an exile wandering the earth in search of a new home, guided by oracles towards the site of a new city. So, with a direct if somewhat sardonic echo of Virgil's *Aeneid* 1.276–7 where Jupiter prophesies the founding of Rome, here Cadmus seeks advice from the oracle of Apollo at Delphi. The oracle is unusually helpful and tells him to follow a cow until it lies down to rest and upon that spot to site his new city – to be named Boeotia (in Greek 'cow land'). Although Ovid's astute readers may suspect that, in the aftermath of another one of Jupiter's bovine-themed rapes, this cow may perhaps turn out to be the girl Europa transformed – particularly as she is described lifting her beautiful head to the heavens and filling the air with her moos (3.20f) – in fact, the terms of the oracle prove to be perfectly straightforward and with a cow, a moo, and a strong sense of anticlimax, Cadmus founds Thebes.

His next task, quite properly and piously, is to make a sacrifice to the gods, so he sends out his companions in search of water. But pious intentions count for little in the world of the *Metamorphoses* and as the men enter an ancient forest, a typical *locus amoenus* (pleasant place) untouched by axe or human hand, their unwitting trespass is figured as a violation (*violata* – 3.28) of the wood's sanctity – for which they must, of course, be punished, despite the piety of their mission. Deep within the primeval forest is a cave where the guardian of the place lives – a gigantic, golden crested, venom-filled serpent of excessively epic proportions. Indeed, this massive dragon-like monster surpasses anything found in Virgilian or Homeric epic, despite borrowing several features from *Aeneid* 2.203ff and Virgil's description of the two snakes that kill Laocoon and his sons. This snake makes short work of slaying Cadmus' men, until our own epic hero, dressed as a Virgilian Hercules setting out to slay the monster Cacus (*Aeneid* 8.252–367), arrives to avenge the deaths of his friends. An epic duel between beast and hero ensues and Cadmus duly slays the monster, finally nailing it through its throat to a tree. But just as Cadmus is on the point of celebrating his victory, standing in classic heroic pose looking down at the fallen body of his foe, he hears a strange voice which offers an unexpected and curious prophecy, predicting Cadmus' own future metamorphosis into a snake.

No explanation is offered either by the voice or by Ovid as to why Cadmus should deserve this particular form of punishment, although it is clear that Cadmus' transgression is to have seen something which he should not – a continuing motif repeated from book 2 that will feature prominently in the rest of book 3.

There then follows a strange episode in which Minerva arrives and commands Cadmus to get on with founding Thebes. He sows the serpent's teeth in the ground like seeds, from which a crop of fully armed soldiers grow, spears first, like figures painted onto the backdrop curtain of a Roman theatre stage-set (3.101–14). This theatrical simile, no less than Ovid's own authorial observation that the thing is 'beyond belief' (*fide maius* – 3.106), reminds us that we are not expected to believe in the veracity of this tale – or, indeed, of any tale in the *Meta-morphoses* – but simply to suspend our disbelief and enjoy the spectacle. Indeed, as these soldier 'brothers' (*fratribus* – 3.118) begin to fight among themselves, driven by a fratricidal mad-ness, Ovid uses the story as a parallel to contemporary Roman politics, describing the fight between the soldiers explicitly as a civil war (*civilibus . . . bellis* – 3.117). Cadmus takes no part in the conflict, remaining an Augustan model for peace and recon-ciliation, but recruits the five survivors of this miniature civil war to aid him in founding Thebes and establishing his new dynasty (3.129–35). But Ovid reminds us that however happy and blessed a man's life may appear, no man can be counted happy until after his death (3.135–37). Given that Cadmus will not die but will be turned into a snake at the end of his life, this homily hardly seems appropriate here. But, as Ovid turns to narrate the numerous troubles that afflict Cadmus' descendents and destroy his dynasty, we are reminded of the particular relevance of this cautionary tale for Augustus himself, whose own attempts to establish a secure line of imperial succession were no less fraught than Cadmus' own. As it was in Thebes, so it is – or will be – in Rome.[35]

Actaeon (3.138–255)

Having mentioned Cadmus' sons and grandsons in passing (3.135f), Ovid now segues neatly into the first of what promises to be a series of stories detailing their troubles (each a subtle variation or metamorphosis of the Cadmus story itself), begin-ning first with Actaeon. Somewhat unusually, Ovid opens this story with a short précis and an authorial commentary, signal-ling clearly from the outset of the narrative that this tale bears particular – and perhaps even personal – significance for him. Indeed, it is tempting to see in Ovid's spirited defence of Actaeon's mistake or *error* here a veiled defence of his own *error* in the mysterious offence he caused Augustus (*Tristia* 2.103ff), making it possible that Ovid added or otherwise revised these lines of the poem after his banishment (3.138–42).

The mistake or *error* that Actaeon commits (echoing that of Cadmus) is to stumble across the naked goddess Diana while she is bathing, and so accidentally to see something that he should not. This unwitting transgression is played out against a backdrop that is full of dark foreboding: a short ecphrasis describes Actaeon and his fellow hunters heading for home in the heat of midday (always a dangerous time in the world of the *Metamorphoses*), their weapons dripping with the blood of the many animals they have killed, the mountainside stained with the gore of their successful day's hunting (3.143–54). The canny reader already knows that the blood of one more beast will be added to that slaughter before too long, as one of these hunters becomes one of the hunted.

A neat narrative tracking shot and a second ecphrasis moves our attention from the mountain, down into its valley, and into an idyllic grotto – a delightful *locus amoenus* (although Ovid's reader has by now learned to mistrust such pleasant places) where nature appears to have imitated art (3.158f), and where the virgin goddess Diana now happens to be bathing.[36] Into this private and sacred space stumbles Actaeon – his sudden, shocking, and unintended interruption signalled by Ovid with a direction to the reader to 'look!' (*ecce* – 3.174). Ovid clearly intends us to view Actaeon as entirely innocent of any intentional harm, trespass, or crime here. Indeed, in Ovid's erotically-charged and minutely detailed description of Diana's bathing preparations – a virtual strip-tease (3.163–72) – it is *we* as the poem's readers who arguably see more of the goddess' naked body than the hapless Actaeon. His sudden appearance at the entrance to Diana's cave produces panic and chaos as the goddess' attendant nymphs try to shield her modesty with their own naked bodies (3.178–81). But, Ovid adds with wry humour, the goddess is so much taller than her nymphs that she stands head, shoulders, and breasts, above them, revealing the upper part of her naked body to Actaeon's eyes – as to ours.[37]

Diana's blushing response is as anticipated: naked and so unarmed, she throws water into Actaeon's face, daring him to tell of what he has seen (3.192f). Clearly, she intends not only to punish Actaeon for his trespass and for seeing that which he should not, but to prevent him from speaking of what he has seen – picking up on the motif that ran through book 2. What happens next is typical of the other metamorphoses we have seen so far in the poem: Actaeon sprouts antlers from his head, and finds his hands changed to hooves, his arms into legs, as his body is transformed into that of a stag. When he sees his new reflection in Diana's pool he finds that he cannot speak, he is afraid both to go home and to stay in the woods. And, despite his physical transformation of external form, his mind remains unchanged (3.203).

As Actaeon hesitates, unsure what to do next, he sees his own pack of hounds approaching – each dog individually and inventively named by Ovid in a mock epic catalogue of which even he seemingly grows tired after twenty lines (3.206–25). Actaeon flees from them, desperate but unable to reveal his true identity. Suddenly, three dogs pounce – their surprise attack striking both Actaeon and the reader with parallel force, as Ovid ingeniously explains that these three hounds had not been named in the catalogue as they had started out after the rest and followed a short cut so as to take their prey (and the reader) unawares (3.232–5). Actaeon's horrible death as he is torn apart by his own hounds, unable to pray to the gods for aid, unable to communicate with his men who join the hunt calling for Actaeon to join them, is then told with considerable pathos (3.235–50).[38] Finally, to balance the prologue with which Ovid introduced this story, the poet offers a narrative postscript, reporting upon the mixed reactions to Actaeon's death. He writes (3.253–5) that:

> Comments varied: some felt that the goddess had overdone
> her violent revenge, while others commended it – worthy,
>   they said
> of her strict virginity. All were prepared to defend their opinion.

Ovid's apparent openness to competing interpretations and readings of this story seems strange given the unambiguous emphasis upon Actaeon's innocence in the telling of it here – and given Ovid's own self-identification with Actaeon as the victim of a cruel deity and an unjust punishment. What then are we to make of these lines? John Heath suggests that Diana's extreme reaction towards Actaeon can be seen as informed by her – and our – own 'reading' of rape stories such as those narrated in the *Metamorphoses* and that she is justified in expecting that Actaeon represents a real threat to her virginity. Alternatively, he proposes that Ovid invites us to see the hunter Actaeon as a male counterpart to those innocent virgin-huntresses whose stories we have already read in the *Metamorphoses*, the girls like Callisto and Io who inadvertently stray into the path of a god and are raped, and that, in this light, Diana can be justly condemned for her cruelty.[39] Perhaps all we can reliably take from this observation upon how to read and respond to the story of Actaeon – and to the *Metamorphoses* as a whole – is the possibility that multiple viewpoints, comments and opinions upon the poem are not only possible, but actively invited and authorized, both here and throughout the poem.[40]

Semele (3.256–315)

That we (and Diana) are quite justified in making such connections between ostensibly different stories in Ovid's *carmen perpetuum* is reinforced by the next tale in Ovid's Theban cycle: the story of Semele who, like Actaeon and Cadmus before her, pays a heavy price for seeing something which she should not – in this case Jupiter's true sexual self. Juno has now transferred her jealous rage from Europa, whose story was told in book 2, towards Europa's family in general and to Semele (who is pregnant by Jupiter) in particular. So Semele, like Io and Callisto before her, although a willing sexual partner in this case and not a victim of rape, becomes the latest victim of Juno's misplaced wrath and Jupiter's misplaced *amor*.[41]

Juno swears that she will give Semele cause to regret her beauty (in Latin, her *forma* – 3.270) and, disguising herself as an old woman – Semele's trusted nurse Beroe – she sets out first to 'transform' (*formarat* – 3.288) Semele psychologically, undermining her trust in her divine lover, and – with comically bad taste – encouraging her to test Jupiter's true identity by asking him to make love to her exactly as he does to his wife.[42] Repeating the same mistake made by Sol in book 2 in swearing an unbreakable oath *and* in attempting a relationship with a mortal, Jupiter is tricked into becoming the agent of Juno's revenge. And although he tries (ridiculously) to lessen the force of his sexual potency by firing off a few thunderbolts before entering Semele's bed, her mortal body cannot withstand such intimate contact with an immortal and he destroys her.

A brief postscript to this story then describes how Jupiter saved Semele's unborn child from its mother's fate, using his

thigh as a womb in which to carry the baby Bacchus to term
(3.310–312). As the *pater omnipotens* (omnipotent father),
Jupiter easily transforms his gendered identity and so prepares
us for the equally easy changes of sexual identity that we witness
in the next story.

Tiresias (3.316–38)

This tale is presented as a light-hearted interlude, introducing
Tiresias into the narrative and preparing us for the key role
he will play as prophet and seer in the longer stories of Pentheus
and Narcissus that follow.[43] For, having lived as both a man
and a woman, Tiresias has unique insights into the sex lives
of both men and women – his sex change(s) resulting from his
seeing and striking two mating snakes with his staff in a violent
act that is significantly described in the Latin as a religious and
sexual violation (*violaverat* – 3.325). When the gods disagree
over who enjoys sex more (Jupiter claims that women do; Juno
disagrees) Tiresias is called in to arbitrate, but when he agrees
with Jupiter, Juno blinds him – in punishment for violating
her divine authority, and for intruding upon the sacred mystery
of sex, perhaps. His blindness is ostensibly ameliorated by the
compensatory prophetic sight that Jupiter bestows upon him,
yet this powers of foresight turn out to bring no benefit either to
Tiresias or anyone else – as we see in the next story.

Echo and Narcissus (3.339–510)

Tiresias uses his newly acquired powers to predict the future of
a new-born babe named Narcissus – the result of yet another
rape of a beautiful nymph, this time by the river-god Cephisus.
Asked by the child's mother if her son will live a long life,
Tiresias replies: 'If he never knows himself' (*si se non noverit* –
3.348) – an ironic inversion of the Greek maxim 'Know thyself'
(*gnothi seauton*) famously inscribed on the temple of the oracle
at Delphi. Narcissus will not live to see a ripe old age (3.347)
because of something he will see that will lead to an early
death, in a variation of the motif of the dangerous gaze that
runs throughout book 3. What Narcissus sees, of course, is
his own reflection in a forest pool. But his obsessive, destructive
self-love also results in the death (of sorts) for his narrative

double, his story *imago* (reflection or echo), the nymph Echo, whose story as told here cleverly intersects with and reflects Narcissus' own tale: she too sees this beautiful boy, falls instantly in love, and then pines away when she finds herself and her love rejected.

The story of Narcissus is now one of the most well-known of all ancient myths, not least of all because of the use made of the story by Freud. But, for Ovid's Augustan audience, the tale of Narcissus and his novel type of madness (*novitasque furoris* – 3.350) is likely to have been an entirely new tale.[44] Indeed, there is much in this characteristically Ovidian new story to appreciate – in particular the reworking (metamorphosing) of motifs familiar from love elegy, interwoven with a witty word-play that makes language itself the subject of a kind of transformation here. When we first meet Echo, she has already lost the power of independent speech, and is able only to repeat the words spoken by others – Juno's punishment for the once talkative nymph's attempts to distract her with idle chatter while Jupiter enjoyed yet another of his adulterous affairs. But this speech impediment does not prevent Echo from (more-or-less) successfully playing the role of an elegiac lover here as she actively pursues Narcissus, repeating his words and in so doing reminding us – as Ovid himself had previously reminded us in his *Amores* – that every lover always already speaks a kind of script, using words that a million lovers have used before them.[45] Narcissus meanwhile, similarly woos his own reflection by playing the role of an elegiac lover: like a stereotypical locked-out lover or *exclusus amator*, he lies on the side of the pool in which his image is reflected, forgetful of both food and sleep (3.437f); inverting the traditional elegiac lover's complaint that oceans, mountains, walls or doors separate him from his beloved, Narcissus complains about the superficial barrier of water that keeps him apart from the one he loves (3.448–50); and, repeating the consolation voiced by every elegiac lover that he and his beloved will be united after death, he comforts himself with the thought that he and his beloved will die together (3.473).

When the paths of Echo and Narcissus finally cross, Echo is unable to initiate the sweet-talk (*blanditiae*) traditionally employed by the elegiac lover to win-over his or her beloved, so instead she waits for Narcissus to make the first move in their one-sided courtship, and then mirrors back to him his words – transforming their original meaning into her own. Here it is worth looking at the original Latin to see how Ovid produces this ingenious echoing effect – Narcissus' words are in bold and Echo's echoes are italicized (3.379–92):

> forte puer comitum seductus ab agmine fido
> dixerat: '**ecquis adest**?' et '*adest*' responderat Echo.
> hic stupet, utque aciem partes dimittit in omnes,
> voce '**veni!**' magna clamat: vocat illa vocantem.
> respicit et rursus nullo veniente '**quid**' inquit
> '**me fugis?**' et totidem, quot dixit, verba recepit.
> perstat et alternae deceptus imagine vocis
> '**huc coeamus**' ait, nullique libentius umquam
> responsura sono '*coeamus*' rettulit Echo,
> et verbis favet ipsa suis egressaque silva
> ibat, ut iniceret sperato bracchia collo.
> ille fugit fugiensque '**manus conplexibus aufer!**
> **ante**' ait '**emoriar, quam sit tibi copia nostri**';
> rettulit illa nihil nisi '*sit tibi copia nostri.*'

Narcissus once took a different path from his trusty companions.
'**Is anyone there?**' he said. '. . . *one there?*' came Echo's answer.
Startled, he searched with his eyes all round the glade and loudly
shouted, '**Come here!**' '*Come here!*' the voice threw back to the
    caller.
He looks behind him and, once again, when no one emerges,
'**Why are you running away?**' he cries. His words come ringing
back. His body freezes. Deceived by his voice's reflection,
the youth calls out yet again, '**This way! We must come together!**'
Echo with rapturous joy responds, '*We must come together!*'
To prove her words, she burst in excitement out of the forest,
arms outstretched to fling them around the shoulders she
    yearned for.
Shrinking in horror, he yelled, '**Hands off! May I die before**
you enjoy my body.' Her only reply was '. . . *enjoy my body.*'

Echo's transformation of Narcissus' words here is both pathetic and brilliant: *veni* (3.382) as spoken by Narcissus, suggests an entirely innocent desire on Narcissus' behalf for Echo to 'come' to him. Interpreted and repeated by Echo, however, *veni* also suggests a desire of a more sexual nature. Similarly, *coeamus* (3.386) as spoken by Narcissus, suggests his wish for them to 'come together'. Interpreted and repeated by Echo, however, *coeamus* euphemistically suggests, once again, a desire of a more erotic nature, as she turns Narcissus' invitation (We must come together – 3.386) into an acceptance (We must come together – 3.387), and his curse (May I die before you enjoy my body – 3.391) into an invitation (enjoy my body – 3.392).

Readers and critics of the *Metamorphoses* are divided in their responses to Echo's echoes. Naomi Segal suggests that however brilliant her twisting of Narcissus' words, Echo remains a passive and pathetic figure.[46] Garth Tissol, on the other hand, sees Echo as a creative force as her punning word-play makes Narcissus' words her own.[47] In fact, in her creative appropriation, translation and transformation of another's words, Echo can be seen as a model for the poet Ovid himself, her words echoing his own poetic project in the *Metamorphoses,* where he too creatively appropriates, translates and transforms the words and stories of others into a text that fully represents his own designs and desires.

So crucial is this metamorphic aspect of the story, and so cleverly interwoven into the texture of the narrative is this motif of linguistic transformation, that the physical metamorphoses of both Echo and Narcissus are tagged on to the end of this tale, seemingly as an incidental and anticlimactic afterthought. So, the lovelorn Echo physically fades away, leaving only her voice and her name – in the form of the echo we find in lonely spots. And the lovelorn Narcissus similarly pines away and dies – leaving only a flower in place of his body (*pro corpore* – 3.509): a strange kind of transformation (if that is what this is). The yellow and white flower that we know as the narcissus seems to be a replacement *for* rather than a transformation *of* the narcissistic boy here – its colours reflecting the similes Ovid uses to describe the marble and ivory whiteness (3.419–23) of his skin, and the yellow of the melting wax to which Ovid likens his wasting away (3.487–93). The Narcissus-flower seems just another metaphor for the boy. After his death we see Narcissus in the underworld, still gazing at his reflection in the pools of the river Styx (3.505) and Echo again echoing the sad laments of the mourners at Narcissus' funeral – a fitting conclusion that figures both continuity and change for these characters.

Pentheus and Bacchus (3.511–733)

After the stories of Tiresias, Narcissus and Echo – none of whom were related to Cadmus – Ovid now returns to his original programme for book 3 with the well-known story of Pentheus, grandson of Cadmus and son of Echion, one of the Thebans born of the dragon's teeth-seeds. According to Tiresias, whose prophecy provides the smooth narrative link back into this Theban story-line, Pentheus will die a violent death after seeing something that he should not (the unifying motif of book 3) – torn into a thousand pieces by his own mother and her sisters after denying the divinity of Bacchus and spying upon the secret and sacred rites of the god (3.516–25).[48] This forecast of the narrative to come suggests an obvious connection with the story of Actaeon, but we will not see Ovid's sympathetic treatment of Actaeon repeated here. What is more, Ovid and his Augustan audience would have been familiar with the tragic tale of Pentheus from Euripides' play, the *Bacchae,* and the Homeric *Hymn to Dionysos,* but – as we have now come to expect from the *Metamorphoses* – Ovid's version of the myth, along with its protagonists, will be presented in a new and unfamiliar form. Indeed, here, it seems Ovid has taken the well-known forms of both Euripides' play and the Homeric hymn, and transformed both.

The story begins with Pentheus declaring his dislike and distrust of Bacchus and his followers in a lengthy speech that is stuffed with allusions to Virgil's epic *Aeneid,* anachronistically contrasting the Roman virtues of manliness, dignity, honour and clashing arms, with the effeminacy, madness, trickery and clashing cymbals of the Theban bacchants (3.531–63).[49] Pentheus then orders the arrest of the 'imposter' Bacchus, but instead his men bring him a sailor who calls himself Acoetes – notionally a priest of Bacchus, but here playing the thinly-disguised role of the Stranger/Dionysos familiar from Euripides' play.[50]

In an extended inset narrative and a speech even longer than that delivered by Pentheus (clearly indicating where Ovid's sympathies lie), Acoetes/Bacchus tells the story of how he first encountered the god on board his ship and, significantly, what happened to his fellow sailors who failed to recognize the god's divinity and attempted to double-cross him. It is here that Ovid introduces the focal metamorphosis of this story, describing how Acoetes' ship was suddenly becalmed, held fast with ivy; how the god Bacchus terrified the sailors with images of tigers, lynxes and panthers upon the ship's deck; and how the men leapt overboard into the sea in panic – where they were all transformed into dolphins (3.658–86). Dismissing both Acoetes and his warning, Pentheus orders the captive to be tortured and killed, but in a miracle that adds further weight to the notion that Acoetes is really Bacchus in human form, the doors to his prison fly open, the chains fall from his arms, and the sailor disappears (3.692–700).

In fury, Pentheus then heads towards Cithaeron (and towards his unavoidable death) to witness the Bacchic revels with his own eyes – not, as in Euripides, led by the god, but by his own blind anger and arrogance. Ovid is careful here to establish Pentheus' act of transgression as entirely his own doing, his crime and his punishment as human rather than divine acts. So, as Pentheus spies with profane eyes upon the sacred rites of Bacchus and is himself first seen and then savagely torn apart by Bacchus' crazed female followers, as he begs his own mother to 'see' that the wild boar she thinks is her prey is really her son (3.725), no blame for this horrific punishment falls to Bacchus. Indeed, as the full horror of his fate becomes clear, Pentheus finally admits his blame and confesses his sin in denying Bacchus' divinity (3.718). But his confession comes too late. As Pentheus reminds his aunts (and us) of the horrible death that befell his cousin Actaeon in a futile bid to avert his own parallel fate, he tries to stretch out his arms to appeal for pity (just as Actaeon had done) only to find that he has no arms – they have been ripped off by the bacchants and he has only bloody stumps to wave instead.[51] And so, with a wholly inappropriate Homeric simile, comparing the tearing of Pentheus to pieces with the shedding of autumn leaves (3.729–31), the story and the book draw to close, as the people of Thebes take heed of this cautionary tale (*exemplis monitae* – 3.732) and worship Bacchus as a god.[52]

Discussion points and questions
1. How effective is the transition between books 2 and 3? Does Ovid maintain the continuity of his *carmen perpetuum*?
2. How does the motif of seeing link the stories narrated in book 3?
3. How important is the theme of physical metamorphosis in book 3?
4. Compare Ovid's treatment of Actaeon's *error* (mistake) and Pentheus' *crimen* (sin).

Book Four

The Daughters of Minyas (4.1–415)

Having focused in the last book upon the tragic consequences of gazing upon a sacred mystery, or simply of seeing something which one should not, Ovid now picks up a motif introduced in the story of Pentheus, to examine the tragic consequences of failing to show due honour and respect to the god Bacchus. Ovid shifts his focus to the daughters of Minyas, who refuse to take part in the local holiday honouring Bacchus, boasting instead of their pious devotion to the goddess Minerva – weaving and telling each other stories as they work. This allows Ovid to introduce the sisters as internal narrators, each telling a tale-within-a-tale in a sophisticated meta-narrative that incorporates some of Ovid's best-known love stories: Pyramus and Thisbe (4.55–166); Venus and Mars (4.167–89); Leucothoe and Clytie (4.190–273); and Salmacis and Hermaphroditus (4.274–388).

We might expect Ovid – the famous love poet – to identify and perhaps empathize with these story-tellers who weave their tapestry just as the poet weaves his text, but it seems obvious from the start of the book that he shares little sympathy with their impious lack of respect for the god. In fact, he explicitly identifies himself *against* these women and *with* the followers of Bacchus, adding his own song of praise to those of the locals, calling upon the god by his familiar cult names (4.13–17) and offering a hymn celebrating the powers of Liber (4.17–30). He presents the Minyeides, in contrast, as kill-joys who spoil the party, thinly disguising their disrespect for Bacchus in a show of respect for Minerva. What is more, although the first sister to take up the role of narrator is represented as an experienced and erudite story-teller who hesitates over which of the many exotic tales in her repertoire to tell (4.42–54), Ovid appears to make fun of her poetic pretensions and her Callimachean preferences for exoticism and novelty – despite the fact that these are the very same literary preferences he himself professes in the prologue to the *Metamorphoses*. The Babylonian love story that she finally chooses, having rejected several other tales of metamorphosis, is unknown before Ovid and is certainly, therefore, both novel and exotic, but has been criticized by several readers as lacking sophistication and subtlety, as saccharine and sentimental, naive and amateurish. Indeed, William Anderson asks: 'Isn't there something rather "spinsterish" in this sentimental tale?'[53] Perhaps. And perhaps this is Ovid's intentional design – to highlight the superiority of his own storytelling techniques in the *Metamorphoses* over those of his imperfect internal narrators. Perhaps there is even a whiff of sexism in Ovid's – or in his readers' – representation of the female Minyeides as inadequate narrators, undermined by their romantic, spinsterish sentimentalism. If so, it is somewhat ironic that the story of Pyramus and Thisbe, narrated by the first of the sisters, should become one of the most popular of all Ovidian stories, later adapted by Shakespeare in *A Midsummer Night's Dream*.

Indeed, Shakespeare's comic treatment of this story of forbidden love releases the humorous potential that lies here: the two young lovers, separated by a family feud – and a wall dividing their two homes – behave like stock characters in a Roman comedy or an elegiac love poem, whispering sweet-nothings (*blanditiae*) through a chink in the wall, while the tragedy and potential pathos of their suicide is undermined by the comedy of errors that brings these deaths about. Even the metamorphosis that is included, almost incidentally, in the centre of the tale – the transformation of the fruits of the mulberry tree from white to dark red – is made bathetic by the extravagantly grotesque description of Pyramus' blood spurting out high into the air, like a jet from a broken water pipe (4.121–7), to spray the fruit of the tree with gore.

After a short break (this is no internal *carmen perpetuum*) a second sister launches straight into her tale – or rather series of tales – concerning the loves of the Sun (*Solis . . . amores* – 4.170). Her narrative is less sentimental and more sophisticated than that which we have just heard, moving deftly between the stories of Venus and Mars' adulterous affair, the Sun's infatuation with and rape of Leucothoe, who becomes a frankincense shrub, and his rejection of a former lover Clytie, whose grief transforms her into a sunflower. The neat transitions between these three stories are worthy of Ovid: Venus blames the Sun for revealing her affair and so punishes him with an uncontrollable desire for Leucothoe; a jealous Clytie informs Leucothoe's father, who reacts to the Sun's rape of his daughter with Juno-like insensitivity and buries her alive; the remorseful Sun then spurns Clytie who becomes a heliotrope. What is more, the unifying motif of passion thwarted, that runs between this collection of stories concerning divine *amor* would not have seemed out of place in the earlier books of the *Metamorphoses*. Only minor hints suggest that here too Ovid may be mocking his internal narrator for her spinster sensibilities: the excessively poor taste shown by the Sun in disguising himself as Leucothoe's mother in order to rape her (4.219, compare Jupiter's rape of Callisto at 2.425); the senti-mental description of Leucothoe's welcome submission to the Sun as he rapes her (4.232f); and the incidental setting for Leucothoe's rape (4.220f) as she sits weaving and spinning at home. As Elaine Fantham suggests: 'is the poet perhaps imply-ing that the spinning Minyeides enjoy the thought of ubiquitous seduction?'[54]

After a brief interruption while the Minyeides discuss the plausibility of the tales they have just heard, the third sister begins the final tale in this sequence. Considering and then rejecting a number of stories as 'too well-known' (*vulgatos* – 4.276), she selects from her impressively broad narrative repertoire a determinedly Callimachean story that, she claims, will delight her audience because of its novelty: the strange story of Salmacis and Hermaphroditus.[55] Pressing her Callimachean credentials perhaps a little too far, she signals further that this will be an aetiological tale, telling how the famous spring of Salmacis originally gained its reputation for emasculating those who swim in its waters (4.285–7).

Enjoying the same literary conceit that we saw in book 1, where a river can be an anthropomorphized god *and* the waters of his own river, Ovid's internal narrator represents the man-eating nymph Salmacis as both pool and as predatory female, who attempts to rape the unsuspecting youth Hermaphroditus who comes to bathe in her. The reader who approaches this story as part of the continuum of Ovid's *carmen perpetuum* will recognize instantly that here is an inversion of the pattern of rape narrative that we have seen in earlier books, and will notice distorted echoes too of the Narcissus story. Like Narcissus' pool where nothing muddies or disturbs the crystal purity of the water, the description of Salmacis' pool here suggests an idealized *locus amoenus* – an idyllic yet menacing spot (4.297–301). Like Narcissus himself, Hermaphroditus is represented as an ivory statue, his skin reflecting the whiteness of lilies, the red blush of ripe apples (4.331f; 354f). And, just like Narcissus, he rebuffs the unwanted amorous attentions of an ardent nymph. But Salmacis is no patient, pathetic Echo, and although she pretends to withdraw at this rejection, it is only to carry on stalking Hermaphroditus from the bushes (4.338–45). Indeed, Salmacis is unlike any nymph we have yet encountered in the world of the *Metamorphoses*: alone of all the nymphs, we are told, she does not follow Diana (and so, we understand, has no interest in preserving her virginity), but instead spends her days lying beside her pool, dressed in a see-through gown, combing her hair and gazing narcissistically at her reflection (4.302–14). Occasionally, she picks flowers (a motif that is often the precursor to rape in the poem), and spying the lily-like beauty of Hermaphroditus one day, she decides to pluck him too (4.315f).

There follows one of the most bizarre – and, frankly, disturbing – accounts of rape found in ancient literature. Unaware that he is being watched, Hermaphroditus strips and dives into the pool. With a wholly unfeminine cry of triumph (4.356; cf. 6.513), Salmacis strips off her (already transparent) dress and dives in after him (4.358–67):

> [She] grabbed hold of his limbs as he struggled against her,
>   greedily kissing him,
> sliding her hands underneath him to fondle his unresponsive
> nipples and wrapping herself round each of his sides in turn.
> For all his valiant attempts to slip from her grasp, she finally
> held him tight in her coils, like a huge snake carried aloft

in an eagle's talons, forming knots round the head and the feet
of the royal bird and entangling the flapping wings in its tail;
or like the ivy which weaves its way round the length of a
   tree-trunk,
or else an octopus shooting all its tentacles out
to pounce on its prey and maintain its grip in the depths
   of the sea.

Outwardly appearing to be the victim and the weaker party in
each of these similes (the snake is the eagle's prey, the ivy far
more fragile and tender than the oak), the very real danger that
Salmacis poses to Hermaphroditus and his virginity is finally
revealed in the image of the octopus: here is a rape achieved by
enclosure rather than penetration. Finally, as the insatiable
Salmacis prays that they may stay physically joined this way
forever, the gods grant her prayer – interpreting it literally – and
the bodies of man and woman merge together in metamorph-
osis, as Hermaphroditus becomes the first hermaphrodite,
cursing the pool that had unmanned him to so weaken every
man that should touch its waters ever after.

It is left unclear how we should respond to this dark tale
of sexual violence perpetrated by a woman, told by a female
narrator to an internal audience of 'spinster' women. Indeed,
we have only Bacchus' response to the hubristic Minyeides to
guide us in an appropriate 'reading' of their strange story-telling:
he turns the threads of their loom into ivy and vine, and turns
the sisters themselves into shrivelled, squeaking bats (4.389–415);
hardly a ringing endorsement for female poetic endeavour.

Ino and Athamas (4.416–562)

The divine power of Bacchus having been firmly established,
Ovid takes up the role of principal narrator again, returning us to
Thebes and to Cadmus' ill-fated family. Playing upon parallels
between the stories of Rome's own legendary foundation and
that of Thebes, he focuses upon Juno's relentless hostility towards
the new race, echoing her part in Virgil's *Aeneid* and transforming
familiar elements of Virgil's epic to his own ends. In the *Aeneid,*
Juno's hostility towards Rome was rooted in her love for Carthage
and for its queen Dido, cruelly abandoned by Aeneas on his path

to Rome and glory. In book 4 of the *Metamorphoses*, Juno's hostility towards Thebes is coloured by her petty jealousy of Semele and the fact that her illegitimate son by Jupiter (Bacchus) is now universally worshipped as a god.[56] Recapping Bacchus' achievements as previously narrated in the *Metamorphoses* (the transformation of the Maeonian sailors, the death of Pentheus, and the metamorphosis of the Minyeides), she swears to out-do Bacchus in the punishment of mortals – selecting for her principal victims two entirely innocent characters, Semele's sister and brother-in-law, Ino and Athamas.

Borrowing freely from Virgil's *Aeneid*, Ovid sends Juno on a mini epic adventure down to the underworld to recruit the hellish Fury Tisiphone to drive Ino and Athamas mad. The grotesque Tisiphone is quick to do Juno's bidding and infects the couple with terror and madness. Thus poisoned, Athamas, believing his wife to be a lioness, his children her cubs, sets out on a crazed hunt for his own family, murdering his baby son in a grisly repetition of the death of Pentheus – although here the innocence of those involved is highlighted by the child laughing and reaching out little hands to his father in the instant before Athamas snatches him from his mother's arms and dashes his head against a rock (4.515–19). As Juno laughs, Ino flees with her second child, leaping from a cliff into the sea, where Venus intervenes and persuades Neptune to grant them immortality. Meanwhile, Ino's companions, who come running after her, are transformed by Juno into sea birds or cliff top rocks – to stand as monuments to her cruelty (4.550). Indeed, Juno's savage cruelty reaches profound new depths in this narrative and although Bacchus has so far been presented as one of the more humane Olympians, his failure to do anything to protect his loyal followers – including his own foster-mother – reminds us that in the world of the *Metamorphoses* the gods follow their own codes of ethical behaviour.

Cadmus and Harmonia (4.563–603)

We now follow the theme of divine anger back to Cadmus to see the fulfilment of the prophecy that he would end his days in the form of a snake. Indeed, Cadmus' story ends back where it began, with he and his wife fleeing the city where they had seen such tragedy and grief to live in exile. Reviewing his early troubles, Cadmus realizes that the snake he speared when he first came from Sidon was a sacred snake and that the troubles afflicting his family ever since have all been part of the gods' vengeance for an unwitting crime. He offers to live in the form of a serpent, and finds first himself and then his wife Harmonia transformed. So ends Ovid's Theban cycle.

Perseus (4.604–803)

But, of course, Ovid's *carmen perpetuum* continues and the narrative moves on – albeit somewhat awkwardly – to introduce the unrelated epic hero Perseus and his adventures; although, the motif of looking at dangerous things arguably continues here too. The transition is not one of Ovid's best: Cadmus and Harmonia continue to be proud of their divine grandson, but one man, Acrisius, denies that Bacchus is the true son of Jupiter, just as he denies that Perseus is Jupiter's son . . . (4.604–14). The abrupt transition does at least allow Ovid to begin his tale of Perseus in true epic fashion *in medias res* – in the middle of things – with Perseus flying over the earth with Medusa's already severed head, bloody drops transforming into deadly serpents as they land in the desert sand below (4.614–20). But it soon becomes clear that Ovid has already transformed the character of Perseus: this familiar epic hero has been softened and will here be concerned less with weapons (*arma*) than with love (*amor*).

Perseus is the perfect hero for Ovid's cinematic narrative style, his magic winged shoes allowing Ovid to give his readers a long aerial tracking shot focalized through the flying hero's point of view as he arrives now at the edge of the world and the lands ruled by Atlas (4.621–30). After a brief and somewhat unsatisfying encounter with Atlas, who Perseus turns into stone using the magic powers of the gorgon's head, we move on. Flying over Ethiopia with Perseus we see a maiden in distress: Andromeda, tied to a rock as a sacrifice (and a meal) for a sea monster. At the first sight of her statue-like beauty Perseus falls in love, and with a brilliant flash of Ovidian humour, almost out of the sky, as – dumbstruck by this vision of helpless, modest, loveliness – he forgets to flap his wings (4.672–7). This comedic and distinctly un-heroic tone continues as Ovid gives an account of Perseus' daring rescue. With the sea monster fast approaching, Perseus takes time out to introduce himself to Andromeda's parents and then to bargain with them for her hand in marriage (4.685–705). Forgetting his most obvious weapon (the gorgon's head), he fights the monster with his famous curved sword, but his wings become drenched with sea spray and the hero is eventually forced to finish off the beast on foot – literally brought down to earth in Ovid's account of this famous adventure.

The sea monster dead, Perseus is feted as a hero and saviour, but Ovid momentarily turns away from the celebrations to offer us an absurdly trivial yet charming background detail concerning Perseus' care of the gorgon's head – and with it an amusing aetiological explanation for the hardness of coral. So that the head might not be bruised on the hard sand, Perseus – somewhat unnecessarily one might think – places a pillow of soft leaves and seaweed under it. The foliage instantly turns to stone, delighting the sea nymphs who come ashore to play with this miraculous thing, and who throw the stony bits into the sea as they play – creating coral (4.741–52).

Celebrations turn into wedding celebrations, and finally Perseus is asked to tell the story of how he came to win the gorgon's head. Ignoring the opportunity to elaborate upon another of Perseus' great adventures, Ovid passes quickly over the details of this well-known backstory, denying it any sense of excitement or suspense by narrating it in indirect speech (4.772–90). He then effectively interrupts Perseus in the midst of his epic narrative to tell (what is, for Ovid) the more interesting and less well-known tale of how Medusa gained her snaky hair. Here he reveals that Medusa, the terrifying gorgon, had once been a great beauty, famed for her lovely hair, that Neptune had raped her in the temple of Minerva, that the goddess had turned away and hidden her eyes behind her aegis, before punishing Medusa for the sacrilege *she* had suffered, turning the girl's beautiful hair into ugly snakes (4.793–803). In the world of the *Metamorphoses* the gods follow their own moral codes – as we have seen. What is particularly significant here, however, is the way in which Medusa is treated by Ovid. In this story, the gorgon responsible for turning so many others into stone has herself been transformed. She has been made beautiful rather than terrible, made a victim rather than a monster, made pitiable rather than fearful, through Ovid's own powers of metamorphosis.[57]

Discussion points and questions
1. To what extent can the inset narrative of the Minyeides be seen as a miniature version of the *Metamorphoses* itself?
2. How does the story of Ino and Athamas revisit and review the stories narrated in books 3 and 4?
3. How – and why – are Perseus and Medusa transformed in Ovid's poem?

Book Five

Perseus (continued) (5.1–249)

While Perseus is telling his wedding guests the story of Medusa's transformation, trouble is brewing and the start of book 5 quickly moves the focus of the poem from *amor* back to *arma*. Before her marriage to Perseus, Andromeda had already been betrothed to her uncle Phineus, it turns out, and he now arrives to avenge his loss, bringing a small army with him. The stage is thus set for an epic battle, reminiscent both of the fight between Odysseus and the suitors in Homer's *Odyssey* and of the conflict between Aeneas and Turnus in Virgil's *Aeneid* – both of which famous clashes were occasioned, of course, by rivalry for the hand of a woman. In the bloody battle described in vivid detail here, Ovid allows Perseus to take part in an *aristeia* or set-piece fight-scene involving the brutal slaying of Phineus' many men. So, with gruesome description, spears strike men full in the face, splattering tables with blood (5.38–40); two best friends, both comrades and lovers (Ovid's substitutes for Virgil's Nisus and Euryalus), are dispatched in swift succession – one with a bone-splintering blow to the face from a wedding torch, and the other with a disembowelling hook from Perseus' famous curved sword (5.47–73); men slip and fall on the blood-drenched floor (5.74–8); they are forced to tread on the bodies of the dying as they fight (5.88); fatal wounds to the face, throat, and groin abound as Perseus heroically takes on a thousand men single-handedly; and through all of this bloody carnage, Perseus remains unscathed, protected like any epic hero worth the name by the divine aid of his sister Pallas Minerva (both have Jupiter as a father). What is more, nobly unwilling to use his secret weapon, Perseus waits until the enemy army are at the point of overwhelming his strength (*virtutem* – 5.177) before picking up the gorgon's head and turning the last 200 of the enemy into stone statues – including Phineus himself, who is frozen forever in the cringing act of supplication (5.210–35).

Ovid's representation of this epic blood-bath, however, is hard to read – in several ways. He uses the language and martial tropes familiar from Homeric and Virgilian epic to present an exciting, if repellent, battle scene in which one man single-handedly defeats an entire army without suffering so much as a scratch. Is this scene unambiguous evidence, then, that Ovid can write epic poetry? That he can take on Homer and Virgil at their own epic game and come out on top? Or has he simply presented us here with a parody of epic conventions and epic characters, transforming Perseus into Aeneas, Phineus into Turnus and Andromache into Lavinia? For, in describing the massacre in such gory detail, and in stacking the odds against his hero so highly, he renders the whole epic enterprise incredible and ridiculous.[58]

Minerva and the Muses (5.250–345)[59]

After the metamorphic conclusion to this battle Ovid next moves on to a very different kind of 'battle': different, at least, in external *forma* but essentially the same in its ongoing concern with storytelling and poetry. Indeed, just as Ovid had emphasized the essential and elemental influence of *amor* in Perseus' epic story, so the Muses of Poetry themselves will now demonstrate the universal power of Venus, Cupid and love, in a mini-epic tale of their own.

Having successfully helped her brother to defeat Phineus and his men, Minerva now flies off for a tour of the region, landing on Mount Helicon to see the fountain Hippocrene, newly created by a stroke of Pegasus' hoof, and to admire the *locus amoenus* (5. 264–6) that is the home of the nine Muses. But as the readers of Ovid's poem are by now all too aware, however beautiful it may be, a *locus amoenus* is not a place of safety, and the Muses tell Minerva of a recent rape attempt made against them by the godless tyrant Pyreneus which they only escaped by 'taking flight' (5.288) – that is, by running away, and not necessarily (as some readers have assumed) by growing wings and *flying* away. This allusion to wings, however, effectively pre-empts the sound of beating wings that now heralds the arrival of the nine daughters of Pierus – once women, now chattering magpies (5.299) – who were turned into birds in punishment for daring to challenge the nine Muses (who they echo in several respects) to a story-telling contest. Indeed, Ovid here deliberately blurs the differences between the Muses and the daughters of Pierus, assimilating the two groups of women by giving one set wings through metaphor, the other wings through metamorphosis, and allowing both the right to claim the name of Pierides – the daughters of Pierus, a cult name often given to the Muses themselves.

Since it is one of the Muses who then gives us an account of the competition – which she describes significantly as a 'battle of voices' (*proelia voce* – 5.307) judged by the local nymphs – we anticipate a degree of bias in her subsequent description of the Pierides' swollen pride and arrogant challenge to the Muses' own poetic prowess. It comes as little surprise, too, that her summary of the Pierides' opening song in the competition is a dull rehearsal of the ancient battle between gods and giants (a precursor to the battle between Pierides and Muses perhaps?), a conventional gigantomachy made interesting only by the Pierides' novel – and potentially blasphemous – claim that the giants had so terrified the gods in this epic battle, that they had been forced to hide themselves in Egypt, taking on the animal forms of traditional Egyptian deities (5.319–31).

Having covered her rival's song in a perfunctory 13 lines of reported speech, the Muse then offers Minerva the opportunity to hear an exact reproduction of the song offered in response, a verbatim miniature epic that takes up the next 320 lines of the poem in an extended inset narrative, a story within a story – containing within it further inset stories, creating the same narrative 'Russian doll' effect we last saw in book 2 (2.531–632).[60]

Calliope's Song (5.346–678)

The Muse Calliope's song is a complex – some might say chaotic – narrative that retells the story of Proserpina's rape by Dis (Pluto), god of the underworld, and her mother's frantic search for her lost daughter, incorporating a variety of secondary stories of metamorphosis along the way: the nymph Cyane into a pool (5.409–37); a cheeky boy into a gecko (5.451–61); the tattle-tale Ascalaphus into a screech owl (5.538–50); the Sirens into birds (5.551–563); the nymph Arethusa into a sacred spring (5.572–641); and the savage king Lyncus into a lynx (5.642–61). Critics of Calliope's song claim that the Muse is a second-rate story-teller, who cannot control her material and is too easily sidetracked by all the irrelevant sub-stories which distract her – and us – from the main narrative concerning Ceres and her daughter. Certainly, Calliope's narrative is convoluted and multifaceted, but so too is the *Metamorphoses* itself. Certainly, we have been primed to see Ovid's internal narrators as flawed story-tellers, vying with Ovid the artist in a metapoetic 'battle of voices' (*proelia voce*), but as the Muse of poetry Calliope is a worthy opponent, not only of the Pierides but of Ovid himself.[61]

Indeed, one of the most significant aspects of Calliope's song is the way in which her story-telling also serves as a kind of critical commentary upon Ovid's own *Metamorphoses*. So, she opens her narrative, after a short invocation to the goddess Ceres, by correcting the blasphemous Pierides' version of the gigantomachy that we have just heard: whereas the Pierid sister had emphasized the heroism of the giant Typhoeus, whose might had forced the gods themselves into flight, Calliope sets the story straight by telling of Typhoeus' subsequent defeat by the gods and his imprisonment under the mountains of Sicily – where his continued fury accounts for Sicily's volcanic, earthquake-prone landscape (5.346–58). This establishes Calliope's role as a poet who, like Ovid, sees and tells things differently – who offers alter-native perspectives and new readings of familiar narratives, including those (like the gigantomachy) that we have heard told (and re-told) in the *Metamorphoses*. Like Ovid, the Muse also seems to favour aetiological – Callimachean-style – poetry, and her opening aetiological account of Sicily's unstable geology provides a neat transition in her mini-epic *carmen perpetuum* into an appropriately novel retelling of the well-known story of Pluto's rape of Proserpina as the cause for Ceres' neglect of her nurturing duties on earth for six months of each year.[62]

Pluto (or Dis) fears for the foundations of his underworld kingdom after Typhoeus' violent resistance to his incarceration, so – like Jupiter after the great fire of book 2 (2.401–5) – he sets out upon an inspection tour of his underground realm. Here, Ovid – through his internal narrator Calliope – transforms the familiar shape of this story, as both we and his Augustan audience recognize it. Introducing an entirely new dimension and agency to the well-known story, Ovid has Venus herself deciding to extend her own powers of dominion by causing Dis to fall in love with the virgin Proserpina, so taking the underworld into her empire – a plan replete with political resonance for Ovid's Augustan audience who would have seen an obvious correlation between Venus' imperialist programme and that of her descendant, Augustus.[63] Cupid duly fires an arrow and strikes Dis in the heart – offering Dis an excuse, of sorts, for the rape of Proserpina that swiftly follows.

Calliope's representation of this rape is, indeed, both more complex and more troubling than that of any of the other rapes and attempted rapes we have so far witnessed in the *Metamorphoses*. In the first place, Proserpina's abduction from the lovely (and familiar) *locus amoenus,* in which she is first seen picking flowers with her companions, is swift and terrifying: in the same instant, Calliope tells her audience, Dis sees the girl, desires her, and carries her away (5.395) as she screams in terror for her mother. Secondly, Calliope takes pains to emphasize that this is not the everyday rape of a nymph by an amorous god: Dis himself is governed by the powerful forces of *amor* (5.396) and Proserpina is both a goddess and a child, who cries out for her mother, and who, in her childish innocence, weeps for the loss of flowers she has been picking as they fall from her lap.[64]

What follows is equally striking. As if unwilling to recount the actual rape of this child, Calliope instead describes a surrogate rape – that of Dis' assault and penetration of the water nymph Cyane, who tries to prevent the abduction by physically placing her body in the way of Dis' chariot. In anger at her interference, Dis strikes her with a phallic blow from his royal sceptre (5.420–3) and carries on down to the underworld straight *through* her, leaving a grief-stricken Cyane to melt into a pool of her own tears (5.425–37). When Proserpina's mother, the grieving Ceres who has been searching across the world for her lost daughter, finally comes across Cyane, the nymph has entirely lost her human shape and can no longer speak or tell what she has witnessed. But floating upon the surface of her transformed waters is Proserpina's girdle, and upon seeing this Ceres is overcome by a fresh wave of grief, blighting the fertility of the earth in her distress and frustration (5.462–86). Ceres has herself been transformed – humanized, we might say – from a goddess into a grieving mother, devastated by the loss of her child.

Calliope's narrative now takes a strange twist, as another river nymph appears to speak to Ceres, apparently a surrogate for the silenced Cyane. The nymph Arethusa describes how she has seen Proserpina with her own eyes, still sad and terrified, but established now as Dis' wife and queen of the underworld (5.487–508): unlike the other rapists of the poem, Dis intended Proserpina to be his consort, not simply to rape her and discard her, it seems – a detail that Jupiter confirms when he intervenes and permits Proserpina to be returned to her mother for six months of each year (5.512–32).

With Ceres now happily reunited with her daughter, Arethusa offers a belated account of her own escape from an earlier attempted rape by the river god Alpheus (5.577–641). Arethusa's first-person account of her own terrified struggles to fight off the shape-shifting Alpheus offers Ceres (and us) an empathetic insight into Proserpina's experiences – a survivor's testimony, unique among the many rape victims of the *Metamorphoses,* that makes a new perspective available from which to review the experiences of Daphne, Syrinx, Io, Callisto, *et al.* Indeed, we might even see in Calliope's song a feminist perspective, in which the bond between women – and particularly between mothers and daughters – is celebrated, and in which women try to help and protect one another, not least of all through the stories they tell each other.[65] It is perhaps unsurprising, then, that the internal audience of nymphs who were established as the judges of this 'battle of voices' should unanimously vote Calliope as the victor (5.663f), and that the talkative Pierides (who turn out to be sore losers) should be punished at the end of this book by the curtailing of their uncontrollable (and stereotypically feminine?) passion for talk (5.678). Story telling is a serious business in the world of the *Metamorphoses.*

Discussion points and questions
1. To what extent does Ovid's account of Perseus' battle with Phineus offer a parody of epic conventions and epic characters?
2. What roles do *amor* (love) and *arma* (weapons) play in book 5?
3. How does the account of Proserpina's rape differ from other rape narratives described in the *Metamorphoses*?
4. Is it legitimate to describe Calliope's song as presenting a feminist point of view?

3.2 BOOKS SIX TO TEN

Book Six

Arachne (6.1–145)

Like its predecessor, book 6 offers particular riches for the reader who has so far followed Ovid's *carmen perpetuum* as a continuous narrative yarn – not least of all because Ovid now makes literal the idea of a poem as something that is spun out and woven like a thread, transforming text into textile and, of course, textile into text. Like Vladimir Nabokov, who wrote in his autobiography (*Speak Memory*) that, 'I like to fold my magic carpet, after use, in such a way as to superimpose one part of the pattern upon another', here we can see Ovid folding his literary tapestry so that stories from the first five books of the *Metamorphoses* overlap with and touch upon this sixth part – notably the stories of gods, rapes, and animal metamorphoses told in the first books, but also the more recent stories of blasphemy and punishment concerning the Minyeides and Pierides.

Inspired, perhaps, by the 'battle of voices' that she has just heard in book 5, Minerva decides to set up a competition of her own, to establish once and for all her divine supremacy in spinning and weaving and to punish the blasphemous arrogance of the low-born mortal Arachne who claims that *her* skills surpass those of the goddess. So, as if engaging in an epic duel, the two women set up their looms and set their skilled (*docta* – 6.60) fingers to work – their skill in blending different coloured threads into a narrative pattern in their textiles (*texta*) reminding us of Ovid's own expertise in weaving together the different stories that make up the text (*textum*) of the *Metamorphoses*.[1]

In an extended two-part ecphrasis, Ovid first depicts Minerva's tapestry (described in competitive, even combative, language as her *argumentum* – 6.69). At the centre of her work, she has chosen to depict an old story telling of her personal victory in a previous dispute with Neptune for control over Athens. Twelve gods, hierarchically ordered, with Jupiter at their centre, look on. As if this were not enough of a salutary warning to her mortal rival in the current dispute, the goddess adds to the corners of her tapestry four smaller scenes depicting the metamorphoses of mortals who have dared to challenge the gods in other minor conflicts. The tapestry is finished off with a neat border of olive branches from Minerva's own sacred tree. As William Anderson suggests, 'the composition of the goddess' work is flawlessly Classical, perfectly centred, balanced, and framed, highly moral and didactic in content.'[2] It is also a piece of highly stylized propaganda worthy of Augustus himself: a fact alluded to by Ovid's suggestive description of Minerva's deities and, by extension, her tapestry as a whole, as *augusta* (6.73).

Arachne's tapestry also depicts a series of metamorphoses. But, in contrast to Minerva's restrained 'Augustan' style, Arachne's style is more 'Ovidian'. In an ordered chaos, recalling books 1–5 of the *Metamorphoses,* she vividly depicts more than twenty scenes of women raped by gods in various metamorphic disguises (among them Europa, Leda, Alcmena, and Danae), edging her work with a border of ivy and flowers (6.103–128). The work is perfect – if potentially blasphemous in its depiction of so many adulterous gods – and the jealous goddess destroys it. As Arachne attempts to hang herself to escape Minerva's wrath, the goddess transforms her into a spider – in which form she ever after continues to spin and weave (6.145).

But it is not clear whether this metamorphosis serves as a punishment or a release for Arachne. The real punishment for her arrogant *hubris* would seem to be the jealous destruction of her marvellous tapestry by an arrogant deity. This has tempted generations of readers to see in Arachne a parallel with Ovid himself, as another talented – and provocative – artist who suffers at the hands of an arrogant authority figure. Indeed, the numerous artists who appear in the *Metamorphoses* are invariably represented as suffering in some way and, given the self-reflexive character of the poem, it is hard *not* to see Arachne's tale as

Sarah Brown does, as 'a kind of commentary on Ovid's own art' and the tales that he weaves together in this poem.[3]

Niobe (6.146–312)

Where Arachne was justifiably proud of her art, her friend Niobe boasts merely of her fertility – swiftly earning the gods' displeasure. Niobe was well-known to Ovid's Augustan audience as the epitome of grieving mother, and her story would have been familiar to them from its retelling in numerous Greek tragedies. Yet Ovid appears to take care to present his Niobe in a new light, stressing her extraordinary arrogance (even when Latona has savagely slaughtered her seven sons, Niobe continues to brag that she *still* has more children than the goddess – 6.285), and allowing us to feel little real sympathy for her. Indeed, as she sits amidst the lifeless bodies of her dead children and husband in stony silence, it is not Niobe (soon to be transformed into rock) but they – innocents punished for the blasphemous impiety of their mother – who really command our sympathies here.

The Lycian Peasants (6.313–81)

The following tale tests our sympathies further still, as an unnamed narrator tells the story of how Latona once turned a rabble of rustics into frogs. But the full significance of the tale only emerges when it is read in sequence with the story of Niobe as part of the patterned magic carpet that is Ovid's *carmen perpetuum*. Here Latona, whom we have just seen orchestrating the slaughter of fourteen children just to punish their boastful mother, has been driven into exile by a spiteful Juno. Parched with thirst, her breast milk dried up and her babies hungry, Latona tries to drink from a village pond but is harassed by an unsympathetic crowd of yokels – who she turns into frogs. Here Latona is figured as a victim worthy of our compassion and the obnoxious Lycian peasants who deny her and her children a drink clearly deserve their punishment. Indeed, their metamorphosis into jumping, croaking frogs hardly seems harsh enough. Yet, as an epilogue to the tale of Niobe, this short story is hard to read, challenging as it does easy assumptions about right(s) and wrong(s), and offering a salient reminder to all Ovid's readers of the important role played by context in shaping meaning.

Marsyas (6.382–400)

The next story presents us with a similar challenge and again returns to the theme of a contest between two artists – although here, as if bored with the contest motif already, Ovid leaves out the details and framing context of the competition and focuses instead upon the grisly punishment that ensues.[4] In this gruesome tale, the satyr Marsyas is skinned alive for challenging Apollo in a musical competition and losing: another artist in the *Metamorphoses* who is punished for his art.

Readers and critics are virtually unanimous in their negative responses to this short episode: Kenney's description of the episode as '(t)he ultimate in gruesome wit'[5] is typical, and reflects a tendency amongst readers and critics of this brief tale to focus upon the surface detail of the narrative and not to look beneath its superficial horror and ugliness. Karl Galinsky claims that:[6]

> Ovid revels in the graphic detail of Marsyas' torture and presents it almost as an anatomy lesson . . . [Ovid's] interest in the physical detail takes precedence over any interest in the suffering Marsyas. Ovid involves the reader more and more: the description progresses from the past tense to the present tense, from the third person to the second person. But it is only the gory details that are brought closer to us, and not the agony of Marsyas.

Certainly, Ovid's detailed description of Marsyas' flaying is the most gruesome scene that we have yet witnessed in the poem, but the pastoral lament which follows and which takes up almost half of this narrative offers a response to this story that suggests Marsyas is what you make of him: despite Ovid's gory description of Marsyas as 'one great wound' (6.388), there is more to Marsyas than his agony. The country people, dryads, fauns, satyrs, nymphs and shepherds who witness or hear his story (6.392–95) weep in response, and it is their tears rather than Marsyas' blood that are transformed into the clear river that takes on the name 'Marsyas'. Their reception and reading of the Marsyas story effectively transforms the satyr into the river that bears his name and so Marsyas – *despite* his challenge to authority and *because* of his resultant punishment – gains fame and immortality by his art. In this context, how can we – or Ovid – fail to sympathize with Marsyas?[7]

Tereus, Procne, Philomela (6.401–674)

The group of Lycian storytellers who have been prompted by Niobe's tragedy to tell each other stories of other ancient blasphemies now bring us back to the present (6.401). Still mourning the loss of their king and his children, they blame Niobe for bringing disaster upon her family (6.402f) – all except for her brother Pelops who, weeping for his sister's tragedy, tells a story of his own. His father Tantalus had once tried to test the omniscience of the gods by cutting up his son into pieces and attempting to feed him to them. When the gods tried to put the child back together again, they found one piece of his shoulder missing but replaced it with a piece of ivory. As William Anderson observes, here 'Ovid is less interested in Tantalus' blasphemy than in the marvellous restoration of Pelops' fragments to a living body' – a perfect analogue to the marvellous joining of narrative fragments that Ovid achieves in his *Metamorphoses*, perhaps.[8]

This extended transition piece (at 22 lines, a larger fragment of the poem than the whole of the Marsyas story) continues, with an epic-style catalogue listing all the cities which sent delegates to express their sympathy for Niobe's tragedy. And, in a transitional device we recognize from book 1 (1.577f) where Daphne's grieving father is visited by all the river gods but one, all the cities but one send their condolences to Thebes: Athens does not come for she is at war. Her ally in this conflict is Thrace and in gratitude for the support of the Thracian king Tereus, Pandion, king of Athens, cements the alliance with marriage to his daughter Procne. So, Ovid completes his narrative transition into the tragedy of Tereus, Procne, and Philomela – a transition that also marks a key shift in the narrative focus of the poem, as we leave behind the cruel, chaotic world of gods, nymphs, and satyrs and move into the cruel, chaotic world of mortal men, women, and children.

Based on a lost tragedy by Sophocles, and replete with dramatic overtones, the story of Tereus, Procne, and Philomela is one of the most shocking and gruesome in the whole of Ovid's poem, involving in one tale the crimes of incest, rape, mutilation, child-murder, and cannibalism.[9] Ovid sets the stage for his horror story with the ill-omened wedding of Tereus and Procne, where the Furies light the ceremony with bridal torches stolen from a funeral (6.428–38). After five years of marriage and the birth of a son, Itys, Procne sends Tereus to escort her beloved sister Philomela back to Thrace to visit her. But the moment he sees Philomela – as beautiful as any woodland nymph (6.453) – he is instantly inflamed with desire for her. Indeed, the nymph simile here foreshadows Philomela's fate as a victim of rape, just like the nymphs encountered in books 1–2 of the poem. Ovid uses exactly the same simile of dry leaves and grass catching fire here as he used in book 1 to describe Apollo's desire for the nymph Daphne (1.492–6; 6.455–7); the same image of predator and prey to describe his advances (1.505–7; 6.515–18, 6.527–30); and, as soon as he has Philomela safely on board his ship, Tereus rejoices with a cry of '*vicimus*' ('I have won!' – 6.513), echoing Salmacis' identical cry of triumph as she attempts to rape Hermaphroditus (4.356). But this is not one of Ovid's characteristic and controversial 'comic' rape narratives involving amorous gods and nymphs; Tereus' all too human cruelty shocks and appals us.

When his ship arrives in Thrace, Tereus drags Philomela off to a remote forest hut where he rapes her – an awful crime made all the more terrible by the familial bonds that connect them and make Tereus' rape of his sister-in-law incestuous. As she recovers and finds the words to curse him for his transgression and confusion of all social and natural laws – calling upon the gods (if there are any gods) to avenge her (6.533–48), he draws his sword to silence her, cutting out her tongue, which wriggles grotesquely at Philomela's feet (6.549–62).

Is this pornography, as some critics have claimed? Does it sadistically glorify the violent abuse and objectification of a woman's body? Or does it accurately and sympathetically represent the harrowing ordeal of rape and sexual assault, as others suggest – highlighting the sense of shame and enforced silence that so many victims experience?[10] Certainly Ovid's attention to gruesome detail in this scene, as in his graphic depiction of Marsyas' flaying, seems designed to shock and horrify his audience. And, there is something inherently disgusting and absurd in his image of Philomela's severed tongue wriggling across the floor towards her, just as there is an inappropriately playful pun in the notion of Philomela calling out to her father Pandion – literally (in Greek) to 'all the gods'. None of whom, of course, come to her aid.

Imprisoned in the forest hut for a year, her sister believing her to be dead, Philomela must save herself. So she weaves a tapestry telling her story and sends it secretly to her sister – although whether she uses images or words in her text(ile) Ovid does not say (6.571–80). Procne's first response upon reading the awful story is shocked silence, an empathetic parallel of her sister's own enforced silence (6.583). But Procne's desire for revenge against Tereus quickly effects a psychological transformation, and her behaviour soon changes to parallel that of Tereus rather than her sister – foreshadowing future horrors to come.[11] So, repeating Tereus' kidnap of Philomela (albeit in reverse and with kinder motives), Procne disguises herself and, under cover of a bacchanal celebration, rescues her sister, her actions described by Ovid as a kind of rape (*rapit raptae* – 6.598) as she literally 'takes the girl who has been taken'. Procne, inflamed with rage just as her husband had been inflamed with desire (6.609, 6.455), swears that, like him, she is prepared to commit any crime, however unspeakable. She considers castrating him with a sword (6.616f) – an option that would offer an appropriate analogue to Tereus' own crimes against Philomela (perhaps Ovid invites us to imagine Tereus' severed penis wriggling across the floor like Philomela's tongue). But upon seeing Itys and his likeness to his father, she decides upon a more unspeakable crime: she kills and butchers her infant son and, with Philomela's aid, cooks the boy's flesh in a kitchen that is 'running with blood' before feeding it to his father (6.636–51). And with an echo of the same black humour that had Philomela calling upon 'Pandion/ all the gods', Tereus calls for his son to join him in the feast – only for Procne to reply darkly: 'Itys is with you already – inside' (6.655). Philomela then joins the fun, throwing Itys' severed head into his father's face (the awful counterpart to her severed tongue) and the revenge – along with the tragic reversal of roles – is complete.

No gods have intervened at any stage to aid or punish any of the victims in this story, and the agency of the gods is again notably absent as Tereus draws his sword and sets out in pursuit of the two sisters. Instead, it is Ovid who draws the story to some kind of morally satisfying close as he transforms metaphor into metamorphosis, changing the fleeing women into birds: 'You could picture the fugitives' bodies suspended on wings. / And they *were* suspended on wings' (6.667f). One sister becomes a nightingale (considered in Greek myth to cry constantly for its children), the other a swallow – traces of the bloody murder they have committed still staining the plumage of both – and Tereus becomes a hoopoe, a sharp beak replacing his long sword (6.668–74). The characters have changed but their characteristics remain the same – much like Ovid's poem, in its own change of focus from the cruel world of gods to the cruel world of men.[12]

Boreas and Orithyia (6.675–721)

After the darkness of this human tragedy, book 6 appears to end on a somewhat lighter note, with a transitional story that allows Ovid to move seamlessly from Pandion's heartbreak at the loss of his daughters, through an account of his granddaughter Orithyia's rape by the Thracian Boreas (a 'lite' version of Tereus' rape of Philomela and a more conventional 'Ovidian' rape in the style of the opening books of the *Metamorphoses*), and finally on to the children of that union growing to manhood. These children then take their places aboard the Argo to set sail over the divide between books 6 and 7 in search of a golden fleece and adventure.

Discussion points and questions
1. How effective is the transition between the first part of the poem focusing on gods, and the start of the second part dealing with mortal men and women? Does Ovid maintain the continuity of his *carmen perpetuum*?
2. How does the motif of weaving link the stories narrated in book 6?
3. What is the significance of the related themes of silence and speech in book 6?

Book Seven

Medea and Jason (7.1–403)

And now (*iamque* – 7.1) we find ourselves sailing straight into book 7 and the heroic adventures of Jason and his Argonauts as Ovid's *carmen perpetuum* continues without a narrative break into the next book. But both Jason and the Argo quickly turn out to be merely the vehicles by which Ovid brings us his most memorable heroine – the witch Medea – whose story takes up almost half of this book. Medea's story would have been only too well-known by Ovid's Augustan audience. They would have been familiar with the adventures of this notorious *femme fatale* from Euripides' famous tragedy, from Apollonius' *Argonautica,* and – most recently – from Ovid's own pen: he had written a tragedy of his own entitled *Medea* (now lost), and had included her as a character in two of his *Heroides* (12 and 6). In the *Metamorphoses*, then, Ovid faces the challenge of making new (*nova*) his favourite mythical figure, of magically rejuvenating and transforming both her and her story.[13]

Ovid's key magical ingredient in effecting this transformation is *amor*. Thus, our first encounter with Medea (signposting the linear chronological treatment of her story that Ovid follows here) is her own first meeting with Jason, with whom she falls in love at first sight.[14] In the first dramatic soliloquy of the poem, Ovid allows Medea to reflect upon her feelings for this stranger, exploring for the first time in the *Metamorphoses* the psychology and pathology of *human* love (7.11–21) as Medea battles with her reason and conscience.[15] She finally decides to turn her back on love and to embrace instead duty, piety and chastity (7.72), but upon seeing Jason again her passion is reignited and her resolve broken. Indeed, Jason is so good looking, Ovid tells us, that we can hardly blame her for this (7.85) – or for using her magic to help Jason complete the impossible tasks that her father has set him (7.100–58: note Ovid's sarcastic authorial aside at this sign of Jason's 'bravery' (7.115–19), protected as he is by Medea's powerful herbs).[16]

Ovid has so far represented Medea as a complex, moral character, deserving of our sympathy. But our empathy abruptly ceases in the next phase of her narrative, as she undergoes a new metamorphosis and the sympathetic and innocent young girl in love seen in lines 7.7–158 is unexpectedly transformed into a monstrous witch, gathering herbs and casting spells to rejuvenate Jason's aged father (7.179–293) and tricking the daughters of Pelias into murdering their father (7.297–349). As Carole Newlands has observed: 'Like many of the metamorphosed characters in Ovid's *Metamorphoses* she has lost her human characteristics, but unlike them she has retained her physical form.'[17] Newlands suggests that Medea has been transformed not only into a witch, but into a one-dimensional character who necessarily fails to hold the reader's interest and sympathy in this second half of Ovid's retelling of her story. However, close reading suggests that Medea undergoes a secondary and more complex metamorphosis in identity, transformed from witch to poet. For, in a characteristically Ovidian play upon the double meaning of the Latin word *carmen* to signify both a magical spell and a poem, Medea's words and spells (*verbis et carmine* – 7.203) here reflect Ovid's own transformative poetics.[18] So, as Medea escapes punishment for the murder of Pelias by flying away in her dragon-drawn chariot, her journey seems to cast a magical influence upon the lands below, where miraculous transformations occur as she passes (7.351–90). Her flight thus provides Ovid with the opportunity to describe a continuous series of fifteen micro-metamorphoses, moving seamlessly from scene to scene almost as a cinematographer might, employing the same long aerial tracking shot that we saw in book 1 (1.566–85), and passing over Medea's most notorious history (the murder of her own children summarized here in just four lines: 7.394–7) as simply another part of this metamorphic flight sequence. Ovid, it seems, has himself fallen under Medea's spell.

Theseus and Aegeus (7.404–52)

Before the full impact of her crimes at Corinth can be realized, Medea is flying off in her magic chariot once more – now headed for Athens. Having poked fun at Aegeus (who was so hospitable that he not only welcomed Medea to Athens but married her as well), Ovid now transforms Medea into that most ancient proxy for the witch, the evil stepmother – the only metamorphosis we see in this bridging story. She attempts to poison Aegeus' son Theseus, but in the nick of time, Aegeus recognizes his lost son and dashes the drink from his hand, as Medea escapes in a whirlwind – never to be seen again.

Minos, Aeacus and the Plague at Aegina (7.453–660)

As Aegeus and his people celebrate Theseus' safe return with a drunken hymn honouring the brave hero's adventures and achievements, Ovid is quick to remind us that there is no such thing as pure, uncomplicated joy in the affairs of men (7.453f) and subtly shifts attention away from Theseus' happy homecoming to Aegeus' fears of imminent war with Minos. There follows an epic-style account of the Cretan king Minos' preparations for war, and his search for allies against Athens. He is successful in winning support from a catalogue of neighbouring states all around the Cyclades, but fails to bring the island of Aegina on side because of their long-standing treaty of friendship with Athens, to whom they now formally offer their allegiance. Aegina is not short of men of fighting age, but their faces are unfamiliar to the Athenian envoy Cephalus who arrives to affirm the alliance, and the king Aeacus tells him of the plague that had recently blighted his island.

The horror narrative that follows is as shocking as that in any modern movie. Aeacus offers a gruesomely detailed depiction of the disease, the death-throes of the dying, the zombie-like half-dead walking the streets, and the piles of rotting bodies that litter the island like fallen fruit (7.552–86). Minor details add to the horror and pathos of his story: the doctors are among the first to fall sick (7.561–3); the animal sacrifices fall dead at the altars before they can be offered to appease the gods (7.593–603); healthy people commit suicide to avoid the sickness of the plague (7.604f); there is no space left for graves, no wood left for funeral pyres, no one left to perform funeral rites, and no one left to mourn the dead (7.606–13). Finally, upon seeing a column of ants crawling beneath a sacred oak, Aeacus prays to Jupiter to be given just as many people to repopulate his empty island. That night he has a prophetic dream in which the ants grow larger and larger before standing up on two legs and taking on human form. In the morning, his dream becomes reality and a new race – the Myrmidons (from the Greek for 'ant') – are born, maintaining continuity through change in their ant-like qualities of thrift and military organisation (7.649–60). Ovid too maintains his own characteristic continuity through change in transforming a suitably epic-style narrative about preparations for war into an episode of metamorphosis.

Cephalus and Procris (7.661–865)

The feasting – a convenient backdrop to the storytelling that is Ovid's main concern here – continues, as the old man Aeacus now falls asleep and his son Phocus takes up the role of host to the Athenian envoys. He notices that Cephalus carries with him an unusual javelin and he asks him for the history of this weapon (7.661– 84). Cephalus' tearful response marks a decisive turning point in the style and content of book 7 as Cephalus responds with the sad story of how his wife, who gave him the spear, came to meet her untimely death. For, in contrast to the epic context of allies preparing for war in which it is narrated, Cephalus' story is markedly elegiac in both its style and content. Indeed, it is worth recalling here that although the elegiac metre in which Ovid usually writes was once associated with everything from mythology and warfare, to love poems and laments, elegy was originally associated with grave dedications and funeral epitaphs. In fact, the traditional etymology of the word was considered by the Roman love poets to derive from the Greek *e legein*, 'to cry woe', and Antimachus, the first Greek poet to produce a collection of elegiac love poetry, dedicated his book to the memory of his dead wife. It is perhaps only fitting, then, that Cephalus should weep as he begins the emphatically *elegiac* tale of his broken marriage and his broken heart.[19]

His story falls into two parts, separated by a purely inconsequential tale of metamorphosis in which Cephalus' favourite hunting dog and its prey are turned into marble statues midchase (7.758–93). Shortly after his wedding, Cephalus goes off on a hunting expedition where he is effectively 'raped' by the goddess Aurora. On his way home – no doubt influenced by his own 'infidelity' with Aurora – Cephalus becomes jealously convinced that Procris has also been unfaithful. He decides to test her, and entering his home in disguise, makes her an indecent proposal. When she hesitates, he reveals his true identity and unfairly accuses *her* of adultery (7.738–42). She flees to the hills to become a follower of Diana until Cephalus convinces her of his deep regret and she consents to come home, presenting him with her own hunting dog and javelin as a gift to cement their reconciliation. They live happily, but not ever after. Off hunting alone, once again, Cephalus seeks out the cooling breeze to refresh his tired body, calling upon it by name – *aura*. But his words betray him (7.808–23): an eavesdropper overhears Cephalus talking to what he imagines to be a lover named 'Aura' and tells Procris. Heartbroken at this evidence of her husband's infidelity, she follows him to the woods to spy upon him, whereupon Cephalus mistakes her for a wild animal and kills her with the famous javelin.

But is this tale a tragedy of misunderstanding or a comedy of errors? Is Procris mistaken in her belief that Cephalus is being unfaithful? And is Cephalus justified in claiming that his words have been misunderstood, that his wife (quite literally in this case) doesn't understand him? Superficially, Ovid has here given us a tragic love story, yet close reading of the narrative suggests that there is another side to this tale and that Cephalus' words really do give him away. The fact that Cephalus is so eager to leave his marriage bed and his wife at dawn each morning to go hunting alone is highly suggestive, as if he is inviting Aurora (the personification of the dawn) to repeat her sexual advances – a notion that is reinforced by the verbal echo of Aura in the name Aurora. What is more, he speaks of 'wooing' and 'wanting' (*petebatur* – 7.811) aura/Aura, of 'waiting' (*expectabam* – 7.812) and 'burning' (*urimur* – 7.815) for aura/Aura, employing language replete with erotic connotations that would have instantly signalled to Ovid's Augustan audience (as they suggest to Procris) that Cephalus' relationship with aura/Aura was not entirely innocent – and his narrative not entirely free of duplicity.[20]

Discussion points and questions
1. To what extent does Medea's character in the *Metamorphoses* reflect Ovid's own role as poet?
2. Assess the 'heroic' roles played by Jason and Theseus in book 7.
3. Is the story of Cephalus and Procris better described as a tragedy of misunderstanding or as a comedy of errors?

Book Eight
Scylla (8.1–151)

The start of book 8 sees the start of a new day in a narrative break that signals both continuity and change, as our attention turns from Cephalus and his allies back to Minos and his war against Athens. While Aeacus and Cephalus have been sharing their stories, Minos has been laying siege to Megara, a city ruled by king Nisus, famous for the magic lock of purple hair that grows upon his head and which guarantees the safe preservation of his power so long as it stays there. His daughter Scylla has fallen in love with Minos after watching him from the palace tower and we first encounter her in the throes of a passion that is described by Ovid as a kind of madness (8.35f) as she envies the javelin and reins that Minos holds – fantasizing that her body might take their place in his hands (8.36), imagining herself in the enemy camp, suggestively willing to open up both the city gates and herself to Minos (8.42). Indeed, the intensity of her desire is such that it comes as no surprise when, having considered the rights and wrongs of her passion (8.44–80) Scylla decides to sacrifice her father's magic lock of hair, her city, and herself to Minos – all in the name of *amor*.[21]

Scylla's situation and soliloquy clearly echoes that of Medea (7.1–403): both girls fall in love with an enemy, both commit an act of betrayal in helping their lovers to obtain a magical talisman (the purple lock and the golden fleece respectively), and both are ultimately themselves betrayed and deserted by the lovers for whom they have sacrificed so much. But whereas Ovid's Medea loses our sympathies as her story unfolds and an innocent girl becomes a murdering witch, Scylla's story follows a reverse pattern, transformed in the course of Ovid's narrative from a foul disgrace (*o nostri infamia saecli* – 8.97), and treacherous monster (*monstrum* – 8.100) into a sympathetic victim.[22] Ovid is clear that Scylla is guilty of an awful crime (*facinus* – 8.85); an enemy within her own walls, she has despoiled (*spoliat* – 8.86) her own father of an unspeakable war-trophy (*praeda . . . nefanda* – 8.86); and, having symbolically executed her father in cutting off his magic lock, betraying both her *pater* (father) and her *patria* (fatherland), she carries her gift to Minos in sinful hands (*scelerata* – 8.94). But although Scylla's betrayal is heinous, she herself is soon betrayed. It is, of course, the cutting rather than the possession of the magic lock that ensures Nisus' downfall and Minos has no need to reward Scylla for her help in effecting the fall of Megara: he condemns Scylla for her aid but takes advantage of it nonetheless, swiftly establishing his rule over the island and then sailing off without her.

Having lost everything, Scylla reacts to Minos' rejection just like one of the deserted women (*deserta* – 8.113) betrayed and abandoned by the men they have loved and helped in Ovid's elegiac *Heroides*. Now a naive victim of *amor* with whom we cannot help but sympathize, Scylla has undergone what Carole Newlands describes as a 'typological metamorphosis', a transformation of type – preparing us for the physical metamorphosis of form that will bring Scylla's story to a morally satisfying close.[23] Leaping into the sea to swim after Minos' ship, Scylla clings pathetically to the prow as she is transformed into a bird, the Ciris (from the Greek *keiro,* I cut) – identified forever by her act of betrayal – while her father, metamorphosed into an osprey, follows her in vengeful pursuit. Unlike Medea, the sky offers no hope of escape for Scylla.[24]

Daedalus and Icarus (8.152–235)

As part of her elegiac complaint at his heartless rejection of her love, Scylla accuses Minos of having been sired, not by Jupiter disguised, but by a *real* bull, and declares him to be the perfect soul-mate (8.131) to Pasiphae – she who had notoriously contrived to have sex with a bull and subsequently given birth to the monstrous half-man/half-beast hybrid known as the Minotaur. As Minos arrives back home, Ovid returns to this strange story (which he had already treated in his *Ars Amatoria* 1.290–327) as an introduction to the character of Daedalus – Minos' architect, who had designed for him a complex labyrinth in which to house the Minotaur.[25]

Daedalus is one of the many human artists who people the *Metamorphoses* and, as such, invites parallels with Ovid himself. Indeed, Ovid's linguistically complicated description of Daedalus' labyrinth could easily be used to describe the complex twists and turns of the narrative structure of the *Metamorphoses* itself, in which it could be said that he too has 'obscured all guiding marks and designed it / to cheat the eye with bewildering patterns of tortuous alleys' (8.160f), in order to house not one but many hybrid metamorphic monsters. So, after following one blind alley in which Ovid very briefly relates the well-known story of Ariadne and Theseus (8.169–182; already treated by Ovid in his *Heroides* 10), too well-known and too like the story of Scylla and Minos to merit a full retelling here, Ovid describes Daedalus' attempts to escape from the bonds imposed upon him by his patron.

Here it is tempting to read Ovid's representation of Minos as a repressive tyrant whose authority and rule governs all things – including the artist Daedalus and his work – as a commentary upon the authoritarian reputation of the emperor Augustus. And it is tempting too to see in Daedalus' frustration at his long exile and his longing to escape from Minos' power a corollary to Ovid's own experience as an artist whose wings were clipped by a disapproving emperor.[26]

With unmistakeable allusions to Ovid's own innovative artistic endeavour in crafting the *Metamorphoses*, then, Daedalus turns his mind to unknown arts (8.188), tying together feathers with twine and wax so skilfully that they look like the wings of real birds (8.195). Indeed, naturalism and the realistic imitation of nature as the epitome of artistic excellence is a *topos* that runs throughout the *Metamorphoses*. In this instance, we might expect such a metaphor to precede a metamorphosis, but there is in fact no physical transformation in this episode: Daedalus and his little son Icarus (who is seen here playing with his father's materials, messing about with feathers and wax, and getting in the artist's way) do not turn into birds. But, by putting on the wings that Daedalus has crafted and flying, they *do* change the laws of nature, overturning the proper order of things by trespassing into a zone properly reserved for gods and birds (recall the careful ordering of these zones in book 1). Underscoring the significance of this transgression to our understanding of the story, Daedalus famously stresses to his son the importance of steering a safe course as he flies, aiming neither too high nor too low but keeping to the middle part of the sky (8.203–8).[27]

However, the tragic outcome of this story is too well-known – to us as to Ovid's Augustan audience – to allow for real suspense, so Ovid colours his narrative instead with the pathos of dramatic irony, foreshadowing the tragedy to come: young Icarus plays with a ball of wax and feathers, unaware that he is playing with the very things that will shortly kill him (8.196); as the old man fits the wings to his only son's shoulders, his cheeks are wet with tears and his hands tremble with fear (8.210f); as he kisses Icarus farewell, Ovid reminds us that Daedalus now kisses his son for the very last time (8.211f); and, as the father instructs his son in the 'fatal arts' of flying (*damnosas . . . artes* – 8.215), Ovid heightens the pathos of the scene by likening him to the bird who nervously watches her fledglings try their wings as they leave the nest for the first time (8.213f) – a lovely simile (a poetic metamorphosis) that also serves as a reminder of the fatal flaw in Daedalus' plan, for birds may fly but men may not.[28]

Icarus, of course, ignores his father's advice and flies too high and too close to the heat of the sun before losing his wings and falling into the sea, calling his father's name as he falls. No physical metamorphosis occurs, but in an incidental, aetiological metamorphosis, the sea in which Icarus drowns and the island on which his father subsequently buries him (Icaria), both take their name from the boy – the change influenced perhaps by the heartbroken father (now no longer a father, as Ovid poignantly reminds us – 8.231) who calls the name 'Icarus' again and again.

Daedalus and Perdix (8.236–59)

As in the story of Phaethon (1.747–2.400), where a secondary tale of metamorphosis is tagged on as a postscript, Ovid adds a less well-known episode to this story, narrating in flashback the story of Perdix, Daedalus' nephew. Jealous of the boy's natural talent, Daedalus pushes him from the top of a tower where Minerva intervenes to turn the boy into a partridge – which, remembering the near-fatal fall, still avoids high places today and still retains the Latin name of *perdix* (8.255–9). This story obviously invites comparison and contrast with the story of Icarus' fall, to which it supplies a useful footnote, its structural similarities and dissimilarities highlighting important facets of the first tale – not least of all, the inherent dangers of artistic competition.[29] Moreover, as one of those occasions identified by Andrew Feldherr where 'the poet can be seen bending over backwards to slip a reference to metamorphosis into a story where it seems to have little place', this tale also draws our attention back to Ovid's own inventiveness and the complex twists and turns of his own ingenious narrative creation.[30]

Meleager and the Calydonian Boar (8.260–546)

The story of Daedalus has taken us along one of the many twisting paths of Ovid's labyrinthine poem, but we now find ourselves back on the main path of book 8, following Theseus as if he himself were Ariadne's guiding thread through Ovid's narrative maze. Theseus' fame, we learn, has spread far and wide after his slaying of the Minotaur and the people of Calydon now look to him to help them get rid of their own monster – sent by a disgruntled Diana to ravage the land and punish the people for neglecting her in their sacrifices. Thus, the Calydonians call for Theseus – along with every other hero worth the name, including their own local champion Meleager, so making Theseus' starring role in the subsequent story immediately redundant (8.270). Ovid gives us a suitably epic catalogue of names to emphasize the heroic nature of this adventure, but undermines his attempt somewhat by the inclusion in his list of the transsexual Caeneus (8.305), the hen-pecked Amphiaraus (8.317), and the tomboy Atalanta (8.317–23) with whom local boy Meleager instantly falls in love (8.324–8) – a romantic detail that Homer leaves out of his own famous account of the adventure in the *Iliad* (9.529–99).[31]

Indeed, the Calydonian Boar-hunt is a delightful mock-epic romp of which any twenty-first century Hollywood director could be proud. It has everything: horror and romance, comedy and tragedy, bloody violence and nail-biting suspense, an exquisitely delivered 'will-she/won't she' dilemma, a fire-breathing, man-killing, giant boar and a magic log. Ovid's highly comedic account of the hunt itself is particularly remarkable for the anti-heroic light in which it casts its famous 'heroes': Nestor pole-vaults into a tree to escape the boar's deadly tusks (8.365–8); clumsy Telemon trips on a tree root and falls on his face (8.378f); only Atalanta manages to wound the boar, to the shame of the other heroes who blush and blunder in response (8.380f); petty Ancaeus, trying to out-do the girl, is gored in the groin (8.391–402); mighty Theseus persuades his beloved Pirithous *against* a show of bravery with a camp cry of (literally) 'Keep back, darling!' (*procul . . . o me mihi carior* – 8.405); and Jason manages to spear an innocent dog (8.411–13). After this unparalleled and extended display of heroic incompetence, Meleager finally manages to hit the boar with his spear, at which the beast spins around, bubbling blood and foam, until it finally falls down dead. The love-struck (*captus amore* – 8.435) Meleager offers the spoils of his victory to Atalanta, to the affront of his fellow Calydonians who snatch back the trophy only to be killed themselves by an equally insulted and infuriated Meleager.[32]

The narrative now moves into its second act and the tone of Ovid's story-telling shifts, as Meleager's mother Althaea, celebrating her son's victory, finds herself mourning the death of her own brothers, her grief quickly transforming into anger when she learns how they have died. She takes from its hiding place an enchanted piece of charred wood which, it is said, the Fates decreed at Meleager's birth would share the same life-span as her child and faces up to her awful dilemma: can she – indeed, should she – end her son's life to avenge the death of her brothers? We have witnessed characters caught up in such moral and emotional quandaries before, but here Ovid offers perhaps his most sensitive and effective dramatization of such a situation. Employing a deft balance of narrative description and dramatic soliloquy, Ovid presents Althaea as torn in two by her competing emotions and between the duties of a mother and a sister (8. 463–77).[33]

She is, Ovid suggests paradoxically, impious in her piety (*inpietate pia est* – 8.477) as she calls upon the Eumenides (the goddesses of vengeance) to aid her and begs the ghosts of her dead brothers to forgive her maternal instincts and her (understandable) reluctance to end the life of her child. At last she takes action and throws the enchanted piece of wood into the fire, causing Meleager to feel himself burn as he endures a most agonising death (8.518). The whole of Calydon laments the tragic death of its hero: his mother commits suicide, his father is prostrated by grief, and his sisters (all except two who have future roles yet to play in Ovid's poem) are so distraught by the loss of their brother that Diana takes pity on them and turns them into guinea-hens (*meleagrides*) – a neat, if somewhat contrived, metamorphic conclusion to the narrative.

Achelous and Perimele (8.547–610)

After this diversion we find ourselves following Theseus once more as he makes his way back to Athens. On his journey he comes upon the swollen river and river-god Achelous (as Ovid once again exploits the conceit that a river-god may exist in both forms) who blocks his way. Achelous persuades Theseus to delay crossing his flooded current and to rest awhile in his home. As they wait, Achelous tells them the story of how he once punished a group of nymphs for failing to honour him in their religious rites by turning them into islands. He then adds, as a contrasting postscript, the story of Perimele, a girl he once 'loved' and raped before she too was transformed into an island.

Philemon and Baucis (8.611–724)

Achelous' two contrasting *factum mirabile* (miraculous tales – 8.611) highlight the way in which transformation serves both as a vehicle for punishment and for reward in the world of the *Metamorphoses* – a motif that is developed further in the following two stories. The first of these is apparently unique to Ovid and its position at the centre of the poem signals that this is a tale of particular significance. After the brutal rapes and tortured passions that represent *amor* in the first half of the poem, Ovid shows another side to love in this key section of the *Metamorphoses*, introducing a rare account of a happy marriage, set in a context of rustic simplicity that recalls his description of the golden age (1.89–112). One of Theseus' companions, Lelex tells the tale of an elderly couple whose generous hospitality towards the gods wins them a deserved reward – another rarity in the world of the *Metamorphoses*. For, when Jupiter and Mercury disguise themselves as mortals and seek a welcome on earth, they find every house but one closed to them. Only Philemon and Baucis in their humble cottage make the gods welcome, sharing with them a simple meal of cabbage and pork, olives, eggs, cheese, nuts, fruits, and honey: certainly not an epic feast, but a pretty full menu nonetheless.[34] When the old couple notice that their wine-bowl keeps magically refilling itself, they realize the divine status of their guests and with pious prayers try comically to catch a goose in order to make a proper sacrifice in their honour. At this point the gods remove the couple to safety while they flood the surrounding countryside and drown its impious, inhospitable inhabitants (compare the tale of Deucalion and Pyrrha at 1.313–415). But, as Philemon and Baucis look on, weeping for the sad fate of their neighbours, they see their little thatched cottage transformed into a temple of marble and gold, and are further amazed when Jupiter invites them to ask for any reward they wish.

In the story so far, Ovid (speaking through the narrator Lelex) has repeatedly stressed the mutual love and equal affection of Philemon and Baucis: they are of the same age (8.631), married in their youth (8.632), have grown old together in their humble home (8.633), and have lived there happily together without children or servants in an equal partnership (8.635f). It is no surprise then, that Philemon and Baucis consult each other before revealing their desire to become priests in service of the gods and to die at the same moment (8.706–10). Their wish is granted and, after years of faithful service, they find themselves turning into two trees, uttering the same words of farewell to each other as the bark closes over their lips.

Set against the other stories of love – and lust – in the poem, this is an extraordinarily beautiful tale in which a loving couple really are permitted to live together happily ever after. It is remarkable then, that no reference to love or *amor* appears anywhere in this narrative and that, although the mutual affection of this partnership is heavily stressed, the relationship between this pious old couple is decidedly asexual (echoing that between Deucalion and Pyrrha in book 1). So, the couple are childless; there are neither masters nor servants in their house – in elegiac terms, neither *domina* (mistress) nor *servus* (slave), so therefore no sexual relationship; the only sparks that the old woman Baucis ignites are used to boil the kettle rather than to inflame any passion; and their mattress and bed are clearly arranged for sitting rather than for sex. Is Ovid here accurately describing a long-term relationship where sexual *amor* has faded? Or is he perhaps suggesting that only a relationship without *amor* can be happy and long-lasting?[35]

Erysichthon (8.725–884)

As Theseus and his companions call for more miraculous stories (8.726f), the river-god Achelous takes over the narrative with the tale of the glutton Erysichthon. This tale offers a pointed contrast to that of Baucis and Philemon: where they were pious, Erysichthon is impious, scorning the gods; where they are turned into sacred trees, he takes an axe to a sacred tree (8.722f; 8.744f), brutally hacking at the wood and murdering the metamorphosed nymph within; where Baucis and Philemon feed the gods with humble abundance and are duly rewarded for their pious hospitality, Erysichthon is punished by the gods for his impiety with all-consuming hunger. At the goddess Ceres' bidding, the personified Hunger (*Fames*) breathes an insatiable craving for food into Erysichthon as he sleeps (8.796–808), so that he wakes to find that there is not enough food in the world to satisfy him: Achelous jokes to his own feasting guests that even when a feast is placed before him, Erysichthon calls for a feast (8.832).[36] Quickly bankrupted by his insatiable gluttony, Erysichthon sells the one thing left to him, his daughter, who uses her transformative powers to escape from each buyer (turning herself into a fisherman, a mare, a cow, a bird, a deer), but only so that her father can sell her again and so feed his voracious appetite – so voracious that the story ends with Erysichthon – horrifically and cannibalistically – eating himself: a dinner-party anecdote that is in decidedly poor taste.

Indeed, this story is itself something of a mixed platter, taking ingredients from a range of different Greek and Roman literary sources – including Callimachus' version of the Erysichthon story as told in his *Hymn to Demeter* – and reflecting mixed tastes in literary style. For, in choosing to place his retelling of this Callimachean tale into the mouth of Achelous, a swollen river in full flood, Ovid is self-consciously and 'tastelessly' transforming one of Callimachus' own stories into a literary form that most disgusted Callimachus himself: according to the principles of Callimachean poetics, the worst form of poetry was that which flowed in a muddy swollen torrent like the river Euphrates (or, here, the river Achelous) – that is, epic.[37] In epicizing Callimachus' Erysichthon, then, Ovid suggests that his own sophisticated Callimachean tastes must sometimes be 'cannibalized' to satisfy his voracious appetite for metapoetic play.

At the end of this tale, Achelous draws his audience's attention to the fact that at present he only has one horn (*cornua* – 8.882f), ending his story – and this book – with a groan as he recalls the loss: an apt response to this 'corny' conclusion, it seems. For, just as at the end of book 2 where the reader found herself along with Europa physically and figuratively holding on to Jupiter's *cornum* (2.874) as well as to the horn book rods (also known as *cornua*) around which books were rolled in antiquity, we again find ourselves faced with the end of another book, and another *cornum*. Indeed, as Achelous points to the horn missing from his forehead (*frontis* – 8.884) and complains that part of him is lacking, he indicates that a part of his story is also missing from this book roll. And so, we must look to book 9, where the river-god's narrative flows on uninterrupted, for the missing part of the story of Achelous' missing horn.

Discussion points and questions
1. To what extent is Scylla an elegiac heroine?
2. How might Ovid's description of Daedalus' labyrinth relate to the narrative structure of the *Metamorphoses* itself?
3. Is Ovid's account of the Calydonian Boar-hunt anti-epic?

Book Nine

Achelous and Hercules (9.1–97)

The start of book 9 continues this corny joke as Theseus asks Achelous to explain the cause of his mutilated forehead (*truncae . . . frontis* – 9.1f), punning upon the fact that the river-god's forehead *and* his narrative have both been mutilated or truncated by Ovid's division of books here. Achelous then obliges Theseus by telling the unflattering story of his fight with the mighty Hercules for the hand of Deianira. Achelous peppers his story with military vocabulary, but his account of the brawl proves to be as unheroic as Ovid's account of the Calydonian Boar hunt in book 8, with which it shares the same comedic, anti-epic tone and the same canonic pedigree. Achelous initially goads Hercules into a fight by taunting him about his heroic credentials, challenging him to admit to being either a bastard or a liar (9.24). He then engages him in a wrestling match which Achelous faithfully describes (or so he says: 9.5, 29, 53, 55), blow by blow and hold by hold – the river-god streaming now not with river water but with *sweat* (9.57f). Realising that Hercules is by far the stronger man, Achelous decides to make use of his metamorphic powers and slips out of Hercules' grip in the form of a snake. But Hercules famously strangled snakes while a mere babe in his cradle and now laughs (with us) as he strangles snaky Achelous. Achelous turns himself into a bull to escape Hercules' throttling grip, but the indomitable hero finally throws him to the ground, tearing off one of his horns in the process, and so mutilating the river-god's forehead (*trunca . . . fronte* – 9.86).

With a final flourish of bad taste, reminding us once more of the satirical flavour that has coloured books 8 and 9 so far, Achelous has one of his nymphs appear with his broken horn, now transformed into a 'horn of plenty' or cornucopia from which to offer his dinner-guests fruit to end their meal. Unsurprisingly, perhaps, his guests do not wait as planned for the flood-waters outside to recede and make an early departure the next morning, leaving Achelous to hide his shamed face beneath his own waves. As well he might.

Hercules and Nessus (9.98–133)

Ovid now picks up the narrative himself, to contrast Achelous' relatively painless encounter with Hercules in which he merely loses a horn, with that of the centaur Nessus who loses his life. Foreshadowing the deadly arrow that will kill him, Ovid describes how Nessus was first (figuratively) pierced in the back by one of Cupid's arrows (9.102) causing him to fall in love with Hercules' new bride Deianira as he meets the couple setting out from Calydon. Just like Theseus and the other heroes leaving Calydon after the boar hunt, Hercules finds his way blocked by a swollen river in full flood, which Nessus offers him help to cross. Swollen with his own heroic self-esteem, Hercules allows the centaur to help Deianira while he himself heroically plunges into the water and wades across to the opposite bank. So absorbed with himself and with defeating the forces of the river is Hercules that he fails to notice the centaur attempting to rape his wife. Hearing Deianira's cries, he slays Nessus with a poisoned arrow to the back (*terga sagitta* – 9.127; notice the repetition of the phrase from 9.102) as the centaur attempts to flee. But before he dies, the centaur swears that his death will not go un-avenged and he offers his cloak, soaked in poison and blood, as a gift to Deianira – pretending that it is a love charm (9.133). *Amor* has brought about the death of Nessus and will soon bring death to Hercules.

The Death of Hercules (9.134–272)

Ovid's narrative passes over the heroic deeds of mighty Hercules, as it had the adventures of Jason and Theseus, and moves straight to the great hero's unheroic death. Rumour (here personified as the goddess *Fama*) brings news to a distraught Deianira that her husband is in love with another woman. Deciding to send Nessus' love charm in the hope of rekindling her errant husband's passion, she unwittingly sends her husband a poisoned robe, and equally unwitting (*inscius* – 9.157), he puts it on.

With a tragic irony that reminds us of the dramatic tradition upon which Ovid draws in his restaging of Hercules' death here (notably Sophocles' *Trachiniae*), Ovid sets the scene in which Hercules puts on the cloak before an altar where, as the poison starts to burn into his flesh, the hero is burning incense to honour the gods. Ovid spares us few details of Hercules' agonising death, describing how his blood boiled, how his bones and sinews cracked and melted in the heat, like an animal sacrifice burned upon an altar. Indeed, as he burns, Hercules calls upon Juno to 'feast' upon his destruction (9.176), imagining that this final torment is another labour (*laboribus* – 9.180) inflicted by the goddess. Raging at (what he perceives as) the injustice of the gods, he lists his successes in the impossible labours set for him by Juno. But his catalogue of superhuman feats only serves to remind us that *amor* and a love charm have finally defeated this 'indomitable' hero.

As a temporary reprieve from this narrative of torment, Ovid introduces an incidental metamorphosis into the story: Hercules catches sight of Lichas, the messenger who brought him the poisoned cloak, and hurls him through the air, the cold air freezing and hardening all the moisture in Lichas' body as he flies, until he falls into the sea transformed into a human-shaped rock – which even now sailors call 'Lichas'. Lichas' swift death through icy metamorphosis (described in chilling scientific detail, 9.220–3) serves as an effective contrast to the drawn-out fiery death of Hercules, to whose agonies Ovid quickly (mid line) returns (9.229). With stoic disregard for his pain, Hercules hands his famous weapons over to his friend Philoctetes, builds himself a funeral pyre, spreads his legendary lionskin on top, puts down his iconic club as a pillow, and lays himself down upon them to await death – already psychologically transformed from the man who had earlier been conquered (*victa* – 9.164) by his agonising pain. Indeed, so impressive is this display of fortitude from the 'Earth's champion' (9.241) that even the gods take notice. Interpreting this rare show of solicitude from his fellow Olympians for his son as a tribute to himself, Jupiter reassures them – and us – that the hero who has conquered everything else in his life will also conquer death (9.250–5).

Hercules' death, then, will not be the end. The first transformation of its kind in the *Metamorphoses*, Hercules will undergo the ultimate metamorphosis, from man to god, so establishing a precedent for deification and apotheosis that will be followed in time not only by Rome's own greatest mythical hero Aeneas, but by its greatest leaders – Julius and Augustus Caesar. For, in his description of Hercules' apotheosis in which the hero dies only to take on an 'august majesty' (*augusta fieri* – 9.270) as he is reborn as a god, Ovid unambiguously foreshadows the future deification of Augustus, whose own apotheosis will mark the climactic end point and the ultimate transformation of the *Metamorphoses*.[38]

Alcmena and Galanthis (9.273–323)
The following story affirms the idea of Hercules' death and apotheosis as a rebirth, by going back in time to tell the tale of his *actual* birth. His mother Alcmena tells her daughter-in-law Iole how Juno, goddess of childbirth, had spitefully tried to prevent the birth of yet another of Jove's illegitimate children by crossing her legs and fingers, and so magically blocking Alcmena's delivery of the baby.[39] Her heroic labour (*labores* – 9.289), lasting seven days and seven nights, is deliberately represented as a corollary to Hercules' own famous labours, her agony in childbirth figured as the equivalent to his agonising death – both victims of Juno's jealousy – in one of Ovid's most persuasive and ingenious emphases upon female heroism.

Ovid concludes the story of Alcmena's 'epic' labour with the metamorphosis of one of her attendants, red-haired Galanthis, who tricks Juno into releasing her spell and with it the baby. For, as Galanthis crows over her success, the goddess grabs her by the hair and turns her into a weasel (9.320f) in one of the many incidental, insignificant transformations with which the poem is patterned.

Dryope (9.324–93)

Bringing the Hercules cycle of stories to a close, Iole responds with a story of her own, telling of another mother and son and another strange metamorphosis. Echoing the stories of rape and transformation in book 1 of the poem, she tells how the nymph Lotis had once escaped the attentions of the lecherous god Priapus by metamorphosing into a lotus flower (9.345–48). Not knowing this story (told at greater length by Ovid in his *Fasti* 1.391–440), Dryope attempts to pick some of the lotus flowers, and is horrified when blood drips from the severed stems. She finds herself rooted to the spot, bark covering her flesh, and her hair turning to leaves, as she is herself transformed into the lotus tree: a familiar metamorphosis lent new pathos here by the description of her baby attempting to nuzzle and feed from his mother's breast, now hard and covered in bark (9.356–8). As her distraught family prostrate themselves at her feet/roots, Dryope begs them to protect her branches from the pruning knife and to teach her infant son never to pick or harm any plant or tree lest he hurt a nymph transformed within. Indeed, the world of the *Metamorphoses* is now so full of such metamorphic hybrids, that her plea is as sensible as it is pathetic.

Dryope's metamorphosis is but one of several tree transformations in the poem (among them Daphne (1.452–567), the Heliades (2.358–63), Baucis and Philemon (8.611–724), Cyparissus (10.86–142) and Myrrha (10.481–502)) and reminds us once more that human bodies are peculiarly tree-like. As Robin Nisbet, echoing Pliny, observes of the symbolism of trees in classical literature:[40]

> Trees are like people. They have a head (*vertex*), a trunk (*truncus*), arms (*bracchia*). They stand tall like a soldier, or look as slender as a bridegroom (Sappho, 115 L-P). Their life moves in human rhythms, which in their case may be repeated: sap rises and falls, hair (*coma*) luxuriates, withers, drops off. Sometimes they are superior and aloof, sometimes they go in pairs, whether as comrades-in-arms (Hom. *Il.* 12.132ff., Virg.

Aen. 9.679ff.) or husband and wife (Ov. *Met.* 8.720). They whisper like lovers (Ar. *Nub.* 1008), embrace, support, cling . . . and, as Dryope's story poignantly illustrates, may also bleed and die.

Iolaus, Callirhoe's Sons and Miletus (9.394–453)

Branching out from these two tales (poems, like people, are also like trees it seems) Ovid tells a second pair of stories similarly concerning parents and children. First Iolaus appears, rejuvenated and primed to help Hercules' sons defend themselves against their father's longstanding enemy Eurystheus. This prompts an allusion to the tale of Callirhoe's infant sons who will one day be prematurely aged by the gods so that they may avenge their father's murder. This material provides Ovid with a (twisted and somewhat tenuous) bridge into his next sequence: the gods each demand the right to rejuvenate their own favourite mortals. Jupiter assures them that only the Fates control this gift, citing his own ageing favourites Rhadamanthus, Aeacus and Minos as examples that he too is subject to this rule; for even at that moment, infirm with old age, Minos lives in fear of an uprising led by Miletus – who has already established a rival city on the shores of Asia and there fathered twins, Caunus and Byblis.

Byblis (9.454–665)

In the following story of Byblis and Caunus we see another side to family relations, as Ovid introduces the first in a sequence of tales concerning forbidden or unnatural love that will continue well into book 10. The shameful and shocking character of Byblis and the passion she feels for her twin brother is signposted by the Ovidian narrator from the outset, presenting Byblis as an *exemplum* – an example and a warning, but also a template for the other girls in this series of tales who, like her, do *not* love lawfully (9.454).

   Byblis finds her chaste, legitimate affection for her twin brother slowly transformed into an immoral, illegal, and incestuous desire. Echoing other women in the poem who are similarly torn by competing forms of familial and erotic love,[41] Byblis first explores her feelings in a soliloquy (9.474–516) before deciding to write Caunus a letter (9.517–63) like one of the epistles collected in Ovid's own elegiac *Heroides*. Caunus responds with disgusted horror and leaves home while Byblis herself, in a frenzy of grief, is transformed into an eternally weeping spring (9.635–65).

Highlighting the literary pun suggested by Byblis' name (Greek for 'book'), several critics have noted the 'literary incest' that infects this narrative, as Ovid represents Byblis' passion as a peculiarly perverse form of literary love. As Shilpa Raval has observed:[42]

> Byblis's monologues and amorous ploys consist wholly of literary tropes and conventions and are modelled upon Latin elegy. Her entire love affair is conducted as if Byblis has "read" all of Latin elegy as well as the *Heroides* and the *Ars Amatoria*.

So, just like Ovid's love-struck Phaedra (*Heroides* 4), Byblis sees the incestuous relationships of the gods as validating her own incestuous desires (9.497–9) and, like Canace in her letter to her brother/lover Macareus (*Heroides* 11), she cites the Homeric Aeolidae (9.507) who notoriously married their sisters, as a mythical precedent for her fantasy. She wonders how and why she knows about these *exempla* (9.508). Clearly, she knows Ovid's elegiac *corpus* only too well.

The bookish Byblis also demonstrates a perverse faith in the power of words, the power of letters and names to shape and reshape reality according to her own desires. Ovid himself alerts us to this in the opening lines of the story, where Byblis' name is repeated three times in as many lines (*Byblida . . . Byblis . . . Byblis* – 9.453–5), highlighting the key role that names will play in this narrative. In fact, Byblis sees language rather than law or morality as posing the main obstacle to her incestuous desires here. In her letter to Caunus, she begins with but then erases the word that identifies her as his sister (*soror* – 9.528f), identifying herself instead as a lover (*amans* – 9.531) who is ashamed to reveal her name, and when she hands the letter to a servant she hesitates for a long time before telling him to take it to her brother (*fratri* – 9.570). Byblis hates to name her brother as such, preferring to call him her master (*dominum* – 9.466) as she linguistically transforms Caunus into the male equivalent of a beloved elegiac mistress or *domina*. In turn, she wishes he would call her 'Byblis' rather than 'sister' (9.467) and longs to be able to change her name (*mutato nomine* – 9.487): a simple metamorphosis that she believes would enable her to realize her desires. [43]

Iphis (9.666–797)

Ovid further exploits the idea that language has its own metamorphic powers in the next story, where once more we see names play a determining factor in shaping character(s) and role(s) in the world of the *Metamorphoses*. We have already seen the 'Wolf-man' Lycaon become a wolf (1.163–252), Narcissus a flower (3.339–510) and Arachne a spider (6.1–145) and in the story of Iphis we again see Ovid play with the idea that (as Stephen Wheeler puts it) 'a *nomen* is an *omen*' – names predict a character's fate and narrative.[44]

In this tale, an impoverished couple are expecting a baby and, in line with ancient Greek custom, reluctantly agree that if the infant is a girl they will have to put her to death. But when a baby girl is born the mother pretends that the child is a boy and rejoices when the father names her 'Iphis' – a suitable name for a girl, a boy, or a girl pretending to be a boy. The female Iphis is raised as a male (9.712) alongside the beautiful girl Ianthe, to whom, at the age of thirteen, she becomes engaged. Ovid carefully stresses the many similarities that the two girls share, enhancing the pathos of their seemingly impossible union (9.718–21), but at the same time reminding us of the parallels between the stories of Iphis (in love with another girl just like her) and Byblis (in love with her own twin). Yet, whereas Byblis had indulged in self-delusion and erotic fantasy, looking for mythical and literary exemplars to help rationalize and legitimize her strange passion, Iphis simply accepts the hopelessness of her own strange love (9.727f), concluding that nothing can be done about it. Taking her examples from the world of nature, she reasons that cows do not mate with cows, nor mares with mares, and that her love is therefore unnatural (9.731–4): her desires are worse even than those of Pasiphae, her fellow Cretan, she concludes – those at least were 'normal' in that they were heterosexual in orientation (9.735–40).

Ovid's sympathy for Iphis here, then, should not necessarily be assumed to demonstrate the poet's approval of same sex female relationships: the maxim repeated again and again in Iphis' soliloquy is that lesbianism is 'unnatural' (9.758). Indeed, rather than allowing Iphis and Ianthe to live happily ever after in a mutually loving same sex relationship, it is significant that it takes a miracle and a sex-change to ensure this couple's married bliss. So, as the day of the wedding approaches and excuses for delay grow increasingly tenuous, Iphis and her mother pray desperately to Isis for help. And lo – Iphis undergoes a miraculous transformation: her stride and her limbs lengthen, her complexion grows darker, her facial features grow sharper, and even her hair shortens as she increases in strength (*vigoris* – 9.790) and turns into a man (9.786–91). As we saw in the transformations of Tiresias (3.316–38), the physical differences between men and women are minor indeed – their essential similarities more striking than their dissimilarities. But here, Iphis' miraculous transformation also reminds us that in Latin, a girl (*puella*) is etymologically the diminutive form of a boy (*puer*).[45] Iphis the *puer*, then, is simply a *puella* with a little more *vigor.*

Discussion points and questions
1. To what extent is Hercules' death anti-heroic?
2. To what degree is it fair to describe the story of Byblis as a tale concerning 'literary incest'?
3. What does the story of Iphis and Ianthe suggest about Roman attitudes to gender difference and gendered identity?

Book Ten

Orpheus and Eurydice (10.1–85)
From the happy wedding of Iphis and Ianthe, Ovid segues cinematically into the next book by following the god of conjugal union, Hymen, tracking the god as he flies on to his next booking at the wedding of Orpheus and Eurydice. But Hymen fails to bring lucky omens or happy faces to this couple (10.4f). In direct contrast to the joyous wedding of Iphis and Ianthe, the union between Orpheus and Eurydice is not a happy occasion, and the spluttering of the wedding torch as it refuses to catch fire (10.6f) adds an unlucky omen to the marriage. After this dark foreshadowing of future disaster for bride and groom it hardly comes as a surprise when Eurydice is bitten by a snake and falls down dead. Sara Mack succinctly highlights the prosaic character of Ovid's description of Eurydice's death: [46]

'Nothing is chosen for emotional effect. Eurydice drops dead, no suspense, no pathos, just *occidit* [she dies], bitten by a snake.' Orpheus then makes his way down to the underworld with (what Ovid represents as) something of a half-hearted attempt to persuade the gods there to give her back (10.12). But, as he makes his way back to the upper-world with Eurydice following behind him – permission for her return granted only if Orpheus does not look back at her (10.50f) – he is unable to control the desire to look and he turns only to see her slip back to Hell, his triumphant quest transformed into a pitiable failure at the climactic moment (10.55–63).[47]

There is no physical metamorphosis here, but this version of the story of Orpheus, narrated across books 10 and 11 of the *Metamorphoses* (10.1–11.84), is effectively a transformation of Virgil's *Georgics* 4, a re-reading that turns tragedy into comedy, and Virgilian pathos into Ovidian bathos.[48] In fact, Ovid seems to challenge every detail of Virgil's famous version of the Orpheus and Eurydice myth: Virgil avoids quoting Orpheus' song to the gods of the underworld, Ovid reproduces it in full; Virgil's Eurydice speaks a lament as she dies for a second time, Ovid's Eurydice says nothing; Virgil's Orpheus mourns Eurydice for seven months, Ovid's Orpheus mourns for seven days; Virgil's Orpheus rejects women, Ovid's Orpheus also turns to boys for his sexual fulfilment; and finally, while the decapitated head of Virgil's Orpheus floats down the river Hebrus calling plaintively to his Eurydice, the head and lyre of Ovid's Orpheus produce an elegiac lament, a pathetic 'weepy something or other' (*flebile nescio quid* – 11.52).

Cyparissus (10.86–142)
Orpheus' grief at the double loss of his Eurydice also prompts a psychological metamorphosis of sorts as the poet rejects the company of women and turns instead to pederasty and the love of boys (10.83f), setting an example to the people of Thrace – and setting both tone and theme for the sequence of tales that follow. It is important to remember here that same-sex sexual relationships – including those between older men and adolescent boys – were not viewed negatively in ancient Greece or Rome. But it is also worth recalling that Ovid's own view on 'the love of boys' was not wholly positive. In keeping with the literary

tradition that expected elegiac love poets to have boys as well as girls as their lovers, Ovid claims to be open to either possibility in the opening poem of his *Amores* (1.1.20): after all, as we saw in the tale of Iphis (9.666–797), there is very little difference between boys and girls. But in his *Ars Amatoria* Ovid claims that the mutual pleasure of heterosexual sex and the satisfaction of mutual orgasm are the reasons why he personally prefers to have sex with girls rather than boys (2.683f).[49] It is possible, then, that the emphasis upon Orpheus' sexuality here indicates a subtle divergence in attitude and identity between Ovid and his character and a hint that the two poets may view the world very differently. As we will see.

Orpheus prepares to sing, sitting himself down on the top of a hill and miraculously creating for himself an audience of trees, which Ovid describes in the form of an epic catalogue (10.86–105). The catalogue of trees (which both Ovid and Orpheus exploit to provide an appropriate pastoral context for the telling of Orpheus' next song) lists many unhappy specimens, including the Heliades (10.91) who, in mourning for the death of their beloved brother Phaethon, were once transformed into poplar trees, their tears into amber (2.358–63). The virgin laurel (*innuba laurus* – 10.92) similarly offers an allusion to Daphne's transformation (1.452–567), and the watery lotus (*aquatica lotos* – 10.96) recalls both Lotis (9.345–8) and Dryope's (9.324–93) recent metamorphoses. The catalogue concludes with a reference to the funereal cypress tree and the story of the metamorphosis of Cyparissus, loved by Apollo, famed for his inconsolable grief at the accidental death of his dearly beloved (and comically pampered) pet deer, and notable here for the parodic comparison that his excessive mourning invites with Orpheus' own grief at the loss of Eurydice. Cyparissus thus provides the ideal narrative link between Orpheus' mourning for Eurydice and his new interest in boys.

The Song of Orpheus (10.143–739)[50]

Strangely, Orpheus' internal audience for his next song is comprised of trees, wild beasts and birds, spell-bound by the power of his music (10.143f). They listen in silent enchantment as he sings to them of 'boys / whom the gods have loved and of girls who have been inspired to a frenzy / of lawless passion' (10.152–54).

But, as one critic has observed, when 'Orpheus proceeds to tell the owl and the wild pussy-cat about Ganymede, Hyacinthus, Pygmalion, Myrrha, and Adonis, there is something comic about the situation, just as there would be about singing true romances to a tortoise'.[51] Orpheus himself, however, seems unaware of any humorous incongruity and sets out his poetic programme with serious intent, calling upon Jupiter and the Muse Calliope to inspire his song (10.148–54).[52]

Ganymede and Hyacinthus (10.155–219)

After his introductory prooemium Orpheus begins his song (as promised) with Jupiter and his infamous rape of the boy Ganymede. The story is covered in just 7 lines, with none of the psychological colour or detail given by Ovid to his own telling of similar Jovian rapes and transformations. Instead, Orpheus moves quickly on to develop a story with more obvious personal relevance: the tale of Apollo and the death of his beloved Hyacinthus. Here Apollo reprises the role he played in the tale of Cyparissus, and here too the same motif of a lover accidentally causing the death of a beloved is repeated as the god Apollo kills Hyacinthus with a deadly discus throw. Apollo's divine arts in medicine fail him and as he laments his loss, holding the dying boy – like a broken flower (10.190–5) – in his arms, he initially blames himself for the tragedy (10.199–201): 'I, I am the cause of your death / Yet how can it be my fault unless to have played a game / or have fondly loved can be called a fault?' Such denial of culpability from a lover sounds oddly familiar. Having sent Eurydice back to Hell with his impatient look, Ovid suggests that she could not blame Orpheus for this second death: 'as she died for the second time, she never complained / that her husband had failed her – what could she complain of, except that he'd loved her?' (10.61f). Orpheus, it seems, is projecting his own experience of tragedy onto his narrative of this story. Indeed, just as Orpheus took up his lyre to sing songs of lament after Eurydice's death, so now Apollo similarly promises to commemorate his beloved in the music of his lyre and in all his future songs (10.204–6). Moreover, he declares that his grief will also be memorialized in the form of a new flower, its petals inscribed with the markings AI AI (a cry of lamentation) that will one day also commemorate the hero Ajax (or Aias).

From the blood spilled upon the ground from Hyacinthus' wounds a hyacinth flower grows (the metaphor of 10.190–5 now refigured as metamorphosis) and on each anniversary of this miracle, Orpheus tells us, the Spartans will celebrate the Hyacinthia in honour of their fallen son. With this aetiology, Orpheus concludes his short sequence of tales concerning 'boys whom the gods have loved' and turns his attention instead to 'girls who have been inspired to a frenzy of lawless passion'.

Cerastae and Propoetides (10.220–42)

At least, that is the expectation formed by Orpheus' programmatic statement of themes at the start of his song. It comes as something of a surprise then when his next story concerns the Cerastae (horn wearers) – a murderous race of both men and women who are turned into bulls by Venus for their impiety (10.220–37). The next story, concerning the infamous daughters of Propoetus, the 'obscene Propoetides' (*obscenae . . . . Propoetides* – 10.238), who deny the divinity of Venus, turn to prostitution and are then turned into statues, accords more obviously with Orpheus' plan – but here too, close reading reveals that the story does not quite fit its billing.

The Propoetides are typically regarded by readers and critics of the poem as hard-faced, hard-hearted prostitutes and their transformation into stone statues is seen as their punishment for this.[53] Close reading of the story, however, reveals that this view of the Propoetides is wrong. They are, in fact, turned into prostitutes as punishment for denying the divinity of Venus (*ausae esse negare deam: pro quo* – 10.238f), *after* which they turn to stone. It is prostitution rather than petrifaction that is their punishment and it is likely that their crime against Venus in the first place is not selling their bodies for sex (if this were the case, prostitution would hardly be a fitting punishment) but rather *refusing* to use their bodies for sex – that is, living their lives in celibacy, denying the power and pleasures of Venus. The second metamorphosis into stone may be seen, then, not as a punishment, but as a kind of self-transformation, the life of prostitution they are forced to lead causing them to become as hard (as) stones. Transformation is often figured in the *Metamorphoses* as a kind of refuge or escape – particularly from undesired sexual experience – and it is feasible to view the transformation of the women into stone as their best means of escaping an enforced life of prostitution. The Propoetides then are hardly 'girls who have been inspired to a frenzy of lawless passion'.

Pygmalion (10.243–97)

The artist Pygmalion, however, confuses both the sequence and the agency of the Propoetides' metamorphoses and misreads their story. He sees the *obscenae Propoetides* as always already prostitutes, turned into stone in punishment for their immodest and immoral sexual behaviour: a warning to himself and others to avoid the 'vices with which the female sex has been so richly endowed' (10.244f). Disgusted by the lifestyle of the Propoetides, Pygmalion himself turns to celibacy, rejecting women in much the same way, albeit for very different reasons, as Orpheus – whose voice and viewpoint continue to colour the narration of this next story.

Spurning women of flesh and blood, Pygmalion sculpts an ivory statue, 'an image of perfect feminine beauty' so realistic that it appears to be alive (10.247f) – so life-like in fact that Pygmalion falls in love with it, the artist himself deceived by his own artistry (*ars adeo latet arte sua* – 10.252).[54] Foolishly, he treats the statue as if it were a real woman, caressing and kissing it, believing that his kisses are returned. Treating her exactly as if she were a hard-hearted elegiac mistress or *dura puella*, Pygmalion himself adopts the pose of an elegiac lover, gently attempting to win her affections. He shows concern that his caresses may be too rough (10.258), he gives her expensive gifts (10.260–5), flatters her (and himself, perhaps) that she is beautiful dressed but even more beautiful undressed (10.266), and he lays her down upon rich coverlets and soft pillows (10.267–9). Indeed, all these behaviours suggest that the artist Pygmalion practises the 'art of love' as prescribed in Ovid's own *Ars Amatoria*. Here, the art of love is taught to the prospective lover according to a series of guidelines in which he is taught 'to woo his mistress with indulgence, compliments, persistent compliance, service, gifts, calculated flattery, and solicitude (*Ars* 2.145–336)'.[55] Pygmalion follows this guide to the letter in his attempts to woo his own *dura puella* – who, as a statue, is both absurdly and literally just like the stereotypical 'hard-hearted' mistresses of elegy.

Pygmalion's comical confusion between representation and reality climaxes at a festival held in honour of Venus. Praying to the goddess of love, not daring to ask to have his ivory statue for a wife – that is, to be allowed to have sex with his statue – he asks instead to have a wife just *like* his ivory statue (10.274–6):

> *constitit et timide "si, di, dare cuncta potestis,*
> *sit coniunx, opto," non ausus "eburnea uirgo"*
> *dicere, Pygmalion "similis mea" dixit "eburnae".*

> . . . Pygmalion stood by the altar
> and nervously asked: "You gods, all gifts are within your power.
> Grant me to wed . . ." – not daring to say "my ivory maiden",
> he used the words "a woman resembling my ivory maiden".

Pygmalion's hesitant, disjointed speech (perfectly conveyed by the tentative Latin here) eloquently expresses his confusion and his inability to make clear distinctions between representation and reality, his perverse desires thinly veiled in the language he uses. This confusion continues when he returns home after the festival to find that his prayers have been answered – literally – and that he has been granted a wife exactly *like* his statue. Feeling a new warmth and softness to the ivory of the statue (10.283–6), Pygmalion touches it as though it/she were still a work of art – the simile describing his touch suggesting that he handles her newly transformed flesh not as a lover caresses the body of a woman but as a sculptor moulds wax (10.284–6). Indeed, in the defining moment of her transformation and vivification, as Pygmalion's statue opens her eyes to see, a clever pun in the word for sky/sculptor's engraving tool in the Latin *caelo* offers a reminder that, in a sense, she now sees the world only because of Pygmalion's artistry as a sculptor (10.294 – *pariter cum caelo vidit amantem*): even as a woman of flesh and blood she remains his creation, his 'living doll', her transformation from 'art-object' to 'love-object' representing little real change. So, Alison Sharrock sees very little difference between the statue and the woman, who she appropriately names Eburna ('Ivory').

For Sharrock, 'Pygmalion plays out to the full the fantasy of creation. He creates a "living" statue which really does come to life, in a vivification which nevertheless maintains the creator's control.'[56] She suggests that there is little change in the metamorphosis of statue to woman, claiming that, 'in the final metamorphosis Eburna becomes even more like an automaton: she now really does move, and gives birth, but she seems barely more alive than she was as a statue'.[57]

This reminds us that the story of Pygmalion and his statue does not necessarily or straightforwardly have a neat, happy ending. Certainly Orpheus presents it as such: as in his telling of the stories of Cyparissus and Hyacinthus, his own narrative of loss imposes itself as this story's subtext and it is easy to see why he might want to celebrate the success of a fellow-artist who, like him, has shunned the company of women, taken sexual satisfaction in a substitute (albeit in a statue rather than in boys) and who has now miraculously brought a woman (back) to life. As Sarah Brown suggests, 'the story might reflect a wish-fulfilment fantasy on the part of Orpheus who is unable to retain his own revived Eurydice'.[58] But as in the tragedy of Orpheus, Pygmalion loses something precious too. In miraculously gaining a wife, Pygmalion loses his miraculous statue: the woman of flesh and blood that the artist's hands now move over is only *like* his ivory Eburna; he has lost his work of art, his perfect, ideal woman. Perhaps this is Venus' idea of punishment for his former celibacy and disgusted rejection of all women.

What is more, the substitution of Pygmalion's work of art for a real woman, the metamorphosis of fetish and fantasy into flesh and blood, reminds us that Pygmalion's earlier behaviours and desires were unambiguously 'unnatural'. That Pygmalion and Eburna become the grandparents of Cinyras (whose daughter Myrrha's story follows next) further suggests that Pygmalion's mode of 'reproduction' is not to be viewed in an entirely positive light. Pygmalion's act of creation might even be seen as the (re)production of a daughter for whom he then conceives an erotic and incestuous desire: certainly, the Latin is pregnant with words which suggest that the statue represents the artist's child.[59] This configuration of the relationship between the artist and his statue as 'unnatural', then, explicitly foreshadows the incestuous relationship between Cinyras and his daughter Myrrha in the next of Orpheus' tales, casting its own dark shadow back upon the 'fairy-tale' fantasy of Pygmalion and Eburna.

Myrrha (10.298–502)

Having strained his audience's credulity with the tale of Pygmalion and his living statue, Ovid (speaking through Orpheus) now explicitly warns us *not* to believe in the horrible story of Myrrha and her incestuous relationship with her father (10.302) that he is about to narrate – the only one of Orpheus' tales that seemingly fits his theme of girls punished for their lusts. Mirroring Pygmalion's disgust at the behaviour of the Propoetides, Orpheus now emphasizes the vileness of Myrrha's behaviour, as if to further validate his own rejection of women and their vices – a rejection that increasingly seems misogynistic in its foundation. Indeed, there are plenty of clues in this narrative that suggest Orpheus is a biased narrator – and that Ovid's sympathies may not necessarily lie in the same direction. The fact that Ovid has himself, in his own voice (*in propria persona*), only recently told a very similar story of incest – that of Byblis in book 9 – suggests that here he is explicitly inviting us to draw comparisons between his own treatment of the theme and that of his character Orpheus.[60]

At the outset, Orpheus stresses that there are no extenuating or mitigating circumstances in this tale, and that Myrrha's 'crime of passion' has nothing to do with Cupid or *amor*; rather, one of the hellish Furies must have fanned the flames of her unspeakable passion. In contrast to Ovid's own sympathetic characterisation of Byblis and her incestuous love for her brother, Orpheus offers no analysis of Myrrha's incipient desire for her father, but presents her already fully conscious of her 'vile passion' (10.319), launching directly into a soliloquy in which she considers her invidious position (10.319–55). Unlike Ovid's Byblis and Iphis, who look to the laws of religion, of nature, and society to prove the impossibility and impiety of their unnatural desires, Orpheus' Myrrha finds a precedent and a model for incest both among the animal world (10.324–9) and among other cultures (10.331–3): both nature and culture endorse her 'unnatural' love it seems.[61] Like Byblis, Myrrha is troubled by the linguistic confusion and perversion of names and relationships that her incestuous desire must entail, constructing in words the fantasy that she longs for in reality (10.346–8):

> 'Don't you see you're confusing all names and natural ties?
> Will *you* play the role of your mother's supplanter and father's mistress?
> Will *you* be known as your own son's sister and brother's mother?'

Amidst all this linguistic confusion and (fore)play, it is interesting to note that in her soliloquy Myrrha refers to herself repeatedly in the second person, as 'you', highlighting the (incestuous?) confusion of linguistic and narrative roles in which Ovid and Orpheus are themselves entwined here. Indeed, this key aspect of Myrrha's tale comes to a twisted high point when her father Cinyras asks her what kind of husband she would like and she responds: 'A man like you' (*similem tibi* – 10.364). Myrrha, it seems, is very like her great-grandfather Pygmalion.

Orpheus, however, is bolder and less prurient than *his* creator and now moves his incest narrative into shocking new territory. Myrrha's nurse agrees to help her – her hesitant promise of support mirroring that of Pygmalion's request to Venus (10.429f):

> *"vive," ait haec, "potiere tuo"—et, non ausa "parente" dicere. . . .*

> "All right," said the nurse, "you must live and shall have
>   your . . ." – she stopped as she couldn't
> say "father", . . .

A religious festival when wives (and their snowy bodies – *nivea . . . corpora* 10.432: a reminder of Pygmalion's own snow-white wife at 10.247) are forbidden to share their husband's beds gives Myrrha and the nurse their opportunity. The nurse tells a drunken Cinyras that she has a girl for him and when he asks her age (why, *we* may ask, does he do this?), she tells him: 'The same as Myrrha's' (10.441). She hands the trembling girl over to him in his dark bedchamber with the portentous words 'Cinyras, take her, she's yours' (10.464); and with a final perverse linguistic twist, we learn that, 'because of her age, he even called her "my daughter" / and she said "father", to put the finishing touch to their incest' (10.467f). In this and in the nights of incest that follow, Cinyras (according to Orpheus) acted innocently, the crime (*crimina* – 10.470) Myrrha's alone.[62] But if we read the nuances of this narrative closely it is impossible not to see Cinyras as sharing his daughter's sin, as acting out his own incest fantasy as Myrrha enacts hers. So when, after numerous nights, Cinyras finally brings in a lamp 'to see his daughter and his crime' (*et scelus et natam* – 10.474) before grabbing his sword to kill her, our sympathies are easily redirected towards Myrrha. It seems as though Orpheus too has softened towards her, perhaps because, in his eager desire to see his lover, Cinyras inevitably reminds Orpheus of himself: Cinyras is 'eager to know' the identity of his young lover (*avidus cognoscere* – 10.472) just as Orpheus was 'desperate to see' (*avidus videndi* – 10.56) his beloved Eurydice. In both cases, the resulting look marks a fatal turning point in the narrative. So, Myrrha, now transformed from villain into victim, flees her home in terror, the dark night that earlier symbolized nature's abhorrence at her unnatural desire (10.446–51) now sympathetically aiding her in her flight (10.476). Orpheus and his treatment of Myrrha has undergone a complete transformation, it seems, and we are invited to pity her as she wanders for nine months, until advanced pregnancy and exhaustion prompt her to pray to the gods for release her from her mental and physical agony. Some god – we are not told which one – takes pity on her and turns her into a tree, her tears ever after trickling from the bark as myrrh, preserving her name and her honour for all eternity (10.500–2).

Venus and Adonis (10.503–739)

Myrrha's troubles do not end with her metamorphosis, however: she has yet to give birth to her ill-conceived child (10.503), now trapped beneath the unyielding bark of the tree that she has become. The goddess of childbirth, Lucina (whose help can ease or prolong the agony of childbirth – as we saw in the case of Alcmena – 9.273–323) pities her and delivers the child: a beautiful baby boy, just like the infant Cupid. Or rather, just like a *painting* or representation of the infant Cupid – but only if you took Cupid's quiver of arrows away from him, or gave some to the baby Adonis (10.515–18). Orpheus' (or is it Ovid's?) equivocation on this point highlights the continuity between this new story and the stories of Pygmalion and Myrrha that have just been told: the child of Cinyras and Myrrha (10.520f, 717, 730), great-grandchild of Pygmalion and Eburna, continues the family tradition of blurring distinctions between representation and reality. Indeed, we may wonder what other family traditions he will also maintain.

The child quickly grows up and, contradicting Orpheus' earlier claim that Cupid and *amor* took no responsibility for Myrrha's unnatural passion (10.311), unwittingly avenges his mother by causing Venus herself to fall in love with him.[63] For (with obviously incestuous overtones) when Cupid happens to graze his mother's breast with one of his magic erotogenic arrows while kissing her, he accidentally fills her with desire for the mortal Adonis – the beautiful boy who (disturbingly) not only looks just like her own son but also looks a lot like Venus herself (10.579).

The narrative now effects an ingenious (albeit incestuous) intermingling of the themes and motifs that have coloured all of Orpheus' strange stories so far. In a reworking of his stated theme and earlier accounts of 'boys whom the gods have loved' and 'girls punished for their lustful desires' (10.152–54), Orpheus tells of a boy loved by a *goddess* and of a *boy* punished for his lustful desires. Employing his own internal narrator to tell a tale-within-a-tale-within-a-tale, Orpheus has Venus tell the story of Atalanta and Hippomenes (10.560–707) to explain the cause (or aetiology) of her own fear and hatred of wild animals – and of lions above all. Seeking to elude an oracle that had predicted she would 'lose herself' if she were ever to marry, the fleet-footed Atalanta had taken great care to avoid marriage – challenging all potential suitors to beat her in a running race, offering herself as the prize for victory and death as the price for failure. With the aid (and detailed racing commentary) of Venus, Hippomenes tricks her into pausing to pick up three golden apples during the race, thereby winning both the competition and Atalanta as his bride. But, in his moment of victory, Hippomenes forgets to pay Venus her due thanks. In retribution, Venus inflames the couple with such sudden passion that they pollute a sanctuary sacred to Cybele by having sex within in its holy precinct and are turned into lions by the outraged goddess in punishment.

Ignoring Venus' warnings to stay away from such dangerous wild animals, Adonis is fatally gored by a boar (*not* a lion), but a flower – the short-lived anemone (ever after planted for the annual festival of the Adonia, the better-known version of the Hyacinthia[64]) – springs up from his blood as an eternal monument to Venus' grief. And so, Orpheus' micro- *Metamorphoses* (a testament to his own grief at the loss of his beloved) comes to its end and we look forward to our imminent reunion with Ovid as he takes up the narrative once more.

Discussion points and questions
1. To what extent does the Song of Orpheus represent a miniature version of the *Metamorphoses*?
2. To what degree does Orpheus' Song conform to its stated intent to tell 'of boys whom the gods have loved and of girls who have been inspired to a frenzy of lawless passion and paid the price for their lustful desires'?
3. How does the theme of incest unite the tales of Pygmalion, Myrrha, and Adonis?

3.3 BOOKS ELEVEN TO FIFTEEN
Book Eleven
The Death of Orpheus (11.1–84)
The many internal narrators and imbedded narratives in the *Metamorphoses* draw attention to the authority and character of the poem's external story-teller – Ovid himself. As Sara Myers suggests:[1]

> Internal narrators bring to the fore the issue of the reliability of the narrator, which has implications for understanding Ovid's authorial posture in the poem as a whole. His embedded narratives provide repeated and contrasting paradigms for the very nature of tale-telling and for audience-response.

Internal narrators, then, invite us to compare Ovid's own narrative style and technique with those of his story-telling *personae*. They challenge us, in particular, to question the extent to which a character like Orpheus can be regarded either as a virtual avatar for his poetic creator, sharing his sympathies and views, or as an alter-ego, inhabiting and expressing a very different viewpoint. As a fellow poet, Orpheus has been seen by some readers as 'virtually indistinguishable from Ovid himself', his embedded narrative viewed as a microcosm of Ovid's own poem.[2] However, audience responses to Orpheus' song reported by Ovid in his own voice (*in propria persona*) at the start of book 11, suggest that the relationship between Ovid and his character is not entirely sympathetic.

An internal audience of trees, wild beasts and birds is charmed by Orpheus' song (11.1f), but a second audience is less impressed.[3] The women of Thrace, offended by Orpheus' treatment of women (that is, his treatment of Eurydice, of the Propoetides, of Eburna, of Myrrha and Atalanta, and his wholesale rejection of the female sex in favour of boys) launch an impassioned attack against him. Initially, the women's weapons are powerless against the poet as the spell-binding power of Orpheus' music renders harmless the rocks and ivy-wreathed spears that they throw at him. But they drown out the sound of the poet's song with their own music: the clamour of flutes and horns, the beating of breasts and drums, and the howling of raging maenads. Unlike the first 'ideal' and undiscriminating audience of dumb animals, this second audience resists Orpheus' poetic authority. As if in response to feminist Amy Richlin's suggestions of ways to deal with male-biased or misogynist classical texts – 'throw them out, take them apart, find female based ones instead'[4] – the Thracian women refuse to listen to Orpheus, they take *him* apart, and they drown out his words with their own. And in so doing, they invite us to do the same: through this internal audience Ovid invites us to become 'resisting readers' of Orpheus and to challenge the biases of every narrator and every narrative.[5]

Indeed, Ovid's own bias in this retelling of Orpheus' death is clear. As the Thracian women tear Orpheus limb from limb, sending his head and lyre floating off down the river Hebrus, the dead poet's lyre and tongue still produce some sounds of lament (11.52f). But Ovid's scathing description of Orpheus' last song as literally a 'weepy something or other' (*flebile nescio quid*) suggests that Ovid here has little sympathy for his character.[6]

It seems almost as an afterthought that Ovid gives one last backward glance at Orpheus finally reunited with Eurydice in the underworld as he draws the story of Orpheus to a close by showing us what it really means to produce poetry in a 'lighter vein' (literally with a lighter lyre or *leviore lyra* – 10.152): as each one of the Thracian women is transformed into an oak tree in punishment for Orpheus' murder, Ovid cheekily observes that, 'You'd suppose that her outstretched arms / were genuine branches – indeed, you'd be perfectly right in supposing it' (*nodosaque bracchia veros / esse putes ramos, et non fallare putando* – 11.83f). Punning on the alternative meaning of the Latin *putando* as pruning, Ovid here jokes that you might test whether or not the women had *really* turned into trees by pruning them.[7] Coming as it does after Orpheus' song, where appearance and reality have continually confused the unwary, Ovid's joke is perfectly timed and with it he conjures up his own metamorphic audience of trees, leaving Orpheus and his song firmly in the shade.

Midas (11.85–193)

This 'light touch' also establishes the tone and link into the next story, in which Ovid offers his audience a gentle narrative interlude before returning again to the theme of married love and loss. Offering little in the way of context or back-story, Ovid launches straight into the well-known tale of Midas and his foolish request to the gods to grant that whatever he might touch should turn to gold. The plot-line in which a mortal comes to regret asking for a gift from the gods has already been developed by Ovid in the stories of Phaethon (2.1–400) and Semele (3.256–315), but in Midas' suffering in the midst of riches, we may also hear echoes of Narcissus (3.339–510), of Byblis (9.454–665), Iphis (9.666–797), Myrrha (10.298–502), and perhaps of Pygmalion (10.243–97) too: all experience psychological torment because they possess the object of their desire but cannot enjoy it. As Midas prays to give up the gift that has become a curse, the gods show uncharacteristic kindness (11.134) and relieve him of his golden touch, instructing him to wash it away in the river Pactolus – thereby establishing the aetiology of its legendary gold-bearing silt, for which it was still famed in Ovid's day.

Midas' legendary stupidity, however, is not so easily washed away: when asked to adjudicate in a music competition between Pan and Apollo, he offends Apollo by ignorantly judging the rustic (*barbarico* – 11.162), pastoral pipe music of Pan superior to the highly refined (*dulcedine* – 11.170) artistry of Apollo's lyre – for which Apollo aptly punishes him with a pair of hairy ass's ears. It is hard not to see in this playful tale a steer from Ovid himself as to whose style of poetry *we* should prefer – lest, in undervaluing Ovid's own highly refined artistry we too deserve to wear a pair of such donkey's ears.

A comic postscript to this story tells how Midas tried to keep these visible signs of his asinine tastes and behaviour hidden under his hat, until his barber caught sight of them while cutting his hair. Unable to keep the secret to himself but forbidden to tell anyone else, the barber whispers the story into a hole in the ground and buries the evidence of his words (*verba* – 11.193). But the rustling reeds that then grow upon that spot unwittingly repeat the tale as they whisper in the breeze – just as the reed papyrus upon which Ovid now inscribes the words of this story reveal Midas' secret to us.

Laomedon's Treachery (11.194–220)

From this tale of accidental betrayal, Ovid moves on to tell of Laomedon's deliberate perfidy – first in attempting to double-cross Apollo and Neptune by withholding payment for their help in building the walls of his new city of Troy, and then in seeking to cheat Hercules out of his promised reward for rescuing Laomedon's daughter from a sea-monster. In retaliation, Hercules leads an army against Laomedon's Troy, aided by the brothers Telemon and Peleus.

These heroic tales are sketched out in only their barest outlines as Ovid uses them as narrative stepping-stones to reach his next story-point and the well-known romance of Peleus and Thetis, parents of the mighty Achilles. However, close (and not-so-close) readers of Ovid's *carmen perpetuum* will have noticed that Hercules died back in book 9 (134–272) and Peleus was already identified as the 'father of mighty Achilles' (8.309) amidst the heroes hunting for the Calydonian boar: how, then, does this sudden flashback to the first foundation of Troy fit in with Ovid's promised scheme to tell a chronologically ordered history of the world (1.1–4)? Hercules' untimely reappearance draws our attention to the fact that both the foundation of Troy and the birth of Achilles are origin stories (*aetia*) which Ovid should already have narrated. So, as Stephen Wheeler suggests, it seems as though 'Ovid's transpositions of the foundation of Troy and the marriage of Peleus and Thetis are a deliberate structural strategy to furnish new points of origin for the narrative of the final books of the poem'.[8] We begin a new phase in the poem, then, from a new starting point promising a new perspective.

Peleus and Thetis (11.221–65)

Of course, the wedding of Peleus and Thetis (well-known to Ovid's Augustan audience from Catullus' epyllion 64) is itself only a well-worn stepping stone on the traditional narrative path leading towards the birth of Achilles and the start of the Trojan War. But Ovid does not retell this familiar story of the wedding here; instead he follows a different narrative route towards the same end, telling in flashback how Peleus first managed to capture the sea nymph Thetis as his bride. The story that he narrates shares many features with the violent rape narratives that we witnessed in earlier books of the poem, as Thetis forcefully attempts to escape Peleus' determined embrace. As the daughter of the metamorphic sea god Proteus, Thetis has protean shape-shifting powers of her own and, when Peleus attempts to rape her as she lies sleeping naked in her favourite cave, she turns herself into various shapes to escape his hold – until, finding herself bound tightly in ropes, snared like a wild animal, she eventually yields. Ovid incorporates little psychological or emotional colour into his narrative but seems to enjoy the opportunity offered by Thetis' shape-shifting powers to focus upon her metamorphoses rather than her marriage to Peleus. Indeed, as with the violent rape stories of the first few books of the *Metamorphoses*, Thetis' rape raises important questions about how we should respond to Ovid's representation of violence against women in the poem: is Ovid's vivid description of Thetis' resistance to her attacker evidence of his sympathy for victims of rape, or does he take 'pornographic' pleasure in detailing her submission?[9] Here we may also want to consider whether Ovid's decision to focus upon the rape rather than upon the wedding of Thetis as the context for the conception of Achilles is unnecessarily salacious, or whether it prepares us to be prepared for further surprises and innovations as we head towards Ovid's unique retelling of the Trojan War.

Peleus and Ceyx (11.266–409)

To begin with, the conception of the epic genre's greatest hero Achilles proves a false start. Instead of following-up this narrative lead, Ovid returns his attention to Peleus and Thetis and, with a familiar transition through reference to an absent presence (the couple's happiness in everything *except* the murder of Peleus' brother, Phocus – 11.266–8), the poem follows them into exile.[10] In Trachin, the peace-loving king Ceyx welcomes them and tells the story of his brother Daedalion and his unfortunate niece Chione (11.291–345) – she, raped by two gods on the same day and killed by Diana, her grief-stricken father transformed into a sea hawk as he threw himself from a cliff-top.[11] As Ceyx finishes his story, news arrives that a monstrous wolf is attacking Peleus' cattle (a clear sign that the gods have not yet absolved Peleus for his part in the death of Phocus) so, turning the wolf into stone, the couple head off to seek final absolution for Peleus elsewhere – leaving us in the company of Ceyx and his wife, Alcyone. Ovid's rationale for including these two brief tales of metamorphosis here seems primarily strategic: the transformation of the grief-stricken Daedalion into a bird foreshadows the metamorphoses of Ceyx and Alcyone that will follow, and the story of the wolf serves as a convenient device to drive the epic characters Peleus and Thetis away into the background and so allow Ceyx and Alcyone to take centre stage in the following narrative in a dextrous swerve that seemingly takes us ever further away from the anticipated build-up to the story of Troy.

Ceyx and Alcyone (11.410–748)

In fact, these seemingly incidental stories of metamorphosis prove pivotal in driving forward the plot of the next story – a romantic epyllion, dealing not with epic *arma* but with elegiac *amor*. Pious Ceyx is so troubled by these strange transformations that he decides to consult the oracle of Apollo at Delphi. Alcyone pleads with him not to travel and offers an impassioned plea begging him to stay with her, the style and content of her entreaty familiar from the world of elegiac love poetry where such appeals (*querellas* – 11.420) from a lover are a literary commonplace.[12] Alcyone's words fail to persuade Ceyx to stay, however, and while she weeps a storm of tears in her bedroom, a storm of epic proportions descends upon him, wrecking his ship and drowning all on board.

Pitying Alcyone, Juno arranges to inform her of Ceyx' death through a dream – allowing Ovid to actualize the abstract concept of 'sleep' in a novel form of metamorphosis:[13] the cave of Sleep (Somnus) is silent except for the sound of trickling waters (11.600–9) and Ovid enhances the drowsy effect of his description (further enhanced in the long vowels and dipthongs of the Latin) with witty detail; as Iris enters the cave, she has to brush aside the dreams that block her way like cobwebs; Somnus repeatedly nods off as Juno's messenger, Iris, delivers her request; and she has to hurry to leave the cave before its sleepiness takes hold of her too.[14] Somnus duly sends the shape-shifting Morpheus (the perfect agent both for Juno's and for Ovid's meta**morph**ic business), here transformed into a perfect likeness of Ceyx, to appear in a dream to Alcyone. And as she wakes and the dream-ghost of her beloved husband disappears, she reaches out to embrace him in vain (just like Orpheus reaching out to hold the ghost of Eurydice at 10.58f) and she begs him to stay or to take her with him – just as she had begged him when he first set out on his voyage. Her moving elegiac lament (11.684–707), echoes both her earlier speech and the elegiac tradition in which such lovers' laments are a common literary *topos*, as she concludes that she will join her beloved husband in death: 'We shall be united, if not in an urn, in the letters / engraved on our tomb – not dust touching dust, but name touching name'.[15]

Returning to the same spot on the shore from which she had watched Ceyx sail away (repetition and return are recurring motifs in this extended narrative, as throughout the *Metamorphoses*), Alcyone catches sight of Ceyx's corpse washed up in the surf. She leaps into the sea to embrace it – only to find herself transformed into a sea-bird and Ceyx himself brought back to life as her mate. So, through the pity (*miserantibus* – 11.741) of the gods (a miracle in itself in the cruel world of the *Metamorphoses*), the two lovers are reunited for eternity, raising their children together on the calm sea waters during the calm 'halcyon' days of each winter.

This story invites comparison with other tales of tragedy and married love in the poem and critics have noted the similarities that this narrative shares with that of Pyramus and Thisbe (4.55–166) and Cephalus and Procris (7.661–865) in particular.[16] Indeed, like the story of Cephalus and Procris, which is set against the backdrop of preparations for war, this story too offers a 'halcyon' interlude of relative calm before the storm of the Trojan War breaks at the start of the next book. Yet the married couple with whom Ovid most obviously suggests that we compare the peace-loving Ceyx and Alcyone is Peleus and Thetis. Indeed, the contrast between the two couples is striking: Ovid deliberately draws attention to the murderer Peleus' blood-stained hands (*fraterno sanguine sontem* – 11.268) as he is welcomed to Trachin by the peace-loving Ceyx, who rules without force or bloodshed (*sine vi, sine caede* – 11.270); Peleus lies about the reason for his exile, namely the murder of his brother (11.280f), Ceyx accepts him with compassionate words (11.282) while grieving for the loss of his own brother (11.273); and (above all) placid Ceyx and Alcyone bring peace to the world and the stormy seas as they raise their children, in stark contrast to Peleus and Thetis, whose marriage brings mighty Achilles into the world and (albeit unintentionally) brings terror to Troy – to the story of which we now (re)turn.[17]

Aesacus (11.749–95)

An old man is inspired by the sight of the Alcyonae – the sea birds into which Ceyx and Alcyone have been transformed – to tell the story of a similar metamorphosis concerning Aesacus, grandson of Laomedon, son of Priam, and brother of illustrious Hector. With unmistakable echoes of the tales of Apollo and Daphne (1.452–567), Eurydice and Orpheus (10.1–85), Ceyx and Alcyone (11.410–748), the old man narrates how Aesacus once fell in love with the nymph Hesperia. Like Daphne, she ran away from him, and like Apollo, he chased after her (11.771f; cf. 1.533–9). But, as at the wedding of Eurydice, a snake hidden in the grass sinks its fangs into the girl's foot and kills her (11.775f; cf. 10.10). Holding the dead girl in his arms, (echoing Alcyone holding Ceyx) Aesacus laments (literally): 'I would be worse than the snake that killed you if I did not send you solace in death with my own death' (11.781f; cf. 11.701–5). But the goddess Tethys pities the tragic lover (11.784; cf. 11.741) and, as he throws himself from a cliff-top, hoping to die, she turns him into a diving sea bird. And so book 11 draws to a close with the metamorphosis of a Trojan prince – unmentioned in either Homer or the traditional epic cycle, but who, Ovid tells us, had he not met such a strange fate, *might* have been as famous as Hector (11.760).

Discussion points and questions
1. To what extent can Orpheus be regarded as a virtual avatar for his poetic creator, Ovid?
2. Compare Ovid's representation of Peleus' rape of Thetis with the rape narratives of books 1 and 2. What features do these stories share and why does this episode provide an effective introduction to Ovid's own 'little *Iliad*'?
3. How does the story of Aesacus and Hesperia rework motifs from the stories of Apollo and Daphne, Eurydice and Orpheus, Ceyx and Alcyone?

Book Twelve
The Greeks at Aulis (12.1–38)[18]
After a series of false leads telling of the misadventures and metamorphoses of unsung epic heroes and lovers, Ovid finally turns his attention to the Trojan War itself – his transformation of this well-known story (often referred to as Ovid's 'little *Iliad*') beginning at the start of book 12 and continuing into the middle of book 13 (where Ovid's 'little *Aeneid*' begins). The introductory stories of married love in book 11, however, have prepared us to look for the continuation of this amatory motif in Ovid's elegiac metamorphosis of this epic subject, so it comes as little surprise when he opens book 12 with Paris and his stolen wife *(rapta . . . coniuge* – 12.5) Helen. Indeed, following the pattern associated with his earlier stories of stolen or raped (*rapta*) women, he joins the abduction of Helen to the story of Aesacus by an ingenious narrative link. Like Inachus, who mourns for a lost daughter not knowing that she has been turned into a cow (1.566–85), Priam holds funeral rites for his son Aesacus, not

knowing that he still lives in the form of a bird. All of Priam's sons are present – *except* for Paris, who is (of course) at that moment elsewhere, seducing Menelaus' wife. The focus of the narrative then cuts to Aulis, where a thousand Greek ships are preparing to set sail in pursuit of the adulterous couple.

But Ovid is not interested in ships or preparations for war – the genre-defining subjects detailed by his epic predecessor, Homer. Instead, he highlights a traditional story that is passed-over in Homer's *Iliad* (although frequently treated in Greek tragedy): the sacrifice of Agamemnon's daughter Iphigenia to appease the virgin goddess Diana and so calm the raging winds that threaten to scupper the Greek fleet before it reaches Troy. In a tragic tableau, we see Agamemnon torn between the duties of a father and a king (*rexque patrem* – 12.30), Iphigenia standing weeping before the altar, and – at the crucial moment – Diana's substitution of a deer in the girl's place. Traditional versions of this miracle represent Diana *replacing* Iphigenia with the animal and so rescuing her from the cruel sacrifice, but Ovid's version hints at a darker end to this tragedy. Diana, the cruel goddess already notorious for having turned Actaeon into a deer, is said here literally 'to have transformed' (*mutasse* – 12.34) Iphigenia, indicating that her intervention may not have been as merciful as some readers – and some translations – would suggest.

Ovid's emphasis upon Iphigenia's transformation, along with the clear signposting of his own intended transformation of the Homeric narrative of the Trojan War, is important here: the story of Iphigenia, in particular, anticipates Ovid's focus upon the female victims rather than upon the male heroes of this traditional narrative. Several readers and critics have noted a major shift in Ovid's narrative at this point in the poem as he moves from overtly mythological to more histori-cally based stories;[19] but, here too, there is evidence of continuity through change.

Rumour (12.39–63)[20]

Having boldly taken on the Greek epic poet Homer in the opening lines of the book, Ovid now challenges a second oppon-ent, his Roman rival Virgil – effectively restaging his telling of the Trojan War as a metapoetic battle of literary rather than military prowess.[21] As the Greek fleet sets sail, reports of the

planned attack reach Troy, allowing Ovid to introduce a personi-
fication of Rumour (*Fama*), based on Virgil's virtuoso portrait
of the same in book 4 of his epic *Aeneid* (4.174–88). In contrast
to the cave of Sleep, the house of Rumour is a place of constant
noise, of echoes and repetitions (12.46–8). In fact, the house of
Rumour, like Daedalus' labyrinth, offers a nice template for the
complex narrative pattern of Ovid's own poem where similarly,
it might be said, there exists 'a flimsy throng of a thousand
rumours, true and fictitious, / wandering far and wide in a turbu-
lent tangle of language' (12.55–8).

Cycnus (12.64–145)

Rumour sees to it that the Trojans are ready to fight when
the Greeks finally arrive, allowing Ovid too to move straight
into battle, and to zoom in upon one warrior in particular –
Neptune's son Cycnus, who has already killed a thousand men
when he meets Achilles.[22] Achilles has been looking for Hector
but Ovid here offers him (and us) Cycnus as a substitute (12.75).
We are prepared for a conventional *aristeia* (a display of an epic
hero's 'excellence' in combat) but instead we are given a display
of Ovid's prowess in transforming traditional epic characters
and tropes: a poetological *aristeia*. Achilles, son of Thetis and
Peleus, and mighty hero of Homer's epic *Iliad*, finds himself
unable to wound his opponent – even when Cycnus takes off
his armour to taunt Achilles with his magical invulnerability.
A furious Achilles, raging, (in a suitably Homeric-sounding
simile) like a bull against a red rag (12.102–4), failing with
both spear and sword to so much as scratch Cycnus, loses his
temper – and his dignity. Jumping down from his chariot, he
beats Cycnus around the head with his shield and sword-
hilt, finally strangling his opponent with the straps of his own
helmet: an inglorious death and an inglorious victory. What
is more, as Achilles prepares to take Cycnus' armour as his
trophy, he finds it empty: Cycnus has been transformed into the
white swan that shares his name (12.143–5). Achilles' victory,
like Cycnus' armour, is hollow, and his famous anger – the
stated theme of Homer's *Iliad* – is transformed here into a
temper tantrum.

   After this ignominious conflict, a truce ensues (presumably
the same one described by Homer in *Iliad* 3) and the Greeks

entertain themselves by telling stories – sardonically characterized by Ovid as prosaic 'conversations' (*sermone . . . . loquendi* – 12.159) quite distinct from the poetic stories or *carmina* (12.157) that he himself tells. Achilles at first dominates these stories of manliness (*virtus* – 12.159), combat (*pugnas* – 12.160), and peril on the battlefield (*pericula* – 12.161). For, as Ovid explains, what else would Achilles and his men tell stories about (12.162f)? Significantly, Ovid leaves these stories of epic bravery and derring-do untold. But the strange tale of Achilles' recent encounter with Cycnus prompts the aged Homeric hero Nestor (famous from the *Iliad* for his experience and his honeyed tongue: *Iliad* I.290–5) to break Achilles' monopoly upon the conversation and to take up the role of internal narrator with a sequence of his own strange tales that run almost up to the end of book 12 (12.169–576).

Caeneus (12.146–209)

Nestor seizes the attention of his audience by comparing Cycnus and his strange powers to another hero he had known long ago, whom he had seen with his own eyes rebuff a thousand blows without a scratch, and who – incidentally – had been born a woman (12.175). Even Achilles shows a prurient interest in hearing such a bizarre story, so Nestor narrates the curious tale of Caeneus – although he distances himself from the strangeness of the tale by stressing *twice* that he is only reporting a story known to him by hearsay or *fama* (12.197, 200). According to these *fama,* Caeneus/Caenis, born a girl, was famed for her beauty and (inevitably, in the world of the *Metamorphoses*) raped by a god – Neptune. Offered a gift by him, she asked to be transformed into a man so that she might never suffer such trauma again. And so Caenis became Caeneus – impenetrable and invulnerable, if not wholly invincible, unmanning and emasculating those heroes who cannot penetrate him with their swords and spears and who can only kill him – in much the same way as Achilles killed Cycnus – by suffocation.[23] As Nestor reveals in his next tale.

The Battle of the Lapiths and Centaurs (12.210–579)

To illustrate Caeneus' prowess as a warrior, Nestor offers an eye-witness account of the infamous wedding celebrations of

Pirithous, King of the Lapiths, to his bride Hippodamia, to which he and Caeneus are invited – along with the centaurs. As the wedding guests recline at their banqueting couches (like Nestor's own internal audience – and, perhaps, like Ovid's Augustan audience too), enjoying the festivities and the free-flowing wine, chaos breaks out. Eurytus, 'the wildest of all the wild centaurs' (12.219), is overcome by drunkenness and lust and grabs the bride by her hair, attempting to rape her, with his fellow centaurs each following suit. The battle of the Lapiths and centaurs, famously depicted upon the Athenian Parthenon to represent the forces of civilization conquering barbarism, order vanquishing chaos, has been initiated – like the Trojan War itself – by a fight over a girl.

Indeed, Nestor's flashback narrative of the drunken carnage that ensues is the central battle scene in Ovid's own miniature *Iliad,* his description of the epic battle between the civilized Lapiths and the monstrous centaurs offering an innovative substitution for the familiar Iliadic battles between Trojans and Greeks which Ovid's readers have been anticipating since book 11.[24] However, Ovid's Iliadic battle-scene – suitably placed in the mouth of his Homeric proxy Nestor – is unlike anything described by Homer: the style of combat and weapons employed are unconventional and unepic, the fatal wounds they deal (predominantly to the head and face) are unheroic and horrifically gruesome.

Theseus hurls an antique wine-mixing bowl into Eurytus' face, causing brains, blood and wine to pour from his wound and his mouth (12.235–40) and the other assembled heroes follow his lead, transforming utensils designed for feasting and celebration into weapons of war and destruction (12.244). A centaur smashes a chandelier into the face of a Lapith, causing his eyes to pop out of their sockets, his cheek bones to crack and his nose to stick in his throat (12.245–53), before meeting death himself at the dangerous end of a table-leg (12.254–7). An altar stone is used to crush two men, but the antlers of a stag's head provide a suitable means of revenge – and a revolting description as the offender's eyes are gouged out (12.268f). A burning log used as a club sets fire to one victim's hair as the bloody wound it causes sizzles in the heat like an iron bar in a blacksmith's bucket (12.271–9). The same grotesque weapon smashes out the brains of a second fatality, and is thrust into the open mouth of a third (12.286–95). Another log crushes the skull of yet another unlucky wedding guest, causing his splattered brains to ooze out of his nostrils, ears and eyes like cottage cheese through a sieve – possibly the most grotesque simile in classical literature (12.434–8), unless that honour should go to Ovid's description of a disembowelled centaur tripping over his own entrails (12.390–2).

Amidst this horror, Ovid's Nestor somehow realizes a moment of genuine pathos in his description of the deaths of two young centaur lovers – Cyllarus and Hylonome – an elegiac couple who seem utterly out of place in this violent epic scene. In fact, the hybrid nature of these sympathetic and attractive centaurs reminds us that, like these horse/men crossbreeds, Ovid's 'epic' poem is itself a hybrid creature – part epic, part elegiac.[25] The female centaur Hylonome, indeed, appears to follow the advice set out in Ovid's own elegiac *Ars Amatoria* in her sophisticated dress and toilette (her *cultu* – 12.408). She does everything possible to make herself look attractive, wearing pretty animal skins over her shoulder, weaving flowers into her hair, and washing her face not once but twice a day (12.406–15). Unlike the typical lovers of Roman elegy, however, this couple love equally (*par amor* – 12.416) and do everything together, the exceptional relationship between them highlighted in the Latin by the repetition of words suggesting mutual sympathy and partnership (*par, una, simul, pariter*). In this respect, they mirror the mutual love or *par amor* shared by other married lovers depicted in the *Metamorphoses* (particularly Baucis and Philemon (8.611–724), Iphis and Ianthe (9.666–797)). And – inevitably – they share the same tragic death, as Cyllarus is felled by a javelin thrown by an unknown hand and Hylonome throws herself upon the same spear, to be united with her lover in a dying embrace.

This elegiac digression comes in the very middle of Nestor's violent narrative and offers a welcome relief from the grotesque horrors of the epic battle that surrounds both this story and its protagonists. Indeed, an experienced story-teller in the epic, Homeric, tradition, Nestor can be seen here to adopt a familiar Iliadic technique, in which the narrator offers his audience periodic relief from the violent battle-scenes that dominate his narrative with brief digressions that offer a glimpse into an alternate world of peace and domesticity – of love (*amor*) instead of war (*arma*).

Throughout his narrative, including his digression, Nestor has been eager to stress his reliability as a narrator, diligently distinguishing between those things that he saw himself, and those that he heard at second hand. So, he does not repeat for us Hylonome's dying words to her beloved because the noise of the surrounding battle prevented him from hearing them clearly (12.426f). And he acknowledges that he is not entirely sure how – or if – Caeneus met his death: some believe he was crushed by the weight of stones piled upon his body by the frustrated centaurs, others that he was transformed into a bird (12.522–32). Yet, he admits at the start of his narrative that his memory is not perfect and that time has impaired his recall of the long ago events of which he now speaks (12.182–8). He shows his audience the scar he received during the battle between Lapiths and centaurs as testimony to the truth of his story about Caeneus, but he immediately undermines the reliability of his narration by reminiscing that, two hundred years ago when the battle took place and he was still in his prime, he might even have been a match for the mighty Hector, the current scourge of the Greek forces at Troy – if Hector had been more than a babe, indeed, if he had even been born back then (12.447f). Yet, as Margaret Musgrove notices: 'why should there be any question about whether Hector was yet alive two hundred years ago?'[26] Nestor's reliability as an epic narrator – and perhaps the reliability of any narrator – is brought into question again as he confesses to certain holes in his memory. Recalling the details of Caeneus' *aristeia*, and listing the centaurs he killed in the battle, he tells us in an aside that he can't remember their wounds or how they died, only their names and number (12.461). Given the catalogue of horrifically detailed wounds, and the blow by blow account of numerous other deaths in the battle between Lapiths and centaurs that Nestor has just narrated, scepticism in his reliability as a narrator seems fully justified. That is certainly the response of Nestor's own internal audience, as Hercules' son, Tlepolemus, politely asks why the old man's story has made no mention of his heroic father – famous for his exploits in the battle of Lapiths and centaurs. But Nestor is unapologetic about leaving Hercules out of his story: he hates him for murdering his brothers and destroying his home, and feels no desire to glorify the deeds of an enemy. All narratives are unreliable it seems, subject to biases and prejudices, inventions and exclusions.

The Death of Achilles (12.580–628)

After Nestor's confession of deliberate omission, selection and suppression in his own storytelling, Ovid takes Nestor's example as he takes up the narrative once more – and boldly skips over *all* the remaining incidents and events of the Trojan War, ingeniously covering the narrative of almost ten years of fighting (and twenty four books of the *Iliad*) in one line (*iamque fere tracto duo per quinquennia bello* – 12.584). Jumping forward to the death of Achilles, an event not narrated in the *Iliad* itself but well-known to Ovid's audience from Homer's *Odyssey* and other non-Homeric epics, Ovid makes one of his own stories (that of Cycnus) central to Achilles' final defeat. Nursing a wrath to rival Achilles' own infamous anger, the god Neptune decides to take revenge for the death of his son, Cycnus. He persuades Apollo to guide one of Paris' arrows and so ensures mighty Achilles' swift and ignominious death at the hand of a cowardly adulterer (12.609).

So Achilles and book 12 come to an end together. Ovid says nothing of the funeral games or elaborate rites that would have accompanied Achilles' cremation, only that the body was burned until all that remained of the once great hero was a handful of dust – scarcely enough to fill an urn (12.612–6). But his immortal fame lives on – enough to fill the whole world. Even his famous armour continues to play its part in a new conflict. For, as book 12 draws to a close the other Greek heroes begin to squabble over who should now wear it and 'arms were taken up for his arms' (12.621).

Discussion points and questions

1. What does Nestor's narrative suggest about the nature of story-telling in the *Metamorphoses*?
2. To what extent is the *Metamorphoses* a hybrid poem?

3. What does the story of Caenis/Caeneus reveal about attitudes towards gender in the poem?

Book Thirteen

The Debate over the Arms of Achilles (13.1–398)

In keeping with its epic subject, book 13 is the longest of the poem, embracing in its ridiculously comprehensive scope the central characters and events of the *Iliad* (postponed from book 12 and narrated now in flashback), the *Odyssey*, the *Aithiopis*, *Cypria* and *Little Iliad* from the (now lost) Epic Cycle, as well as the *Aeneid.* Callimachus would, no doubt, have been appalled by such a torrent of epic material. In addition to this 'epic' range of epic intertexts, numerous tragedies inspired by the Epic Cycle are also touched upon along the way (including Aeschylus' lost drama the *Judgement of Arms*, Sophocles' *Philoctetes*, and Euripides' *Hecuba*) as Ovid continues to explore the variety of different forms into which familiar narratives can be meta- morphosed, and the transformations that inevitably reshape a story through the act of its retelling.

Aptly enough, given the chronological and narratological compass of his own epic *carmen perpetuum*, Ovid is also par- ticularly interested here in the minor episodes that occur before, after, or in-between the principal happenings featured in the Greek and Roman epic tradition – prompting him to summarize (or simply ignore) well-known details and events and to elab- orate upon less celebrated aspects of familiar tales. In fact, this practice of variation (known to the classical schools of rhetoric as *variatio*) was a technique widely employed in the standard oratorical debates of Ovid's own time – debates, moreover, in which the argument or *controversia* between Ajax and Ulysses (Odysseus) over who should inherit the arms of Achilles had become a well-rehearsed commonplace.[27] Ovid's challenge in this debate, then, is to make his own variation of that argument persuasive and to turn it successfully to his own ends as an innovative new form of epic storytelling.

He achieves this by using the debate as an ingenious means of compressing the extended narrative of the Trojan War into a few lines, summarising key episodes both in and leading up to the conflict, as first Ajax and then Ulysses offer their own checklists of salient events. Ajax speaks first, offering the following (distinctly biased) summary of reasons why he and not Ulysses deserves to inherit the great Achilles' armour (13.5–122):

1. Ulysses ran away when Hector tried to torch the Greek fleet, while Ajax stayed to fight and saved them.
2. Ajax is the son of Telemon (who helped Hercules to defeat Troy in an earlier conflict), Achilles' own cousin *and* descendent of Jupiter, whereas, Ulysses is a nobody, fathered by the notorious trickster Sisyphus.
3. Ajax was one of the first to take up arms, whereas Ulysses tried to avoid the war by feigning madness.
4. Ulysses left his comrade Philoctetes to die alone, falsely charged his friend Palamedes with treason, and even deserted faithful old Nestor in his hour of need.
5. Ajax once saved the cowardly Ulysses' life on the battle-field.
6. Ajax once threw a boulder at the mighty Hector.
7. Wily Ulysses has no need of armour as he avoids hand-to-hand combat in favour of tricks, and Achilles' heavy shield and spear will only weigh the weakling down as he tries to run away from the enemy.
8. Ajax needs a new shield as his own is full of holes from all the action it has seen in combat, whereas battle-shy Ulysses' rarely-used shield is undamaged.

Emphatically a man of action (*agendo* – 13.120) rather than of words (*verbis* – 13.120), Ajax finally suggests that the two men should fight to decide who should have the arms, confident that he can beat Ulysses in a brawl if not in a debate. The common crowd (*vulgi* – 13.123) of Greek soldiers applaud Ajax' short speech, but when Ulysses steps up to respond he directs his words towards the more critically discerning Greek leaders (*proceres* – 13.126) and it is towards this audience (in which Ovid includes *us*) that he aims the full force of his famous eloquence. In his version of events, Ulysses claims that (13.128–381):

1. Ulysses discovered Achilles hiding on Scyros and person-ally brought him to join the Greek force, so therefore, Ulysses can indirectly claim Achilles' victories as his own.

2. Ulysses is also descended from Jupiter *and* claims descent from Mercury on his mother's side – but if Achilles' arms are to be claimed by a blood relative, they should be given to his son.

3. Ulysses convinced Agamemnon to make the human sacrifice (Iphigenia) that guaranteed the Greek fleet's safe arrival at Troy.

4. Ulysses tried to persuade Priam and Antenor to return Helen to her husband and so resolve the conflict peaceably without need for war.

5. During the first nine years of the war, Ajax did nothing, while Ulysses worked hard as an ambassador and spy, boosting the morale of the troops.

6. Ulysses persuaded Agamemnon *and* Ajax not to give up and go home, so therefore, Ulysses can indirectly claim Ajax' victories as his own.

7. Ulysses killed Dolon the Trojan spy.

8. Ulysses has received battle-wounds, whereas Ajax has none.

9. It was Patroclus disguised as Achilles who saved the fleet from fire, not Ajax.

10. Ulysses carried Achilles' dead body from the battle-field – armour and all – so clearly has strength enough to bear his arms. Moreover, Ulysses has the intellect to appreciate their artistry, whereas Ajax is too stupid to realize their aesthetic and symbolic beauty.

11. Ulysses admittedly entered the war after the others, but so too did the great Achilles.

12. The Greek leaders themselves approved his treatment of Philoctetes and Palamedes – and still require Ulysses' help to bring back Philoctetes and so slay Paris with Hercules' bow.

13. Ulysses will recover Philoctetes just as he once captured the seer Helenus and the 'Palladium' statue of Minerva.

The Greek leaders are persuaded by Ulysses' words and award him Achilles' armour: as we might expect, words (*verba*) carry more weight than deeds (*acta*) in the world of the *Metamorphoses*. In fact, that is perhaps how Ovid himself triumphs in his own literary battle of words here: where the narratives of his epic predecessors offered us tales of heroic deeds, Ovid simply gives us two heroes and their words – that is, their own speeches claiming the right to Achilles' arms. It is significant, moreover, that Ajax' traditional and rigidly narrow conception of the proper form of the epic hero (along with his biased 'misreading' of the *Iliad* and the Epic Cycle) is challenged and successfully bested here by Ulysses' more creative, flexible and intellectual model. Wily Ulysses, the skilful liar, storyteller and man of many ways (his standard Homeric epithet is *polytropos*) serves – in many ways – as an appropriate model for Ovid's own storytelling technique in the *Metamorphoses*.[28]

Indeed, at this point Ovid's polytropic, epic narrative takes a new turn – or, rather, *return* – towards the elegiac theme of commemoration and lament. When Ulysses wins this war of words, Ajax commits suicide by falling upon Achilles' sword, a purple hyacinth flower springing up from his blood (just it had at Hyacinthus' death – 10.206–19), its petals bearing the pattern of AIAI. Thus, an elegiac cry of lament (13.398) stands as the final, fragile memorial for this mighty epic hero.

The Sorrows of Hecuba (13.399–575)

The theme of commemoration continues to drive the narrative in the next episode, as Ovid turns from the Greek victors of the war to remember and honour the Trojan survivors as they, in turn, struggle with their own tributes to the dead. And again, the next story sees him once more summarizing or ignoring well-known details and events and elaborating upon those that are less familiar. So, passing quickly over the deaths of Paris and Priam, the burning of Troy, and the enslavement of the Trojan women, this episode focuses upon the experiences of the Trojan queen Hecuba, treating her personal bereavement as a form of synecdoche for the fall of Troy itself – the ashes of Hector (all that Hecuba can carry as she is dragged into captivity) serving as a metonymic substitution for the ashes of Troy.

Here, the dead impose a dreadful duty upon the living, as the angry ghost of Achilles rises from the grave to demand a share of the captured Trojan women, ordering the sacrifice of Hecuba's sole surviving daughter to his memory (13.445–8). In an echo of Iphigenia's cruel sacrifice at the start of the Trojan

War, Polyxena is duly torn from her grieving mother's arms to face death, which she meets like a true (male) epic hero, both bold (*fortis* – 13.451) and fearless (*intrepidos* – 13.478), bravely offering her throat to the knife, preferring death to a life of slavery. In stark contrast to the petty squabbling of Ajax and Ulysses and the petulant anger of Achilles, Polyxena here demonstrates epic *virtus* or 'manly' heroism in a new – and improved – feminine form. Ovid has not only metamorphosed the form of Homeric epic here, it seems: he has also transformed the very gender of epic *virtus*.

Echoing the paired speeches of Ajax and Ulysses at the start of the book (13.5–381) and eloquently illustrating the fearless heroism that women may show in war, Ovid follows Polyxena's bold suicide address (which moves the assembled Greeks to tears) with Hecuba's own poignant list of the many sorrows she has herself endured (13.494–532). But, like 'the man of many sorrows', Ulysses himself, there is yet more suffering in store for Hecuba: as she collects water to wash her daughter's corpse, she finds the murdered body of her youngest son Polydorus (sent to stay with an ally, the Thracian king Polymestor, at the start of the war) washed up on the seashore. The profundity of her grief strikes her dumb and she is frozen to the spot like a rock (13.538–40). The transformation that Hecuba experiences here, however, is not physical but psychological, not a turning of flesh to stone (as in the case of Niobe at the death of her children – 6.146–312) but rather a turning of grief into rage: like a female Achilles, she 'arms' herself with anger (13.544) and sets out to take her revenge. But, as she bites and howls at her enemies, she is miraculously transformed into a dog, forever after howling out her sorrows in a place named Cynossema, the Dog's Tomb – the name of the place serving as a memorial to her undeserved suffering and her strange transformation (13.575).

Memnon (13.576–622)

So sad is the story of Hecuba that it moves not only her fellow Trojans, but her Greek enemies and all the gods as well. All, that is, but Aurora, who has sorrows of her own. In a neat transition through absence or exception, Ovid thus moves from the tale of one mother's grief to another's, to remember the story of

Memnon, son of the goddess of the dawn.[29] Here, once again, we see Ovid experimenting with the traditional form and content of the epic tradition as he picks upon a minor character who, according to later retellings of the story of the Trojan War, succeeded Hector as leader of the Trojan forces.[30] Ovid now follows that variant upon the Homeric tradition in his own *variatio* upon the themes of commemoration that dominate this book. Like Hecuba, Aurora is overwhelmed by grief at the death of her son – killed years before by Achilles – and begs Jupiter for some compensatory honour. Jupiter agrees to her request and, as Memnon's body burns on its (long overdue) funeral pyre, the smoke and ashes that swirl up from the fire take on the appearance of a bird and then – as metaphor becomes metamorphosis – turn into real birds (13.607), the Memnonides: a neat aetiology that prepares us for the following account of new life arising from the ashes of Troy, as we follow Aeneas in his escape from the fallen city.

The Wanderings of Aeneas I (13.623–968)

As both a Trojan-Roman and a Homeric-Virgilian figure, hero both of Homer's *Iliad* and Virgil's *Aeneid*, Aeneas is already a metamorphic character, eminently suitable as one of the heroes of Ovid's epic, and we now follow him (as he himself follows the wandering homeward journey of Odysseus) as he sets out to found a new Troy – to found Rome.[31]

Aeneas, famously carrying his household gods and his father upon his shoulder and leading his son Ascanius by the hand, flees with the rest of Troy's refugees. But Ovid suggests that in *choosing* (*eligit* – 13.626) these companions and leaving his wife Creusa to die forgotten and unmentioned behind him, pious Aeneas perhaps fails – like the epic tradition itself – to pay due consideration and honour to the women in his story: a neglect, of course, to which Ovid's own retelling of the aftermath of the Trojan war has offered some kind of corrective in its distinctive focus upon the impact of the war upon Troy's women. Indeed, this focus continues into the next story as we follow Aeneas, Anchises and Ascanius to Delos, where an old friend of Anchises, the Delian king Anius, entertains the Trojans with a banquet. To Anchises' inquiries as to the health of his children, Anius tells how his four daughters – who each possessed the metamorphic power to turn whatever they touched into wine, corn, or oil – had themselves transformed into doves when Agamemnon had tried to force them to use their gifts to aid the Greek forces at Troy (13.632–74).

According to custom, the visitors and their host exchange gifts as well as stories, and Anius then presents Aeneas with an intricately decorated bowl, depicting the story of the daughters of Orion (13.675–99). In an extended ecphrasis Ovid describes for us the narrative of this tale, illustrated in sequential scenes around the bowl: a city with seven gates (Thebes), a plague, the desolation of the city and its countryside, the self-sacrificing suicides of the daughters of Orion, their funeral and, arising from their pyre, two sons, the Coronae. The story on the bowl neatly rehearses a parallel to the story of Anius' own self-sacrificing daughters, as well as recalling those of Memnon and Polyxena, thereby illustrating the themes explored across the interwoven narratives of book 13: in particular, female sacrifice and new life born from the ashes of death and defeat – presaging Troy's own revival and rebirth from the ashes as Aeneas (and Ovid) head for Rome.[32]

Ovid next moves swiftly over an eventful itinerary that took Homer's Odysseus and Virgil's Aeneas several books to traverse (13.705–29) as the Trojan refugees quickly take their leave of Crete, Ithaca, Ambracia, Dodona, Chaonia, the utopian fairyland of Phaeacia, and the Trojan theme-park of Buthrotos, before arriving at the shores of Sicily. Here, the monstrous Scylla (*not* the same Scylla as the girl featured in book 8, even though Minos refers to her there as a 'monster' (8.100)) threatens to destroy every approaching ship. But, instead of sailing heroically past this notorious obstacle (as did Homer's Odysseus and his crew), Ovid here slows down his narrative to take a closer look at the terrifying Scylla, now a monstrous creature with snarling dogs from the waist down but once a beautiful girl (13.730–7) who loved to tell stories of her former lovers (*narrabat amores* – 13.737). Ovid's sympathies for this fellow narrator of elegiac love-stories (Ovid's own first collection of poetry was, of course, his *Amores*) – and his intention *not* to follow in the footsteps of his literary predecessors but to allow female voices to be heard in his version of epic – could hardly be indicated more explicitly.

Galatea and Polyphemus (13.738–897)

Before we hear one of Scylla's love stories, however, we are first introduced to one of her sister nymphs, Galatea, who now tells Scylla (while combing her hair, in a metapoetic activity often associated with elegiac poetic composition[33]) the tale of her own *amores*. Galatea's story involves a love-triangle – the first of several in this part of the *Metamorphoses* – comprising her lover Acis and the monstrous Cyclops, Polyphemus.[34] Already familiar to Ovid's Augustan audience as the lovesick buffoon (hairy but harmless) of Theocritus' *Idyll* 6, the Polyphemus described by Galatea is a very different creature, at whose monstrous appearance the very woods shudder, who despises the gods, and terrorizes hapless strangers. Venus and *amor*, however, transform the wild Polyphemus, causing him to take a new care in his appearance. Like a pupil of the 'love doctor' or *praeceptor amoris* of Ovid's elegiac *Ars Amatoria,* the Cyclops combs his shaggy locks with a rake, trims his beard with a scythe, and checks his face in pools of water, giving up his old violent pursuits and neglecting the care of his sheep, instead playing his giant pan-pipes and singing songs in praise of Galatea.

The Cyclops' song configures Galatea as a stereotypically hard-hearted elegiac mistress or *dura puella* (13.789–807), and there is something undeniably comic about the presents he promises his love if only she will return his affection – apples, grapes and strawberries, milk and cheese, and even a pair of baby bears (13.810–37). How could a girl resist? Yet, the baby bears (*now* cute and cuddly but destined to grow up hairy and wild) are only one of many clues in Polyphemus' song that hint towards the presence of a dark side to this would-be lover: in narcissistic self-regard he boasts of his size and his hairiness as surpassing even that of Jupiter, likens his one eye to the all-seeing sun, and threatens to tear his rival Acis limb from limb as the passion that he feels for Galatea boils up in his heart like molten lava (13.840–69). The Theocritean gentle giant is transformed into his violent Homeric counterpart in the course of his song, as pastoral motifs give way first to elegiac and then epic conceits.[35] Giants in epic, of course, scorn the gods and tear up mountains (as we saw in Ovid's own gigantomachy – 1.151–62) and upon seeing Galatea in the arms of her beloved Acis, this is precisely what Polyphemus does next – crushing Acis to death with a giant boulder torn out of a mountainside (13.882–4). Galatea saves her lover by transforming him into a river-god, before swimming away to join her sister nymphs in the sea.

Ovid then temporarily takes up the narrative, and returns to Scylla wandering along the shoreline. There she is spied by the sea-god Glaucus, who sets out to woo her by telling the story of his own transformation from man into merman (13.917–65). But, just as Galatea had been disgusted by the hairy giant Polyphemus, Scylla too is repulsed by Glaucus' fishy form and runs away – leaving Glaucus to set out to seek a love-potion from the witch Circe. At this crucial point, the longest book in the *Metamorphoses* ends, and we follow the story of Scylla and Glaucus across the break and into book 14.

Discussion points and questions
1. How do Hecuba and Polyxena transform the standard model of epic heroism and *virtus* in this book?
2. What themes unite the tales of Polyxena, Memnon, the daughters of Anius, and the daughters of Orion?
3. How does Ovid transform the Cyclops Polyphemus?

Book Fourteen

Glaucus and Scylla (14.1–74)

Best known for her transforming role in Homer's *Odyssey*, where she uses her magic to turn Odysseus' men into pigs, Circe is an obvious candidate for inclusion in Ovid's *Metamorphoses* – although it is noteworthy that here her place in the narrative of Ovid's 'little *Aeneid*' (like that of the Cyclops) chronologically *precedes* her famous encounter with Odysseus. It is as if Ovid's retelling of these well-known tales places Homer and Virgil as Ovid's epic successors rather than his poetic predecessors – an ingenious move on the part of this belated poet.[36] In her encounter with Glaucus and Scylla, Circe herself is now transformed – turned by Ovid into a jealous lover who instantly falls in love with Glaucus when he asks her for a love potion or spell to win Scylla's affections. When he refuses her, Circe is enraged and, like Polyphemus in book 13, turns her spiteful anger towards her rival in love. She poisons one of Scylla's favourite pools with magic herbs so that when Scylla wades waist-deep into the pool to bathe, she finds her lower body horrifically transformed into a mass of monstrous, barking dogs' heads (14.59–67). This partial transformation – mirroring that of the merman Glaucus – is a novelty in the world of the *Metamorphoses* and allows Ovid to reclaim some of the shocking psychological impact that metamorphosis held both for its victims and for the poem's readers in earlier books as Scylla attempts to run away from the monstrous creatures that snarl around her waist, only to take them with her as she flees (14.61–7).

The Wanderings of Aeneas II (14.75–608)[37]

Narrating the more famous of Aeneas' adventures only in out-line (just as he had the key events of the Trojan War) and elaborating only upon those episodes that provide an opportun-ity to explore a tale of metamorphosis, Ovid merely summarizes the next few stages of Aeneas' journey towards Italy, condensing the role played by Aeneas himself in his narrative to that of a minor bit-part (on stage for less than a fifth of the 953 line 'little *Aeneid*'), and allowing him to speak only once (14.123–8). So, in marked contrast to Virgil's treatment of the same episodes, Ovid compresses the Trojan voyage from Sicily to Carthage (taking up most of *Aeneid* 1) to just three lines (14.75–7); reduces the infamous and ill-fated romance between Dido and Aeneas (taking up all of *Aeneid* 4) to another four lines (14.78–81); and cuts the events of *Aeneid* 5 (including the attempted burning of the Trojan fleet and the loss of Aeneas' helmsman, Palinurus) into a brief seven lines (14.82–88). The only story on which he elaborates here is an episode unmen-tioned by Virgil – the transformation of the cheeky Cercopes into cheeky monkeys (14.89–100): a nice example of Ovid himself making a monkey out of his epic predecessor in this 'little *Aeneid*'.

In fact, the first – and only – Virgilian episode on which Ovid lingers at any kind of length is Aeneas' visit to the Sibyl at Cumae, the prelude to Virgil's celebrated journey to the underworld where Aeneas is shown a parade of Rome's future heroes (14.101–53). However, in direct contrast to Virgil's treat-ment of the same episode, in this heavily edited, truncated account of Aeneas' underworld adventure, there is no sense at all of the manifest destiny of Aeneas himself, of his descendents (among which Augustus counted himself), or of the future Roman race. Instead, Ovid's Aeneas is made to seem a mere refugee, driven to Italy by the winds of chance rather than divine providence: a provocative re-telling of Augustus' favourite foundation myth.

Following Aeneas on his onward journey from Cumae to Caieta – but effectively doubling-back upon his own narrative journey – Ovid continues to be brief where Virgil is expansive and expansive where Virgil is brief, focusing next upon two discarded comrades of Ulysses and their less-than-heroic adventures. As the two friends bring each other up-to-date about their separate exploits, Achaemenides first tells (in flash-back) of his awful experience hiding from the monstrous Polyphemus, watching his companions being eaten by the Cyclops, their bones sucked clean of marrow, while he himself lived on acorns and grass until his rescue by Aeneas (14.167–222). Macareus then takes up the narrative with an abbreviated account of his own adventures on board Ulysses' ship – a 'little *Odyssey*' inset within Ovid's 'little *Aeneid*'. Macareus' story condenses the events of Homer's *Odyssey* book 10, detailing (once more in flashback) his encounters with Aeolus (14.223–32), and with the cannibalistic Laestrygonians (14.233–42), before bringing us (again) to Circe's enchanted island: Circe's magical powers hold particular charm for Ovid, it seems, and a second visit to her island allows him to retell (alongside the story of Picus and Canens – 14.318–434[38]) the story of her most infamous metamorphosis, the transformation of Ulysses' men – incidentally, the oldest account of a human transformation in the canon of Western literature.

Uniquely in the poem, this allows us the opportunity to hear at first-hand (and in the first-person) a survivor's account of the experience of metamorphosis – although Macareus' report lacks any psychological or emotional depth and is typical of the hundreds of other metamorphoses we have already witnessed as he describes how (14.279–85):

> (I tell the tale to my shame) I started to prickle all over
> with bristles. My voice had deserted me; all the words I could
> utter

were snorting grunts. I was falling down to the earth, head
first.
I could feel my nose and my mouth going hard in a long round
snout;
my neck was swelling in folds of muscle; the hands which had
lifted
the cup just now to my lips were marking the soil with hoof
prints.
Others had suffered the same (those charms are so strong!)
and I joined them,
penned in a sty.

Luckily for Macareus and his fellow pig-men, Ulysses persuades
Circe to undo her spell and with it the transformation of his
men – allowing Ovid to exploit another rare opportunity and to
describe a reverse metamorphosis, with both Circe and Ovid
employing words in reverse (*contraria verbis* – 14.301) until the
pigs regain their former shapes (14.299–305).

We set sail with Aeneas once more – albeit following his
journey at something of an emotional distance, paying attention
only to the major stops on his well-known itinerary, and easily
distracted by any incidental metamorphosis that might occur
along the way – until we reach the coast of Italy and Latium.
Here, in the fourth love-triangle of Ovid's 'little *Aeneid*', Aeneas
must fight against Turnus for the hand of Lavinia. But, instead
of focusing upon the conflict that had so occupied Virgil's
attention, Ovid follows his own narrative tangent. So, as Aeneas
seeks support for his campaign from his old friend Evander,
Turnus sends his ambassador Venulus to ask for aid from the
Greek Diomedes – only to hear the tale of Diomedes' own
troubled journey back from Troy, during which his men had
been turned into seagulls (14.464–511). On the way home,
Venulus passes a hillside cave, now occupied by Pan but once
inhabited by woodland nymphs. This provides Ovid the
opportunity to relate the incidental story of a local Latin
shepherd who had once mocked the nymphs and had found
himself transformed into a wild olive tree for his insult – the
sharpness of his tongue preserved in the taste of its berries
(14.512–26). Neither of these insignificant incidents receives
much attention from Virgil, but both illustrate perfectly the style

of Ovid's own 'transformation' of the *Aeneid* itself – downplaying major events and actors while highlighting those that are incidental and (ideally) metamorphic.

Ovid *does* elect to highlight and transform one major Virgilian episode, however: aptly enough, the transformation of Aeneas' ships into nymphs (*Aeneid* 9.72–122; 10.230–5), one of the rare metamorphoses to appear in Virgil's epic. Readers of Ovid's *carmen perpetuum* are by now used to nymphs turning into plants, trees and other inanimate objects, but the reversal of this trend marks an unusual variation in Ovid's already extensive register of different transformations. Indeed, the transformation of the wooden ships into nymphs neatly inverts the pattern of metamorphosis with which we have become familiar. So (14.549–56):

> As the wood in them gradually softened, the boats were changed into bodies,
> the rounded sterns were transformed into heads, and the oars vanished into
> the legs and toes of a swimmer. The sides continued as sides, and the keel down the middle below was altered to serve as a backbone.
> Rigging became soft hair, and arms appeared on the sail yards.
> The colour was still sea-green. The ships were nymphs of the ocean,
> girlishly playing among the waves which had formerly scared them.

This strange and beautiful transformation, Ovid suggests, should have warned Turnus to give up his fight against Aeneas but stubbornly, Turnus determines to fight on: to the death.

This key event, the bitter climax of Virgil's epic, is reduced by Ovid into a few short lines and the ultimate in condensed narratives, as he reports simply that 'Turnus fell' (*Turnusque cadit* – 14.573). Virgil's own narrative ends abruptly at this point with Turnus' angry ghost descending into Hell, but mid-line and mid-sentence Ovid carries on his 'little *Aeneid*' without a break, with the fall of Turnus' own city Ardea and a heron (in Latin, '*ardea*') rising from its ashes.[39] As Ovid's own narrative continues far beyond that of Virgil, we finally see Aeneas, with his Trojan settlement on Italian soil well established, become ripe for translation (14.584) into the place reserved for him in heaven. Thus, with the democratic consent of all the gods, Venus administers Aeneas' apotheosis, giving him a new identity and name (Indiges). And thus the Trojan hero whose role in Ovid's 'little *Aeneid*' has been distinctly underwhelming becomes a god – paving the way for his ancestors Julius and Octavian (who will orchestrate his own name-change to Augustus) to follow in due course.[40]

Aeneas' Descendants (14.609–851)

His poem now firmly located in Rome, Ovid skips quickly over the successive reigns of Aeneas' descendants – including that of his son Iulus Ascanius, later claimed by the Julian clan (among them Julius and Augustus Caesar) to be their own eponymous ancestor. He moves swiftly from the apotheosis of Rome's illustrious founding father Aeneas through a roll-call of its early kings, pausing at the name of the otherwise undistinguished king Proca to tell the love-story of Pomona and Vertumnus (14.623–771) and within it the inset tale of Iphis and Anaxarete (14.698–764). The reason for this digression and the significance of these parallel tales soon becomes clear, as the god Vertumnus sets out to woo the wood nymph Pomona who loves only her garden, by telling her the cautionary tale of hard-hearted Anaxarete whose rejection of her would-be-lover Iphis resulted in his suicide and her own transformation into stone.

The tale of Pomona and Vertumnus is both the *last* love-story and the *first* authentically and exclusively Roman story in the poem, at the same time both Italian, homespun and rustic, *and* Alexandrian, fine-spun and sophisticated. The story is emphatically Roman in its setting, its characters, and its literary influences (namely Virgil's *Georgics* and Propertius' elegy 4.2), thus marking an important transformation in the overarching narrative style of Ovid's *Metamorphoses*. Some critics have seen this move as representing the final stages in the poem's own gradual transformation and transition from the aboriginal chaos depicted by its first few books into the ordered cosmos promised by the Age of Augustus – as suggested by the ordered garden setting of the story, its emphasis upon consensual love rather than rape, and upon words rather than violence as a means of achieving an object of desire.[41]

This story and its tale-within-a-tale are more complex than this, however. Certainly, Vertumnus' attempt to seduce the confirmed virgin Pomona using words rather than force looks at first blush very different to the violent attempts of Apollo, Jupiter, Pan, et al to rape wood and water nymphs in the first books of the poem (1.452–746). But if we look again at these rape narratives we notice that here too the gods initially attempt to use verbal persuasion to seduce their nymphs into consensual sex, only resorting to violence and rape when words fail them. This is the case in the story of Vertumnus and Pomona too, where Vertumnus tries various narrative and metamorphic strategies to seduce the nymph, including disguising himself as a woman (who, like Jupiter in book 2.430f, kisses Pomona inappropriately – 14.658f) before dropping his disguise and preparing to rape her (14.770). But rape proves unnecessary when Pomona experiences a last-minute change of heart upon seeing just how handsome the god is in his authentic form. The motifs of deception, violence and violation, the objectification and silencing of a female victim, are present in this tale as in many of Ovid's earlier rape narratives and, although a vein of humour runs through Vertumnus' various transformations into a hay mower, a cattle herder, a vine pruner, an apple-picker, a soldier, a fisherman, and an old woman in his attempts to gain admittance into Pomona's garden (and into her 'lady garden'?), his many disguises do not hide the fact that underneath lies a lustful god whose intention is to have sex with Pomona either with or without her consent.

In his concerted attempts to seduce Pomona, and in his willingness to use force when all else fails, Vertumnus reveals himself to be another apt pupil of Ovid's own elegiac Ars Amatoria, applying several of the same techniques and arguments employed by the poem's 'love doctor' or praeceptor amoris as he tries to persuade Pomona to give sex and marriage a try (14.659–68). Similarly, his Iphis and Anaxarete story which, in contrast to the rural Roman context of its external frame narrative is both Greek and urban in its setting, draws heavily upon the figures and tropes of Roman love elegy – in particular, the hard-hearted mistress or *dura puella* and the shut-out lover or *exclusus amator.* Both stories are emphatically elegiac in content and tone then – as if Ovid, like Vertumnus, is finally throwing off his epic disguise to reveal the irresistibly seductive qualities of his true identity as an elegiac love poet.

Indeed, like the reverse metamorphoses that have already featured in book 14, this story (and its inset narrative) reverses the epic direction in which Ovid's poem has been heading and looks back to Ovid's own metamorphosis from elegiac to epic poet at the start of the poem. What is more, it seems highly appropriate that it is Vertumnus, whose name recalls both the Latin word *vertere* (to turn) and the transformative theme of Ovid's *Metamorphoses*, who *turns* Ovid's narrative in this reverse direction. In this respect it is particularly significant, then, that Vertumnus refers to Pomona as his first and last love (*primus et ultimus illi / ardor* – 14.682f), echoing Ovid's programmatic allusion in the first book of the *Metamorphoses* to Daphne as both his and Apollo's first love (*primus amor* – 1.452), and neatly linking the end of the *Metamorphoses* to its beginning. So, just as the transitional and programmatic Apollo and Daphne story first introduced the elegiac and amatory themes that play such a key part in the rest of Ovid's epic, we can agree with Sara Myers that, 'The story of Pomona and Vertumnus . . . also functions in a similarly programmatic way in introducing themes which are important in the remainder of the poem, namely, Italian and Roman religious and topographical aetiologies.'[42] To which we turn in Ovid's next story.

Romulus (14.772–851)

After this romantic digression, Ovid returns to the history of Rome's early kings, outlining briefly some of the stories told at much greater length by Rome's Augustan historian Livy, in a narrative summary which swiftly covers the conflict between Proca's sons, Romulus' rise to power, the rape of the Sabine women, Tarpeia's infamous betrayal of the citadel, and the 'civil war' between Romans and Sabines (14.801f) – an obvious allusion to Rome's more recent civil war. He pauses only to elaborate upon Romulus' apotheosis in a detailed account (which closely mirrors that of Aeneas earlier in the book) describing how the *other* founder of Rome took his deserved place among the gods under the new name and identity of Quirinus (14.818–28), to be joined shortly afterwards by his wife Hersilia (flying up to him on the train of a shooting star or comet, her hair ablaze), similarly transformed (*mutat* – 14.851) and 'translated' into the goddess Hora.

The Hersilia/Hora postscript to Romulus' own apotheosis is lent particular significance by its position as the final episode of this book, but the full force of its meaning here is ambiguous. Is this to be read as a romantic or amatory footnote to the story of Romulus, reunited with his beloved wife in death (a common elegiac trope) to live together forever-after as immortal gods? Or does Hersilia's apotheosis rob her husband's deification of some of its special distinction? Having so far reserved only a few seats in heaven for their mortal favourites – the heroes Hercules, Aeneas and now Romulus – the gods, it seems, are now allowing entry to their favourites' relatives.[43] Where will this all end?

Discussion points and questions

1. How does Ovid compete with Virgil in his re-telling of Aeneas' adventures?
2. What is the significance of the motif of 'reverse' metamorphosis in book 14?
3. Why does it matter that the tale of Pomona and Vertumnus is the first 'Roman' story in the *Metamorphoses*?

Book Fifteen

Myscelus (15.1–59)

With the death and deification of Romulus and his wife, Ovid's narrative moves one step closer to the history of his own time, where men are turned into gods, political chaos transformed into imperial order, and war into peace. Any reader who has followed the twisted thread of Ovid's epic narrative from the beginning up to this final chapter of his *carmen perpetuum* might, at this point, have reached the same dangerous boredom threshold that proved so fatal for Argus back in book 1 (1.713–20). But Argus' *exemplum* warns us to stay awake and pay close attention until our storyteller reaches the very end of his story.

Yet, having promised us in his opening lines that his *Metamorphoses* would offer a continuous narrative from the world's beginning down to his own lifetime (1.3–4), he now appears to avoid following the chronological march of history towards his own Augustan age, and instead temporarily suspends the forward momentum of his narrative to follow Romulus' successor Numa as he seeks enlightenment from the exiled philosopher Pythagoras on 'the nature of things' (*rerum natura* – 15.6). A chronologically contorted and backward looking narrative follows, in which Ovid seems determined to avoid following his own poetic programme, and on his way to meet Pythagoras, Numa is told the story of Myscelus and Hercules. In a dream, Myscelus had seen a vision of Hercules, telling him to leave his native city – something forbidden by penalty of death. As he prepared to do the demi-god's bidding, he was captured and tried for his attempted crime but a miraculous transformation of the jury's voting pebbles from black (denoting a guilty verdict) to white (for innocence) assured Myscelus' acquittal and so he survived to leave his homeland and build his new city. In the world of the *Metamorphoses*, it seems, even when a crime (in Latin, *scelus*) has clearly been committed (as in the case of Myscelus), we can be persuaded that black is white, the guilty innocent.

Pythagoras (15.60–478)[44]

In Myscelus' city (and in possibly the most tenuous link between stories in the whole poem), lived Pythagoras who explained to Numa 'how the universe first began, / discoursed at length upon causes, [and] defined what Nature and God were' (15.67–9). Like Mercury, Ovid seems determined to send his audience to sleep here. There are, however, distinct parallels between Pythagoras' themes and those of Ovid's poem – particularly in their shared concern with origins and causes – and Pythagoras' interest in the nature of divinity reflects one of the primary motifs of Ovid's final books, where we have already seen Hercules, Aeneas, Romulus and Hersilia transcend their physical mortality to become gods. In many respects then, Pythagoras' sermon can be read as summarising and commenting upon the themes of Ovid's

Metamorphoses, inviting us to look back and to reconsider our own reading of it as we approach its conclusion.

Pythagoras begins his commentary with a lesson on the virtues of vegetarianism (15.75–142), emphasising the bounty of nature and the quasi-cannibalism that is entailed when any animal consumes the flesh of another. He cites the man-eating Cyclops (cf. Polyphemus at 13.738–897) as his monstrous model for such behaviour, but in his allusion to a lost golden age in which mankind lived on fruit and herbs until someone opened the floodgates to criminality, impiety and decline by first eating meat, we may also be reminded of Lycaon (1.163–252), who defined the debased iron age of man with his impious cannibalism. He follows this sermon against meat-eating with a didactic lesson condemning the cruel use of animals in sacrifice, observing that it is always the most beautiful creatures who are selected for such sacrifice to the gods: 'A victim unblemished and perfectly formed (its beauty its downfall)' – *victima labe carens et praestantissima forma / nam placuisse nocet* (15.130f). How many times in the poem have we read of a beautiful girl or boy 'sacrificed' to satisfy the desires of a cruel god, their victim selected solely on the grounds of his or her outstanding beauty or *forma,* paying the price of pleasing a god's eye, their beauty their downfall? Yet, although Pythagoras concludes his diatribe with the warning that when we eat oxen we should be mindful that we are eating our own fellow farm-workers (15.142), he makes no direct reference here (as some critics suppose) to the idea that when we eat an animal we might be eating a human soul in animal form. This view is certainly expressed elsewhere in the teachings of Pythagoras, but it is noticeable that here – at the end of a poem in which hundreds of human souls have been transformed into animals – Ovid's Pythagoras makes no explicit connection between vegetarianism and metamorphosis or metempsychosis (the Pythagorean belief that a human soul might be reborn in animal form). In any case, in the world of the *Metamorphoses*, a human soul might just as readily be contained within the form of a tree or plant, making nothing safe for human consumption.

Pythagoras next tackles mankind's superstitious fear of death, advising us not to fear old age, the funeral pyre or the underworld, since our souls are immortal and move on to inhabit new forms after our deaths (15.165–172):

> All is subject to change and nothing to death. The spirit
> in each of us wanders from place to place; it enters whatever
> body it pleases, crossing over from beast to man,
> and back again to beast. It never perishes wholly.
> As pliable wax is easily stamped with a new impression
> and never remains as it was nor preserves one single shape,
> but still is the selfsame wax, so I say that our souls are always
> the same, although they move from home to home in different
>   bodies.

Pythagoras' teaching that 'everything changes' (*omnia mutantur* – 15.165) represents the defining/mutating theme of Ovid's poem and suggests that his lecture may offer other significant insights into Ovid's *Metamorphoses*.

Turning his attention to time and temporality (15.176–236) – but ignoring the temporal impossibility of his ever meeting the addressee of his lecture, the Roman king Numa who died almost a century before Pythagoras' birth – the philosopher continues to elaborate upon his theme of universal flux.[45] According to Pythagoras (reiterating the philosophy of Heraclitus – and the start of Ovid's poem), '"In the whole of the world there is nothing that stays unchanged. / All is in flux. Any shape that is formed is constantly shifting"' (15.177f). Time, he says, is also constantly changing and so changing things, turning day into night, spring into summer and youth into old age, ultimately transforming and destroying all things. Time in the disordered chronology of the *Metamorphoses* has certainly played a major role in transforming the shape of Ovid's epic – not least of all in Ovid's retelling of familiar stories from the epic tradition to suggest that his own narratives chronologically *precede* that of his literary predecessors.[46]

From the theme of time, Pythagoras turns to cosmology – recalling the cosmological beginnings of Ovid's poem. The poem began in chaos and disorder (1.5–7) from which it has appeared to move towards stability and order – epitomized by the Augustan Peace. Yet, here at the end of the poem, chaos returns to the cosmos (or at least demonstrates that it was and is ever present) as Pythagoras foresees an eventual return to cosmic disorder and chaos. In this vision, the fundamental elements of earth, air, fire and water – separated at the start of the cosmos and at the start of the poem (1.5–88) – are confused and in a constant state of flux once more (15.244–53) as Pythagoras argues that the cosmos is, in effect, a 'chaosmos' in which the forces of order and disorder eternally compete and in which nothing stays the same forever.

Indeed, Pythagoras' description of the metamorphic universe might serve just as well as a description of Ovid's metamorphic poem – particularly as he goes on to describe some of the changes that the world has experienced over time: the gradual transformation of the golden age into the iron age (15.260) echoing Ovid's own description of the four ages (1.89–150); land turned into sea and sea into land (15.262–9), again echoing Ovid's own description of cosmic flood and fire (1.253–312 and 2.167–320). Pythagoras describes the creation and drying-up of springs and rivers (15.268–306), recalling the many rivers and springs that have been subject to or agents of metamorphosis in the poem. He lists some of the transforming powers that even in his own time were attributed to various bodies of water (15.307–36), among them the pool of Salmacis (recall the story told at 4.285–7). He goes on to conclude his catalogue of geographical metamorphoses with references to floating Ortygia, the clashing rocks of the Symplegades, and other phenomena of the natural world (15.336–55), recalling not only the second transformation of Scylla into rock (14.70–4), but the voyages of Leto (6.333–6) and the Argo (7.1–7). His passing reference to strange customs practised by the Hyperboreans and Scythians which cause them to grow feathers (15.356–60) brings to mind the many bird transformations featured in Ovid's poem, but also serves as an effective transition into a zoological catalogue of well-known transformations in nature that offer a neat précis of Ovid's poem.[47]

The climax of Pythagoras' speech offers a catalogue of the changing fortunes of great cities, the rise and fall of great civilizations and cultures: Troy, Sparta, Mycenae, Thebes, Athens and – of course – Rome, destined to become the capital city of a world empire according to the prophecy that Pythagoras claims (in a past life) to have heard the Trojan prophet Helenus give to

Aeneas (15.418–52). The emphasis upon Rome's rise to glory as a world super-power is significant here, as is Pythagoras' reported prophecy that the city of Rome will one day be 'greater than any that is or has been or shall rise hereafter' (15.445) and that (15.446–9):

Other leaders, over the centuries, will render her powerful;
but one man born of Iulus' blood will make her the mistress
of all the world. When the earth has enjoyed his presence, the realms
of the sky will enjoy him too; he is finally destined for heaven.

The prophecy looks forward not merely to the rise of Rome but to the ascendancy and apotheosis of Augustus – the highpoint of Rome's destiny and the endpoint of Ovid's poem. Yet, implicit in Pythagoras' account of this stellar rise is the spectre of Rome's fall: like Troy, Thebes and Athens (cities whose rise and fall we have seen charted in the course of Ovid's *Metamorphoses*) is Rome too destined to one day fall? If, as Pythagoras contends, everything changes (15.165) and nothing stays the same forever (15.259), then this is the only coherent conclusion we may draw. Indeed, it is significant that although Ovid claims that Rome will be greater than any city 'that is or has been or shall rise hereafter' (15.445) he does not claim that her power will be eternal or unchanging. In contrast to Virgil, who famously claimed that Rome had been granted by the gods 'an empire without end' in either time or space (*Aeneid* 1.257–96), Ovid makes no such claim for Rome's power to resist the power of time and transformation.

Egeria and Hippolytus (15.479–546)

Numa, they say, took Pythagoras' teachings to heart and used them as the principles with which he ruled the Latin state, teaching the arts of peace to a warlike nation (15.479–84). But, as Pythagoras taught us, things change, and Numa eventually died. His grief-stricken wife, the nymph Egeria, fled into the woods where her weeping disturbed those worshipping at the shrine of Diana – among them Hippolytus, son of Theseus, who attempted to distract Egeria from her woes with a tale of his own suffering. Ovid, it seems, shows no signs as yet of moving his narrative any closer to its long awaited conclusion in his own time. Indeed, the introduction of the tragic Greek hero Hippolytus as an internal story-teller at this point in Ovid's Roman narrative is somewhat unexpected, until we realize that Ovid has here already Romanized Hippolytus. His multiple transformations, first of his mangled body into 'one wound' (15.529), then his resurrection by Apollo and Diana (15.533–7), his metamorphosis into a new physical form with unrecognisable features (15.539), and finally his change of identity into Virbius, a Latin name meaning 'the twice-born man' (15.542–4), transform a familiar Greek tale of tragedy and suffering into a very Roman narrative presenting an edifying *exemplum* of Roman endurance and fortitude.[48] Thus, as Philip Hardie has observed, this metamorphosis can be seen to represent 'one of the culminating moments in the accelerating movement of the last books of the poem from the Greek to the Roman world'.[49]

Cipus (15.547–621)[50]

Like so many of the other stories in the *Metamorphoses* that are told by an internal narrator to some purpose, the sorrows of Hippolytus do not make Egeria feel any better about her own and she continues to weep until she dissolves into her own tears (15.551). Hippolytus and Diana's nymphs are amazed at Egeria's transformation, and Ovid uses this *topos* to jump – somewhat clumsily – first to the story of the country ploughman who was just as amazed when he saw the Etruscan prophet Tages emerge as a fully grown man from a clod of earth (15.553–9), then to Romulus' equal amazement at seeing his spear turn into a tree (15.560–4), and finally to Cipus who was amazed one day to see horns growing out of his head. This is hardly the most elegant of transitions into a retelling of the myth of Cipus, and its clumsy introduction here only serves to draw attention to the incongruity of its inclusion at this point in Ovid's history of early Rome: we too are 'amazed' to see this odd thing emerging from the *caput* (meaning both 'head' and 'end') of Ovid's poem.[51]

Ignoring the succession of Roman kings after Romulus and Numa, the expulsion of Rome's last king, and the creation of the Roman republic, the narrative jumps unexpectedly to a much later period in Rome's republican history to tell the bizarre tale of a legendary Roman general who refused to accept the title of king. Returning from a victorious military campaign, Cipus sees horns sprouting from his forehead and, upon seeking an interpretation of this from a seer, is hailed as Rome's new king. But the staunch republican Cipus rightfully prefers exile to the status of king and elects instead to live outside the city walls, rewarded by the people for his sacrifice with as much land as he can plough and a memorial carved upon the city gates.

In keeping with the Callimachean tone of this final book, the strange story of Cipus is clearly aetiological in character, explaining the origin of an ancient Roman monument. With its motif of the partial transformation of a semi-mythical figure, it also clearly fits with the metamorphic character and theme of Ovid's poem. However, it is for the story's historical parallels no less than for these aetiological and metamorphic connections that it seems to deserve its place at this particular point in Ovid's poem. For, just as Ovid introduces the tale of Cipus through a series of unlikely analogies, Cipus himself serves to introduce by analogy the long anticipated figure of Julius Caesar – the popular Roman general who, like Cipus, had famously refused to accept the crown of Roman kingship before his assassination (although he did, of course, graciously accept the role of dictator). We are at last moving closer to Ovid's own times, it seems – the *mea tempora* (my times) promised in the proem, albeit with all the personal bias that the personal pronoun (**my** times) suggests.[52]

Aesculapius (15.622–744)

A clear narrative break – the first of its kind in Ovid's *carmen perpetuum* – prefaced by a new invocation to the Muses (15.622–5), introduces the final phase of the poem and the story of the man-made-god Aesculapius, famed in Rome for once healing the Latin people of a deadly disease that threatened to destroy the race. The god (in the symbolic form of a golden serpent) is welcomed into Rome with all the pomp and ceremony associated with a Roman general returning from an overseas military campaign to receive an official 'triumph' – just like those famously celebrated by Julius Caesar. The entire population, including Rome's Vestal Virgins, throng to meet their saviour, filling the city with the smell and smoke of burning incense and sacrifice as the god puts off his snaky form and heals the city of its disease (15.729–44) – just as Julius Caesar ('god in his native city' – 15.745f) would later help to heal the Roman body politic.[53]

The Apotheosis of Julius Caesar (15.745–870)

Ovid has almost reached the end of his epic and we have only just now entered the Age of Augustus – Ovid's own time (*tempora*). Much remains to be told of the adventures of Julius Caesar – and of Augustus – but Ovid seems reluctant to tell them. In his *Fasti* – Ovid's elegiac treatment of the Roman calendar (his *Tempora*), written at the same time as the *Metamorphoses* – Ovid had ingeniously avoided treating the politically sensitive months of July and August by simply refusing to write about them, ending his poem at the end of June, without having to deal with the next two months, respectively dedicated to *Julius* and *Augustus* Caesar. Here at the end of the *Metamorphoses* too, he seems to circumvent the narration of Caesar's celebrated deeds, moving straight on to the only achievement that interests him here – Caesar's metamorphosis.

In fact, Ovid provocatively claims that Caesar owes his deification not to his own achievements in war and in peace, but to those of Augustus. For, Ovid reminds us, it was not his many victories in Britain, Egypt, Numidia, Libya, and Pontus but *Augustus* who made Caesar a god – both literally and figuratively (15.757–61). Reversing the pattern of apotheosis that we have so far seen in the stories of Hercules, Aeneas, and Romulus, who were all transformed into gods because of their divine parentage and their own heroic achievements, Caesar is made a god because of the achievements of his divine offspring: like Hersilia, he is made a god because of his divine family connections.[54] The logic of Ovid's analysis – that Augustus must be the son of a god, therefore Caesar must be made a god – is both irrefutable and ridiculous. Even more so when we remember that Augustus was not, in fact, the son of Caesar but his *adopted* heir. Ovid has suddenly brought his narrative into his own politically sensitive times but, in keeping with the motif of continuity through change that has run throughout the poem, his irreverent treatment of material so far continues (apparently) unchanged.

So, as Ovid turns to Venus (in Augustan mythology the *genetrix* or founding-mother of the Julio-Claudian line and therefore divine ancestor of Julius and Augustus Caesar) his representation of her motherly concern for her Roman son Caesar directly echoes her earlier concern for her Trojan son Aeneas. Foreseeing Caesar's murder, she complains to Jupiter that this represents yet another episode in the (epic) catalogue of wrongs done to her – the wound she received from Diomedes during the Trojan War, the fall of Troy and the subsequent wanderings of her beloved Aeneas. Venus herself attempts to rescue Caesar from the conspirators' swords as she had once tried to rescue Aeneas from the battlefield at Troy by wrapping him in a cloud – but she too is bound by the decrees of the Fates and can do nothing to save him (15.803–6). Reprising the speech written for him in the first book of Virgil's *Aeneid*, Jupiter reassures Venus that the glorious destiny of her descendents is guaranteed in the written tablets of the Fates: that, after Caesar's death he will be made a god, and that Augustus will enjoy great triumphs and achievements of his own, including a world empire, an imperial dynasty, and eventually his own apotheosis and deification (15.807–42). If this encomium or praise for Augustus were not enough (and more), Ovid further embroiders his panegyric by adding that, just as the mighty heroes of epic and myth often surpassed their fathers in glory and greatness, so Augustus surpasses Caesar (15.852–60), calling in prayer upon all the gods of Rome to honour Augustus as he deserves (15.861–70). And so ends Ovid's epic.

But how are we to respond to this conclusion and its seemingly sycophantic praise of Augustus?[55] Does this represent a sudden and embarrassing change in Ovid's political sympathies and stance? Such an ideological transformation on Ovid's part would certainly be in keeping with the unpredictable and ever-changing programme of the *Metamorphoses*. Perhaps the final transformation offered by the poem is that of the poet himself: is this a change from anti- to pro-Augustan in the closing lines of the final book, to correspond with the change of elegiac to epic poet enacted in the opening lines of the first? It is certainly the case that, in keeping with the wider pattern of book 15, Ovid's treatment of Julius and Augustus Caesar in the final lines of the poem recalls its first book: here he compared Jupiter to Augustus, likening a council of the gods to the Roman senate, and Olympus to the Palatine (1.173–6), comparing Lycaon's impious crimes against the gods to the assassination of Caesar (1.199–205), all within an ostensible context of encomium or praise. His enthusiastic praise for both Augustus and Caesar in the final book balances that in the first, then, in a form of ring-composition that encloses the poem within what critics have recognized as an encomiastic frame.[56]

However, pairing the Augustan panegyric of the first book with the Augustan panegyric of the last does far more than lend a cyclical structure to the *Metamorphoses* in which the end returns us to the beginning – however much such an inconclusive conclusion might suit a *carmen perpetuum*. Rather, the encomiastic frame recalls two books of Callimachus' *Aetia* – the *Victory of Berenice* and the *Lock of Berenice* – which are similarly framed by passages of praise for a ruler, reasserting Ovid's literary credentials as the 'Roman Callimachus' at the end of the *Metamorphoses* in the same way that his promise to spin out a *carmen perpetuum* established that claim at its start.[57] The end of the *Metamorphoses* reminds us, then, that we have been reading an aetiological poem, a poem explaining the origins and causes (*aetia*) of Ovid's own times – an *Aetia* for the Age of Augustus.

Epilogue (15.871–9)

But, just as Pythagoras taught us, the end is not really the end. Ovid adds a brief epilogue to his epic, in which he describes the poem's final metamorphosis. And, like the final transformations of Aeneas, Caesar and Augustus, this too is an apotheosis – of Ovid himself. He proclaims that because of his poetry – because of his *Metamorphoses* – his death will not be his end, but that 'the finer part' of himself (15.875) will be raised above the stars where his name will last forever in its immortal fame. It is significant that he sees here his transformation into his own words, the metamorphosis of poet into poetry: 'Wherever the might of Rome extends in the lands she has conquered, / the people shall read and recite my words' (*quaque patet domitis Romana potentia terris, / ore legar populi*) – or, more literally, 'I will be recited on the lips of the people' (15.877f): the people will read and recite *Ovid*. The poet will become his own poetry then, and this transformation, like so many others in the poem, will offer him not only immortality but protection from harm, from Jupiter's anger, from fire, sword, and devouring time (15.871f).[58]

And, as the poet continues to live throughout the ages in this new form, so he will continue to change, to be transformed in and by each new reading of his poem, finally achieving permanence and immortality through change and through his *Metamorphoses. Mutatis mutandis.*

Discussion points and questions
1. To what extent does Pythagoras' lecture represent a summary of the *Metamorphoses* as a whole?
2. How does Ovid present himself as a Roman Callimachus in book 15?
3. How does the final book of the poem represent Ovid's own metamorphosis?

CHAPTER 4

RECEPTION AND INFLUENCE

Wherever the might of Rome extends in the lands she has conquered,
the people shall read and recite my words. Throughout all ages,
if poets have vision to prophesy truth, I shall live in my fame.
Ovid, Metamorphoses *15.877–9*

Ovid ends his *Metamorphoses* with a bold epilogue declaring that, even after death, he will live on – that his epic poem and his name will live forever. Nearly two thousand years after his death, Ovid's confidence in the power of his poetic *corpus* to survive the death and destruction of his physical *corpus* appears to have been justified. And although we may be far from living in a new 'Age of Ovid' or *aetas Ovidiana* – as the medievalist Ludwig Traube described the flourishing of Latin literature in the twelfth and thirteenth centuries, few classical authors continue to make such an enduring impact upon the literary, artistic, and imaginative landscapes of Western Europe as Ovid. Although we may not always recognize its indirect influence upon our culture, the stories that make up this epic poem are – as Ted Hughes has pointed out – 'inseparable from our unconscious imaginative life'.[1]

Indeed, the *Metamorphoses* was an almost immediate 'classic' – as influential as Virgil's *Aeneid* in shaping the poetry of the next generation of Roman writers, Lucan, Statius and the younger Seneca. Ovidian graffiti discovered on the walls of Pompeii offers further evidence to his popularity in the ancient world. And since Ovid's death, the *Metamorphoses* has become 'one of the cornerstones of Western culture'.[2] Its encyclopaedic collection of Greek and Roman myths has been successively plundered by writers, artists, and musicians for the past two thousand years – each one adding to no less than taking something from this extraordinary work.

Textual illustrations from the middle-ages to the present day have frequently sought to capture the dramatic high-point of each myth, often the very moment of metamorphosis itself. So, in the borders of richly illustrated manuscripts of the fourteenth century *Ovide Moralisé*, grotesque creatures – half human, half animal, bird, or insect – were painted to depict characters clearly recognizable as Actaeon, Tereus, or Arachne at the mid-point of transformation. Elaborate woodcuts illustrating episodes in early modern editions and translations of the poem modified this approach, showing, for example, a bear flying up into the sky to illustrate Callisto's second metamorphosis into the constellation Ursa Major, or Daphne as a Renaissance maid with flowing hair and branches for arms. However, artistic decorum prevented illustrators in the early modern period from depicting the human body being deformed by the actual process of metamorphosis. So, Daphne in Florentine dress might be rooted to the spot and given leafy branches for arms (as in Pollaiuolo's *Apollo and Daphne*) or Actaeon depicted as a tunic-clad knight sprouting horns (as in Spreng's woodcut for the *Metamorphoses Illustratae*), but Renaissance illustrations and paintings that capture the drama of metamorphosis – and so of the *Metamorphoses* itself – are rare.[3]

In fact, it could be argued that, in the Renaissance, only Bernini comes close to translating Ovid's poetry into art with his sculpture *Apollo and Daphne*. Here, as in other representations of the period, Daphne's hands sprout leaves, but – caught by Apollo (and Bernini) at the moment of metamorphosis – her lower half appears partially encased in wood, which seems (even in marble) to be rapidly creeping up her back to complete the transformation of nymph into tree. Just as Ovid describes (1.548–51):

She had hardly ended her prayer when a heavy numbness came over her body; her soft white bosom was ringed in a layer of bark, her hair was turned into foliage, her arms into branches. The feet that had run so nimbly were sunk into sluggish roots . . .

Bernini illustrates exactly this moment: Daphne's arching back and Apollo's flying drapery emphasizing the precise point at which metamorphosis overtakes the nymph. More than simply illustrating a scene from the *Metamorphoses*, Bernini's sculpture here seems to be 'reading' Ovid's poem, translating into marble Ovid's own linguistic emphasis upon this pivotal moment (*pes modo tam velox pigris radicibus haeret* – 1.551): note the midline juxtaposition between *velox* (swift) and *pigris* (sluggish), the paradoxical state that Bernini's sculpture performs. Charles Martindale observes that:[4]

> There is an intense, tactile, almost surreal concentration on the details of metamorphosis, particularly marked in the treatment of fingers and toes, the latter becoming, horribly, claw-like at the tips as they put down roots. Daphne's face seems to express fear and horror, which could be as much in response to her metamorphosis as to the imminent approach of the lustful god. . . . In general, the sculpture embodies a characteristic baroque paradox, on the one hand sweeping theatrical movement creating an impression of careless ease, on the other a technical perfection in the surfaces and a mastery of precise detail, not in the least impressionistic. The paradox is perfect for the combination of movement and stasis as the fleeing Daphne becomes 'root-bound', as Milton puts it in *Comus* (661). The witty, the erotic and the grotesque are miraculously fused as in the original, in an image at once polished and fluid, sprightly and troubling.

Bernini's *Apollo and Daphne*, then, illustrates much more than an individual moment of metamorphosis – of Daphne into laurel: it illustrates the spirit of the *Metamorphoses*. And this – whether or not they also show us a moment of metamorphosis – is characteristic of all the best artistic transformations of Ovid's poem, from the grotesque illuminations on medieval manuscripts, through Titian's erotically charged, technically brilliant, darkly witty *Poesie*, to the surrealist images of Dali.[5]

Indeed, in literature as in art, the transforming spirit of the poem and its theme of 'continuity through change' can be clearly felt. During the medieval *aetas Ovidiana*, Ovid's poetry was far and away the most popular of any classical – or contemporary – writer. Ovid was everywhere. His love poetry was used in the medieval schoolroom to teach literary and rhetorical style, the *Fasti* was used to teach history, the *Heroides* and *Tristia* were widely copied as templates for poetic letters, the *Remedia Amoris* was consulted for medical advice, and – however strange this may now seem – several of Ovid's writings, particularly the *Metamorphoses*, were regarded as authoritative works of philosophy, and were consulted by medieval experts for advice on Christian morality, ethics and the good life. So, in medieval works such as the *Ovide Moralisé* Ovid's stories of the Creation and Flood were seen as pagan parallels to the biblical tales in *Genesis*. In the same religious vein, Deucalion and Pyrrha were viewed as the equivalents of 'Mr and Mrs Noah'; the story of Actaeon was read as an allegory of Christ's suffering and death; Daedalus became a sinner attempting to escape the devil – as represented by Minos; Alcyone became a good Christian devoted to Christ – as figured by Ceyx; Daphne and (more bizarrely) Myrrha were transformed into prototypes of the Virgin Mary; and Ovid himself transformed into a proto-Christian, martyred by Augustus. The allegorical tradition of *Ovide Moralisé* may seem strange to anyone who has ever read the original *Metamorphoses*, but it has been argued that some of the more recent literary critical approaches – Freudian, Lacanian, Feminist, Marxist, *et al* – offer effectively the same sort of allegorical interpretation of the poem, seeing in the story of Narcissus an expression of the Freudian narcissistic ego or the Lacanian 'Mirror Stage', or in Arethusa a proto-feminist.

In the Renaissance, the *Metamorphoses* was itself transformed into a kind of 'secular bible', its tales of transformation providing a rich source of inspiration for the many writers and artists whose genius flourished in this period. A close reader of the original Latin, Milton made careful use of this pagan poem for his own epic, *Paradise Lost*, transforming and absorbing Ovidian motifs into his Christian narrative, as in the direct 'echo' of *Metamorphoses* 3.339–510, when Milton's Eve first sees her reflection in a clear pool (*Paradise Lost* 4.460–8). Here Milton offers us a female Narcissus and an unambiguously Ovidian allusion but, unlike the pagan world of the *Metamorphoses*, here in *Paradise* there is a Christian author and a Christian God to set everything straight. Ovid's Narcissus does not hear or heed his author's advice (3.432 – 'Trusting fool, how futile to woo a fleeting phantom') – with tragic consequences. Milton's Eve gains knowledge about herself and her world in God's timely warning and so avoids Narcissus' fatal error. Indeed, in a celebrated description of the Garden of Eden, Milton explicitly acknowledged both his debt and his resistance to Ovid and the *Metamorphoses*, famously declaring that (*Paradise Lost* 2.268–75): 'Not that fair field / Of Enna, where Proserpine gathering flowers / Her self a fairer flower by gloomy Dis / Was gathered . . . / . . . might with this Paradise / Of Eden strive . . .'. But Milton's very boast that his own poem *surpasses* Ovid's draws attention to the Ovidian contours of the Renaissance literary landscape in which he writes.

Perhaps the most prominent landmark in this Renaissance landscape was Shakespeare, of whom Francis Mere wrote in 1598: 'as the soul of Euphorbus was thought to live in Pythagoras, so the sweet witty soul of Ovid lives in mellifluous and honey-tongued Shakespeare: witness, his *Venus and Adonis,* his *Lucrece*, his sugared sonnets . . .'. Witness also Shakespeare's *Titus Andronicus, Romeo and Juliet, A Midsummer Night's Dream,* and his *Tempest*: all pluck ideas (or Ovid's 'odiferous flowers of fancy' as Holofernes calls them in *Love's Labours Lost*) from the fertile fields of the *Metamorphoses*. Transplanted, translated and transformed in Shakespeare's own work, Ovidian characters and stories flourished there – as in the reworking of the 'most lamentable comedy and most cruel death of Pyramus and Thisby' by the mechanicals in *A Midsummer Night's Dream*, where the play within the play and the play without are both wholly Ovidian in character(s) and tone. 'Bless thee Bottom, bless thee! Thou art translated!' is Quince's poignant cry upon discovering Bottom's transformation into an ass (3.1.93): a cry that speaks for Shakespeare's Ovid too.

Such translation – both literally (of Ovid's Latin into English) and figuratively (of Ovid's stories into new forms) – has been essential in enabling Ovid's *Metamorphoses* to assert its influence upon the worlds of art and literature. In fact, the first complete English 'translation' of the poem was itself closely based on another translation: when Caxton first translated the *Metamorphoses* into English in 1480, he turned not to the Latin original but to a 1460 French translation *Métamorphoses moralisées* (itself a reworking of Bersuire's Latin text *Ovidius moralisatus* from the 1330s) as the base for his own version.[6] Caxton followed the early medieval tradition of *Ovide Moralisé* that shaped his source-text, and didactically moralized his *Metamorphoses*, Christianizing the pagan poem and its poet in the process. So, Caxton had Procne slaughter Itys and feed him to his father not because she sought revenge, but because 'the deuyl counceylled her' to do so. And he transformed Actaeon, not into a stag, but into a lazy beggar who is eaten by his hungry hounds – a salient moral lesson for the work-shy. For, as he asserted in his Preface, 'the trouth thereof lyeth coverid under fables.'

Golding's Preface to the next complete English translation of the *Metamorphoses*, published less than a century after Caxton's, shared his view that Ovid's poem 'with leesings and with fables shadowed so / The certeine truth' – but there the similarity ended. Golding's Renaissance version (famously described by Ezra Pound as 'possibly the most beautiful book in our language') was the first authentic translation of the complete *Metamorphoses* ever produced and with it, according to Christopher Martin, 'Golding provided his contemporaries with a delightfully readable version of Ovid that was also faithful to the original sense and spirit'.[7] Indeed, among those Elizabethan contemporaries who were inspired by Golding's Ovid were Marlowe, Spenser, and, of course, Shakespeare – who, with his 'little Latin', would have struggled to read the *Metamorphoses* in the original and would have turned instead to Golding's translation. His use of Golding's version is perhaps nowhere better illustrated than in the *Tempest*, in Prospero's valedictory incantation – a transformation of Medea's speech in the *Metamorphoses* (7.192–219) – where Prospero invokes 'Ye elves of hills, brooks, standing lakes and groves' in echo of Medea's invocation of 'Ye Ayres and Windes; ye Elves of Hills, of Brookes, of Woods alone / of standing Lakes, and of the Night'.

Perfectly suited as it was to the Elizabethan Age, Golding's translation did not itself translate well, however, and barely sixty years later its fourteener couplets already seemed old-fashioned and fussy, its rhymes ridiculous. Sophisticated seventeenth century tastes demanded that Ovid and his *Metamorphoses* be translated into yet another form, and in 1626 Sandys obliged with a witty new version of the poem, and reintroduced an appropriately urbane Ovid to his contemporaries. But to the next generation, inevitably, this translation too appeared anti-quated, and a new Ovid was once again required to coordinate with the other neoclassical fashions of the new Augustan Age. Dryden proved the perfect man for the job: as Ted Hughes would later suggest of himself and of Ovid – 'the right man had met the right material at the right moment'.[8] And although Dryden did not complete a full (or literal) translation of Ovid's text, his words were added to those of Congreve, Addison, Pope, and Gay in Garth's definitive edition of all fifteen books of the *Metamorphoses* in 1717 – the text that would effectively fix the poem in its English form until the late twentieth century and the transformations of a new Ovidian Golden Age.

In 1994 – the same year that saw the publication of David Slavitt's famously idiosyncratic translation of Ovid's epic – the poetic collection *After Ovid* appeared: a collaboration of sixty translations of individual tales by 42 eminent poets, mirroring the collaborative translation of the complete poem by Garth, Addison, Dryden, Gay, Pope and their contemporaries some three centuries earlier. The introduction to *After Ovid* reiterated the idea first mooted by Caxton and Golding and repeated by Garth, that Ovid's poem contains hidden truths about humanity, suggesting that:[9]

[Ovid's *Metamorphoses*] offer a mythical key to most of the more extreme forms of human behaviour and suffering, especially ones we think of as peculiarly modern: holocaust, plague, sexual harassment, rape, incest, seduction, pollution, sex-change, suicide, hetero- and homosexual love, torture, war, child-battering, depression and intoxication . . .

This perhaps offers one explanation for the renewed popularity of the *Metamorphoses* at the end of the second millennium. But if the *Metamorphoses* does provide such a key to modernity and its horrors, it does so in the teeth of its (often dark) humour. Poet Laureate Carol Ann Duffy's contribution to *After Ovid* recognized this crucial aspect of Ovid's modernity in her 'Mrs Midas', which expertly captured the wit and pathos that is characteristic of Ovid – and of the new perspectives upon old myths that he so often presents through the eyes of marginalized female characters in the *Metamorphoses*. In *The World's Wife*, Duffy added other Ovidian companions to her 'Mrs Midas', and her invention 'Mrs Icarus' (recalling the famous depiction of this scene in Pieter Brueghel's painting *Landscape with the Fall of Icarus*) adopts the same position of witness that is given to the fisherman, shepherd and ploughboy who, in Raeburn's translation of Ovid's original, 'All watched in amazement, thinking, "They certainly must be gods / to fly through the air!"' (8.217–20).

Duffy's up-dating of Ovid shares much with that of her fellow poet laureate and co-contributor to *After Ovid*, Ted Hughes, whose *Tales from Ovid*, the award-winning translation (or, better, transformation) of 24 selected episodes from the *Metamorphoses* similarly grew out of his contribution to *After Ovid* to become the most influential of all modern metamorphoses of Ovid's poem. Like Duffy's, one of the most striking elements of Hughes' translation of Ovid is his modernization: Jupiter destroys Semele with the 'nuclear blast of his naked impact' (19), Phaethon wears sunblock (29) to protect him from the Sun, Tiresias sees into the future using his 'inner eye, like a nightscope' (73), and Pygmalion's fear and disgust of women is described in terms of a twentieth-century 'phobia' (145). But in these obvious anachronisms, Hughes faithfully echoes Ovid's own practice in the *Metamorphoses*, for Ovid too (as he had promised in his proem) brought his tales of transformation bang up to date (1.4). With playful, even satirical anachronism, he likens the homes of the gods on Mount Olympus to Augustus' marble residences on Rome's Palatine Hill (1.176), and in one darkly comedic scene describing the death of Pyramus (4.121–4), he even evokes a simile drawn from contemporary Roman plumbing. Hughes' modern rendering of Ovid's poetry into twentieth-century English reveals a powerful affinity with Ovid and with the tone and spirit of the *Metamorphoses*, then. And this, indeed, is what the best translations – like the best illustrations – of the *Metamorphoses* can offer: a reading of the text that transforms our understanding of the poem, and brings the poet and his 'wonder-tales' (as Hughes called them) alive.

Hughes' revivification and transformation of Ovid into a postmodern contemporary was not the first such twentieth-century metamorphosis to reshape the poet and his epic into a new form. Kafka's *Metamorphosis*, David Garnett's *Lady into Fox*, and Virginia Woolf's *Orlando* had each already renewed the Ovidian theme of bodily transformation. James Joyce had prefaced his *Portrait of the Artist as a Young Man* with a quotation from the *Metamorphoses* – *et ignotas animum dimittit in artes* ('and he put his mind to unknown arts' – 8.188) and named his Ovid-reading protagonist Daedalus. And in a famous note to line 218 of *The Waste Land*, T.S. Eliot had identified his Ovidian Tiresias as 'the most important personage in the poem, uniting all the rest . . . What Tiresias *sees*, in fact, is the substance of the poem', illustrating this claim with a quotation from book 3 of the *Metamorphoses*. Ovid's twentieth-century presence – including that of Hughes – became mediated and shaped by each of these modernist works, so that Ovid and his work began to seem always already modern – even modernist.[10]

In 2000, a number of popular authors contributed to a sparkling collection of innovative and original stories on Ovidian themes in *Ovid Metamorphosed*, experimenting with and reshaping the form of the modern short story – just as Ovid had transformed the traditional genres of epic and elegy two thousand years before. Several of these stories took their inspiration directly from Ovid's *Metamorphoses*, reworking and recasting Ovid's work into new forms, and in so doing offering fresh insights both into the poem and – significantly – into the history of its reception. Here, Nicole Ward Jouve restages the story of Narcissus and Echo at a scholarly conference where a pool of academics and psychoanalysts find their narcissistic tendencies reflected – and where Jouve cleverly engages the modern reception of Ovid's story in Freudian and Lacanian psychoanalytic theory. Here A.S. Byatt, weaving her short story from a variety of different generic threads – including autobiography, art history, and natural history – involves herself in a new competition with Ovid and his Arachne. Her interwoven narrative interconnecting the story of Velázquez's painting *Las Hilanderas* (*The Spinners* – inspired by Ovid's *Metamorphoses* book 6), descriptions of real and literary spiders, her own childhood encounters with Greek goddesses and with

Ovid, spins a complex spider's-web of a tale, ingeniously and in miniature reflecting both Ovid's poem and its prismatic influence.

Here too M.J. Fitzgerald 'translates' the horror-story of rape, mutilation, infanticide and cannibalism that is played out by Tereus, Procne, and Philomela in book 6 of Ovid's poem – reflecting upon a story that has already been metamorphosed and re-translated in numerous literary forms. Fitzgerald's work gives the impression of a faithful translation, but in its small deviations from the original narrative it offers a salient reminder that all translations are also transformations, and that the mute text of the *Metamorphoses* – like Philomela herself – tells its stories intertextually, speaking to us in words that are necessarily mediated through others and through other texts.

Similarly concerned with the theme of translation, David Malouf's poetic novella, *An Imaginary Life*, focuses upon Ovid's own metamorphosis as an exile. In his first year in Tomis, still unable to speak or understand the local dialect, Ovid finds himself transformed into an infant again 'discovering the world as a small child does, through the senses, but with all things deprived of the special magic of their names in my own tongue' (22). Memories of his childhood nightmares – and of his *Metamorphoses* – prompt him to fear werewolves in the Tomitian forests and when locals capture a feral child (who has been raised by animals and is uncivilized even by the standards of Tomis) suspicions arise that the child is a Lycaon-like lycanthrope. Ovid attempts to teach the boy to speak, but when fearful villagers drive both Ovid and the boy into the wilderness Ovid must learn from the child how to make animal and bird sounds. In the wilderness, in 'the Child's world' (143), and in the last days of his life, Ovid finally achieves peace. Echoing Pythagoras' speech at the end of the *Metamorphoses*, he finally realizes that: 'We are continuous with earth in all the particles of our physical being, as in our breathing we are continuous with sky. Between our bodies and the world there is unity and commerce' (147).

In his poem 'Ovid in Tomis', the Northern Irish poet Derek Mahon uses Ovid's exile as a foil for his exploration of the metamorphosis of the post-modern world, particularly the sense of alienation and personal exile that is seen to characterize life in the late twentieth-century. Exiled from Augustan Rome, where his name has long since become 'A dirty word', Mahon's Ovid seems peculiarly at home in our post-modern brave new world. Although Mahon's poem focuses ostensibly upon Ovid's exile, it is with his *Metamorphoses* and the metamorphosis of the poet himself as a result of this banishment that the poem seems principally concerned. According to Hugh Haughton: 'The poem imagines a new metamorphosis of Ovid, a portrait of a metropolitan sophisticate adrift on the outermost margins of his culture and an intellectual coming to terms with the exilic nature of modernity. For this is an Ovid also exiled to the twentieth-century, whose monologue begins with reflections on the metamorphosis of "nature" itself.'[11]

This reflection on the metamorphosis of nature turns into a reflection on the nature of the metamorphosis of the *Metamorphoses*, as Mahon's Ovid considers the marsh reeds that grow around him, remembering Syrinx and her transformation. But Syrinx and her fellow nymphs are no longer afraid of Pan, but of the pulping machines that will turn them into paper. In contrast to Malouf's Ovid, who finally reconnects with his *Metamorphoses*, with nature and with himself at the end of his life, Mahon's Ovid ultimately fails to make that connection. In the end, a textured blank sheet of paper, 'woven of wood-nymphs', seems to the poet to possess more eloquence than any poem that he might write upon it.

Ovid is a potent yet absent presence in Christoph Ransmayr's award-winning novel, *The Last World,* which focuses instead upon the character of Cotta, Ovid's friend and addressee of six of the letters collected in the *Epistulae ex Ponto.* Hearing rumours of Ovid's death, Cotta travels to Tomis in search of the poet and the manuscript of the revised *Metamorphoses* that he is supposed to have left behind. There Cotta finds a land that seems to have been transformed by Ovid's presence and poetry, and whose storytelling inhabitants not only relate episodes from Ovid's epic, but appear to have taken on themselves the identities of characters from the *Metamorphoses.* The grisly deaths of Hector, Hercules, and Orpheus are shown on movie-reels projected (aptly enough) onto the whitewashed walls of the village slaughterhouse. Jason and the crew of the Argo arrive to trade with the locals. A new volcanic mountain near the village has become known as Mount Olympus – although no gods appear to live there. Ovid's former servant is a Greek named Pythagoras, who claims to have been reborn in various lives as a salamander, a soldier, and a pig girl. The village shop where Cotta hears the local gossip is run by Fama. Cotta rents a room from an old man called Lycaon, who he sees running across the mountainside dressed in a wolf-skin. The local prostitute (who is good at keeping Cotta's secrets) is named Echo. The old lady who weaves stories of metamorphosis into her tapestries is, of course, called Arachne. The village undertaker is named Thies (Dis), his wife Proserpina. And the local butcher is Tereus – whose life-story tragically and brutally follows that of his Ovidian namesake. Traces of Ovid and his *Metamorphoses* are everywhere in this story.[12]

In *The Last World*, Ransmayr describes a land that mirrors the intellectual, literary and artistic landscape of our own post-classical world. Here too, Ovid and his *Metamorphoses* are everywhere – an absent presence. Mediated through the writings of Chaucer and Shakespeare, Ovid's Pygmalion is visible in *Frankenstein*, *My Fair Lady*, *Vertigo*, and *Blade Runner*. His Philomela appears in Chaucer, Shakespeare, but also in Peter Greenaway's film *The Cook, The Thief, His Wife, and Her Lover*.[13] Ovid's Orpheus and Eurydice can be seen in opera, ballet, film, in a Japanese animated version of the *Metamorphoses – Winds of Change* (or, in a more literal translation of the Japanese title, *Orpheus of the Stars*) – and in Salman Rushdie's *The Ground Beneath her Feet*. As Ovid himself tells us, speaking through the metamorphic river god Achelous (*Metamorphoses* 8.728–30: my translation):

> . . . There are those who,
> once changed, remain forever in their new form;
> but there are others who have the power to transform into
> many shapes.

CHAPTER 5

FURTHER READING

Our modern *aetas Ovidiana* has seen a wealth of material published on Ovid and his *Metamorphoses*, and these suggestions for further reading are necessarily highly selective. Sara Myers offers a useful survey of recent scholarly work on Ovid in her bibliographical essay 'The Metamorphosis of a Poet', and readers will find further ideas for reading and research on the *Metamorphoses* there. Full details of each work recommended here can be found in the bibliography.

Two recent and broadly comprehensive works on Ovid, *The Cambridge Companion to Ovid* and *Brill's Companion to Ovid*, both contain important essays on the *Metamorphoses* and on general Ovidian themes. These books are designed as reasonably accessible handbooks for readers who want to learn more about Ovid, but contain some provocative contributions also aimed at academics and students. H. Fränkel's *Ovid: A Poet Between Two Worlds*, Sara Mack's *Ovid* and L.P. Wilkinson's *Ovid Recalled* (abridged as *Ovid Surveyed*) all provide good starting points for those looking for a more general overview of the poet and his work. The entries on 'Ovid' included in *The Oxford Classical Dictionary* and *The Cambridge History of Classical Literature* are also well worth consulting.

On the *Metamorphoses* itself, there are several works that offer invaluable insights into the poem and its major themes: Otto S. Due's *Changing Forms*, Karl Galinsky's *Ovid's Metamorphoses: An Introduction to the Basic Aspects*, Elaine Fantham's *Ovid's Metamorphoses,* Brooks Otis' *Ovid as an Epic Poet*, and Joseph B. Solodow's *The World of Ovid's Metamorphoses* are essential (and accessible) reading for anyone who wants to continue their study of the *Metamorphoses*, each offering a broad overview of the poem, its structure, and motifs. More challenging (but particularly rewarding) works that draw upon the insights offered by contemporary literary theory and criticism in their analyses of Ovid's poem include Philip Hardie's *Ovid's Poetics of Illusion*, and his co-edited collection of *Ovidian Transformations: Essays on the Metamorphoses and its Reception,* Stephen Hinds' *Metamorphosis of Persephone: Ovid and the Self-Conscious Muse,* Stephen Wheeler's *A Discourse of Wonders: Audience and Performance in Ovid's Metamorphoses*, and Garth Tissol's *The Face of Nature: Wit, Narrative, and Cosmic Origins in Ovid's Metamorphoses.*

The best textual commentary on the complete Latin text of the *Metamorphoses* is (unfortunately for most English readers) in German – Franz Bömer's *Metamorphosen, Kommentar.* However, books 1–5 and 6–10 are superbly supported by the two commentaries of William S. Anderson, and books 13 and 14 are covered, respectively, by Neil Hopkinson and Sarah Myers as part of the Cambridge Greek and Latin Classics series. Donald Hill's commentary in four parts also offers an accessible and helpful treatment of the text – along with a facing English translation. Whether or not you can read Latin, the line-by-line analysis of the *Metamorphoses* that is offered in these commentaries can help to illuminate and explain nuances and details in the text that might otherwise be missed and are therefore useful to any close reader of Ovid's poem.

Some readers may want to pursue a particular interest in one of the *Metamorphoses*' individual books or themes and there are plenty of articles and monographs available to satisfy that interest. Notes to each section of this *Reader's Guide* will direct you to the most relevant secondary scholarship concerning each book of the poem, its contexts, characters, intertexts and themes.

Finally, essential reading for anyone interested in the reception and influence of the *Metamorphoses* must include Charles Martindale's *Ovid Renewed* and Sarah Brown's brilliant study of *The Metamorphosis of Ovid: From Chaucer to Shakespeare.* I would also recommend Leonard Barkan's fascinating account of Ovid's influence upon Renaissance literature and culture, *The Gods Made Flesh*, Jonathan Bate's *Shakespeare and Ovid*, and Theodore Ziolkowski's *Ovid and the Moderns* – the best work available on Ovid's place in modern literature, right up to the third millennium.

NOTES

CHAPTER 1: CONTEXTS

1 On the theme of *amor* in the *Metamorphoses* see Anderson (1995).

2 According to Holzberg (1999) 60, 'It is actually possible to read Ovid's works from the *Heroides* through to his exile poetry as a series of "metamorphoses" of the elegiac discourse found in the *Amores*.'

3 On parallels between the two poems see Hinds (1987).

4 On the mystery of Ovid's exile see Thibault (1964) and Williams (1994).

5 Kenney (1982) 444n.1, suggests that 'It is possible that our text of the *Metamorphoses* goes back to a copy revised (like the *Fasti*) by Ovid in exile, and that one or two apparently "prophetic" touches . . . were introduced by him during revision'.

CHAPTER 2: OVERVIEW OF THEMES

1 Anderson (1997) and (1972), and Bömer (1969–86) offer excellent commentaries on the Latin text of the *Metamorphoses*, while Boyd (2002) and Hardie (2002a) both make fine 'companions to Ovid'. Fantham (2004), Fränkel (1945), Galinsky (1975), Glenn (1986), and Solodow (1988) present intelligent and accessible overviews of the poem.

2 On Ovid's 'changes' see Anderson (1993) and (1963), Due (1974), and Fantham (2004) 3–20.

3 For a nicely nuanced close reading of the proem see Wheeler (1999) 8–33.

4 On Ovid's gods see Feeney (1991).

5 On the narrative and structure of the poem see Coleman (1971), Crabbe (1981) and Wheeler (1999) and (2000). Wheeler (2000) 23 notes the echo of Virgil's *Aeneid* 1.372 ('*O dea, si prima repetens ab origine* . . .) in Ovid's claim to tell the history of the world from its first origins (*primaque ab origine mundi*).

6 Suetonius (*Div. Aug.* 69, 71) describes Augustus as a shameless womanizer who employed his own wife to procure young virgins for his use.

7 On Ovid's Augustanism see Knox (1986), Curran (1972), Davis (2006) and, for an argument challenging the validity and use of terms such as pro- and anti- Augustan in analyses of Ovid, especially Kennedy (1992).

8 See Barchiesi (1991) 6–7, and Feeney (1999). Feeney (1999) 13, links Ovid's reference to 'my times' here with the *Fasti*, composed at the same time as the *Metamorphoses*, which opens with the word '*Tempora*' (*The Times*) – the alternative name by which it was known in antiquity.

9 On Ovid's Callimachean influences see Graf (2002).

10 On Ovid's *carmen perpetuum* see Hofmann (1985). On Ovid's use of lost Hellenistic sources – notably Callimachus' *Aetia (Causes)*, Nicander's *Heteroioumena (Transformations)*, and Boios' *Ornithogonia (Origins of Birds)* – see Forbes-Irving (1990) 7–37.

11 Otis (1970).

12 Ludwig (1965).

13 See Anderson (1997) 13 and Feeney (2004) xxi.

14 See Wheeler (1999) 207–10 for a complete catalogue of all forty internal narrators and narratives in the poem.

15 See Wheeler (2000) 93 and Brown (2005) 36f.

CHAPTER 3: TEXTUAL READINGS

3.1 BOOKS ONE TO FIVE

1 For similar creative artists in the poem see the tales relating to Prometheus (1.76–88), Deucalion and Pyrrha (1.313–415), Arachne (6.1–145), Daedalus (8.152–235), and Pygmalion (10.243–97).

2 See Tissol (1997) on the humorous subtext to Ovid's narrative of cosmic and human origins in the *Metamorphoses*. See Liveley (2002) for a fuller discussion of mankind as the re-embodiment of chaos.

3 On Ovid's creation of cosmos from chaos see Wheeler (1995), McKim (1985), Liveley (2002), Helzle (1993), and Myers (1994b).

4 See Anderson (1989) for an alternative reading.

5 For similar accounts of gods transforming themselves see Mercury disguised as a cow-herd in the stories of Io (1.668–746) and Battus (2.676–707), Jupiter disguised as Diana in the story of Callisto (2.401–530), Jupiter disguised as a bull in the story of Europa (2.833–75), Juno as the nurse Beroe in the tale of Semele (3.256–315), and Bacchus as the sailor Acoetes (3.511–733).

6 Feldherr (2002) 170.

7 For similar accounts of transformation of inanimate objects into human form see the creation of mankind (1.5–88), the race born of blood (1.162), Cadmus' dragon-teeth men (3.101–14), Pygmalion's statue (10.283–6), and Aeneas' fleet (14.549–56).

8 On the Daphne story as a template upon which subsequent rapes in the poem are patterned see Davis (1983) and Salzman-Mitchell (2005) 29–38, Parry (1964), Nicoll (1980), and Nagle (1988a).

9 In the opening poem of his *Amores*, Ovid complains that Cupid wants everyone, everything, and everywhere to belong to him

(1.1.13–15). Apollo's suggestion that Cupid should keep to his own specialist sphere (*Met* 1.456–62) echoes that complaint.

10 In Latin, *amor* covers a wide semantic range and can have different meanings in different contexts. In Ovid's *Metamorphoses, amor* can refer to *Amor* or Cupid; to a 'beloved'; to feelings of erotic or 'romantic' love; and to sex.

11 In his *Ars* 1.665f Ovid teaches his male readers that women pretend to be indifferent to male attention only to make themselves more desirable, and secretly wish to be taken by force – that is raped. See Brown (2005) 45–66.

12 See Feldherr (2002) 173 for the view that in appropriating Daphne's leaves for his 'laurels' Apollo effectively 'epicizes' her tale, transforming an elegiac love story into something more appropriately martial and epic in tone.

13 On Ovid's ingenious transition from Daphne to Io, see chapter 2.

14 Compare Juno's anger towards Io here to her anger and jealousy in the tales of Callisto (2.401–530), Semele (3.256–315), Ino and Athamas (4.416–562), and Alcmena (9.273–323). Juno's anger is a standard *topos* in Greek and Roman epic and a prominent motif in Virgil's *Aeneid* but in the *Metamorphoses* Ovid repeatedly trivializes her anger as prompted by sexual jealousy.

15 Compare Io's frustrated attempt to stretch her arms out and beg the gods for mercy (according to the standard rules of supplication in the ancient world) with that of Callisto (2.401–530), Actaeon (3.138–255) and Pentheus (3.511–733).

16 For similar accounts of gods transforming themselves see Jupiter disguised as a mortal in the story of Lycaon (1.163–252), Mercury disguised as a cow-herd in the story of Battus (2.676–707), Jupiter disguised as Diana in the story of Callisto (2.401–530), Jupiter disguised as a bull in the story of Europa (2.833–75), Juno as the nurse Beroe in the tale of Semele (3.256–315), and Bacchus as the sailor Acoetes (3.511–733).

17 On audiences and narrators in the *Metamorphoses* see Wheeler (1999) and (2000) and Konstan (1991).

18 Brown (2005) 30.

19 Cahoon (1990) 163. On reading Ovid's rapes see also Richlin (1992) and Salzman-Mitchell (2005).

20 See Keith (1992) for a detailed overview of book 2.

21 On the epic qualities of this ecphrasis, akin to the representations of Achilles' and Aeneas' shields in Homer and Virgil, see Brown (1987).

22 On the structure of this episode see Bass (1977) and Brown (1987).

23 For a nicely nuanced reading of the Phaethon episode see Salzman-Mitchell (2005) 101–4.

24 See Gildenhard and Zissos (1999) for this ingenious solution to Ovid's chronological blip.

25 For similar accounts of gods transforming themselves see Jupiter disguised as a mortal in the story of Lycaon (1.163–252), Mercury disguised as a cow-herd in the stories of Io (1.668–746) and Battus (2.676–707), Jupiter disguised as a bull in the story of Europa (2.833–75), Juno as the nurse Beroe in the tale of Semele (3.256–315), and Bacchus as the sailor Acoetes (3.511–733).

26 On the rape of Callisto see Johnson (1996) and Curran (1978).

27 Compare Juno's anger here to her anger and jealousy in the tales of Io (1.568–746), Semele (3.256–315), Ino and Athamas (4.416–562), and Alcmena (9.273–323). Juno's anger is a standard *topos* in Greek and Roman epic and a prominent motif in Virgil's *Aeneid* but in the *Metamorphoses* Ovid repeatedly trivializes her anger as prompted by sexual jealousy.

28 Compare Callisto's frustrated attempt to stretch her arms out and beg the gods for mercy (according to the standard rules of supplication in the ancient world) with that of Io (1.568–746), Actaeon (3.138–255) and Pentheus (3.511–733).

29 For similar accounts of gods transforming themselves see Jupiter disguised as a mortal in the story of Lycaon (1.163–252), Mercury disguised as a cow-herd in the story of Io (1.668–746), Jupiter disguised as Diana in the story of Callisto (2.401–530), Jupiter disguised as a bull in the story of Europa (2.833–75), Juno as the nurse Beroe in the tale of Semele (3.256–315), and Bacchus as the sailor Acoetes (3.511–733).

30 Compare the visualization of Envy or *Invidia* (2.760–832) with that of Rumour or *Fama* (9.137; 12.39–63), Hunger or *Fames* (8.784–822), and Sleep or *Somnus* (11.586–649).

31 For similar accounts of gods transforming themselves see Jupiter disguised as a mortal in the story of Lycaon (1.163–252), Mercury disguised as a cow-herd in the stories of Io (1.668–746) and Battus (2.676–707), Jupiter disguised as Diana in the story of Callisto (2.401–530), Juno as the nurse Beroe in the tale of Semele (3.256–315), and Bacchus as the sailor Acoetes (3.511–733).

32 See Henderson (1979) for a detailed overview of book 3.

33 On Ovid's 'Theban Cycle' see Janan (2009).

34 Compare the paradox of Agenor's 'criminal piety' with that of Tereus (6.473f), Philomela (6.635), Aeetes' daughters (7.339f), Althaea (8.477), and Myrrha (10.366f).

35 See Hardie (1990) for a discussion of Ovid's Theban narrative as an 'anti-Aeneid'.

36 On the role of landscape – and particularly of the *locus amoenus* as a frame for violence in the poem see Segal (1969b) and Hinds (2002). Hinds (2002) 131 suggests that '[i]nasmuch as the ideal landscape pattern functions in the *Metamorphoses* as a recurrent setting for episodes of erotic desire and violence, such landscapes come to provide a narratological "cue" for such action, especially in the poem's first five books'.

37 See Salzman-Mitchell (2005) on the significance of the gaze in Actaeon's story.

38 Compare Actaeon's frustrated attempt to stretch his arms out and beg the gods for mercy (according to the standard rules of supplication in the ancient world) with that of Io (1.568–746), Callisto (2.401–530), and Pentheus (3.511–733).

39 Heath (1991) 242.

40 See Schlam (1984).

41 On Juno's jealousy see Wheeler (2000) 73, Hardie (1990), and Janan (2009) 87–113. Compare Juno's anger here to her anger and jealousy in the tales of Io (1.568–746), Callisto (2.401–530), Ino and Athamas (4.416–562), and Alcmena (9.273–323). Juno's anger is a standard *topos* in Greek and Roman epic and a prominent motif in Virgil's *Aeneid* but in the *Metamorphoses* Ovid repeatedly trivializes her anger as prompted by sexual jealousy.

42 For similar accounts of gods transforming themselves see Jupiter disguised as a mortal in the story of Lycaon (1.163–252), Mercury disguised as a cow-herd in the stories of Io (1.668–746) and Battus (2.676–707), Jupiter disguised as Diana in the story of Callisto (2.401–530), Jupiter disguised as a bull in the story of Europa (2.833–75), and Bacchus as the sailor Acoetes (3.511–733).

43 For a reading that highlights the more serious side to this episode see Liveley (2003).

44 A contemporaneous account of Narcissus also appears in Conon's *Narrationes.*

45 See Kennedy (1993).

46 Segal (1988) 7. For general analyses of word play in this narrative see Knox (1986) 19–26, Solodow (1988) 46f, Tissol (1997) 15–17.

47 Tissol (1997) 16.

48 See Janan (2004).

49 For a detailed commentary on the Virgilian allusions in Pentheus' speech, see Anderson (1997) 389–96. On allusion and intertextuality in the poem, see also Janan (2009) *passim* (but especially 10–21), Hardie (1993) *passim*, Hinds (1998) 104–22, and Thomas (2001) 78–83. On Ovid's debt to Virgil here and throughout the *Metamorphoses* see Huxley (1996) and Weiden Boyd (2002).

50 For similar accounts of gods transforming themselves see Jupiter disguised as a mortal in the story of Lycaon (1.163–252), Mercury disguised as a cow-herd in the stories of Io (1.668–746) and Battus (2.676–707), Jupiter disguised as Diana in the story of Callisto (2.401–530), Jupiter disguised as a bull in the story of Europa (2.833–75), and Juno as the nurse Beroe in the tale of Semele (3.256–315).

51 Compare Actaeon's frustrated attempt to stretch his arms out and beg for mercy (according to the standard rules of supplication in the ancient world) with that of Io (1.568–746), Callisto (2.401–530), and Actaeon (3.138–255).

52 For a (rare) sympathetic reading of Pentheus' story see James (1991).

53 Anderson (1997) 417.

54 Fantham (2004) 47.

55 See Robinson (1999).

56 Compare Juno's anger here to her anger and jealousy in the tales of Io (1.568–746), Callisto (2.401–530), Semele (3.256–315), and Alcmena (9.273–323). Juno's anger is a standard *topos* in Greek and Roman epic and a prominent motif in Virgil's *Aeneid* but in the *Metamorphoses* Ovid repeatedly trivializes her anger as prompted by sexual jealousy.

57 See Segal (1998) on Ovid's 'metamorphic bodies'.

58 See Keith (1999).

59 For a detailed survey of Ovid's 'Musomachia' see Johnson and Malamud (1988).

60 See Wheeler (1999) 207–10 for a complete catalogue of similar inset narrators and narratives in the poem.

61 On the theme of artistic failure see Leach (1974).

62 Ovid's Augustan audience would have been familiar with the *Homeric Hymn to Demeter*, which – as Stephen Hinds (1987) has shown – provides the central form of the story that Calliope here transforms into a new shape. Ovid also repeats a different version of this story in his *Fasti*.

63 On Ovid's political motivation for representing Venus and Cupid as 'Empress and Commander in Chief of an empire' in book 5, see Johnson (1996).

64 See Zissos (1999).

65 For a particularly insightful response to Calliope's song, see Cahoon (1996).

3.2 BOOKS SIX TO TEN

1 For similar creative artists in the poem see the tales relating to the divine creator of the cosmos (1.5–88), Prometheus (1.76–88), Deucalion and Pyrrha (1.313–415), Daedalus (8.152–235), and Pygmalion (10.243–97).

2 Anderson (1972) 160. Minerva's tapestry also recalls the style of art favoured by Augustus as sanctioned by him for the panels of the Ara Pacis.

3 Brown (2005) 105. On the function and significance of metaphors of weaving and spinning in the poem see Rosati (1999).

4 Tissol (1997) 126 suggests that, 'without such a context, the violence of [Marsyas'] fate becomes the more harrowing and repulsive.'

5 Kenney (1986) 411. See also Anderson (1972) 202 who describes the episode as 'grotesquely vivid'; Galinsky (1975) 134 who criticises the 'graphic detail' of the torture; Leach (1974) 118 and 127

who refers to the 'grotesque horror' of this 'brutal tale'; and Tissol (1997) 125–29 who labels Marsyas' representation as 'harrowing and repulsive'.

6 Galinsky (1975) 134.

7 See Feldherr and James (2004).

8 Anderson (1972) 204.

9 Compare the paradox of Tereus' 'criminal piety' with that of Agenor (3.5), Philomela (6.635), Aeetes' daughters (7.339f), Althaea (8.477), and Myrrha (10.366f).

10 See Richlin (1992) and Curran (1978). For a persuasive feminist re-reading of this story – and of Philomela's web – see Joplin (1984).

11 Compare the paradox of Philomela's 'criminal piety' with that of Agenor (3.5), Tereus (6.473f), Aeetes' daughters (7.339f), Althaea (8.477), and Myrrha (10.366f).

12 On the violence of this narrative – and the voyeuristic role played by the reader in witnessing it – see Segal (1994).

13 On Medea as an intertextual heroine see Hinds (1993) and Newlands (1997).

14 Medea's passion is portentously described by Ovid as a kind of madness (*furorem* – 7.10). Love is similarly described in the stories of Narcissus (3.350, 479), Scylla (8.35f), Byblis (9.512, 541, 583, 602.), Myrrha (10.355, 397), Glaucus (14.16), and Iphis (14.701).

15 On the interwoven themes of *amor,* metamorphosis and magic in this story see Rosner-Siegel (1982).

16 Like the gods in books 1–5 of the poem, Medea's desire is inflamed by the sight of Jason. On the importance of the gaze in the *Metamorphoses* see Salzman-Mitchell (2005).

17 Newlands (1997) 189.

18 Ovid even puts into Medea's mouth an elaboration of his own words (*Amores* 2.1.23–6) celebrating the magical power of poetry.

19 On Cephalus' narrative technique here see Tarrant (1995).

20 See Davis (1983).

21 Compare Scylla with Propertius' elegiac heroine Tarpeia (4.4) who also betrayed her city for love.

22 This reference to Scylla as '*monstrum*' suggests that Ovid also has Scylla, the monstrous figure of books 13 and 14, in mind here. He also conflates the two Scyllas in his *Ars Amatoria* 1.331f.

23 Newlands (1997) 197.

24 Compare the bird transformations of Scylla and Nisus with that of Tereus, Procne and Philomela (6. 667–74).

25 For similar creative artists in the poem see the tales relating to the divine creator of the cosmos (1.5–88), Prometheus (1.76–88), Deucalion and Pyrrha (1.313–415), Arachne (6.1–145), and Pygmalion (10.243–97).

26 See Wise (1977).

27 Recall Sol's identical advice to Phaethon at 2.136f.

28 Ovid had previously told the same story at some greater length in his elegiac *Ars Amatoria* (2.19–98) to demonstrate his point that it is futile to attempt the control or restraint of winged Amor. Ovid has here 'transformed' the story as it is narrated in the *Ars* from elegiac verse into the hexameter of epic, retaining several lines of poetry exactly as they appear in the *Ars*. See Anderson (1972) 348–55 for details of this linguistic metamorphosis.

29 On the parallels between these tales see Faber (1998).

30 Feldherr (2002) 164.

31 See Keith (1999) 223–9.

32 See Horsfall (1979) on the comic burlesque of this story.

33 Compare the paradox of Althaea's 'impious piety' with that of Agenor (3.5), Tereus (6.473f), Philomela (6.635), Aeetes' daughters (7.339f), and Myrrha (10.366f).

34 A menu possibly inspired by Callimachus' *Hecale*.

35 For a detailed overview of this story see Griffin (1991) and Gowers (2005). See Hallett (2000) for a reading that views Baucis and Philemon as the ultimate 'green' couple.

36 Compare the visualization of Hunger or *Fames* (8.784–822), with that of Envy or *Invidia* (2.760–832), Rumour or *Fama* (9.137; 12.39–63), and Sleep or *Somnus* (11.586–649).

37 See Murray (2004) and Hinds (1987) 19.

38 See Wheeler (1999) 135–9 and Hardie (1993) 65–7. Compare Hercules' apotheosis here with that of Aeneas (14.581–608), Romulus and Hersilia (14.772–851), Julius and Augustus Caesar (15.832–870), and Ovid himself (15.871–9).

39 Compare Juno's anger here to her anger and jealousy in the tales of Io (1.568–746), Callisto (2.401–530), Semele (3.256–315), Ino and Athamas (4.416–562). Juno's anger is a standard *topos* in Greek and Roman epic and a prominent motif in Virgil's *Aeneid* but in the *Metamorphoses* Ovid repeatedly trivializes her anger as prompted by sexual jealousy.

40 Nisbet (1987) 243. See also Gowers (2005).

41 Compare Byblis' illicit passion with that of Medea (7.1–403) and Scylla (8.1–151).

42 Raval (2001) 286. See also Janan (1988) and Nagle (1983).

43 On writing in the Byblis episode see Jenkins (2000).

44 Wheeler (1997) 192.

45 On the etymology of *puella* see Watson (1983) 123.

46 Mack (1995) 281.

47 On Orpheus' failure as poet and lover see Leach (1974), Heath (1994), Elsner and Sharrock (1991).

48 See Anderson (1982) 25.

49 On Orpheus' sexuality see Makowski (1996), and on Ovid's see Liveley (2005) 52–4.

50 For a detailed overview of Orpheus' song see Janan (1988).

51 Glenn (1986) 136.

52 Orpheus' literary *recusatio* here (the poet's standard rejection of epic in favour of lighter poetry) reminds us that Ovid too once claimed to have been prompted by the loss of a girl to turn his attention from epic and gigantomachies to elegy and love poetry (*Amores* 2.1.11– 22).

53 Segal (1998) 14. For similar views see also Galinsky (1975) 87, Downing (1990) 59, and Elsner and Sharrock (1991) 160. See also Liveley (1999).

54 For similar creative artists in the poem see the tales relating to the divine creator of the cosmos (1.5–88), Prometheus (1.76–88), Deucalion and Pyrrha (1.313–415), Arachne (6.1–145), and Daedalus (8.152–235).

55 Myerowitz (1985) 93.

56 Elsner and Sharrock (1991).

57 Elsner and Sharrock (1991) 174. For an alternative reading see Liveley (1999).

58 Brown (2005) 127.

59 Several readings highlight the language of procreation that is used to describe Pygmalion's 'relationship' with his statue*: nasci, concepit, plenissima, plenus.* See Leach (1974), Elsner and Sharrock (1991) 179.

60 See Nagle (1983) and Leach (1974).

61 Compare the paradox of Tereus' 'criminal piety' with that of Agenor (3.5), Tereus (6.473f), Philomela (6.635), Aeetes' daughters (7.339f), and Althaea (8.477).

62 Anderson (1972) 501.

63 As Nagle (1983) 315, observes: 'Here Orpheus is clearly sympathetic toward Myrrha, since vengeance implies a victim and a culprit responsible for that victim's suffering; now Orpheus implicitly blames Venus for Myrrha's passion.'

64 Compare this story with that of Hyacinthus (10.155–219).

3.3 BOOKS ELEVEN TO FIFTEEN

1 Myers (1994b) 70. Specific studies of internal narrators in the *Metamorphoses* include: Hoffman (1985), Knox (1986), Leach (1974), and Nagle (1988b).

2 Knox (1986) 62. See also Leach (1974) 106 who sees the song of Orpheus as a microcosm of Ovid's poem.

3 On the theatricality and 'amphitheatricality' of Orpheus' death see Hinds (2002) 139f.

4 Richlin (1992) 161.

5 See Liveley (1999).

6 See Farrell (1999) for the view that Orpheus' head singing on after the poet's death anticipates Ovid's own survival after death, as 'predicted' in the poem's epilogue.

7 See Wheeler (1999) 153.

8 Wheeler (1999) 138.
9 On the politics of reading Ovid's rapes see Richlin (1992), Barsby (1978) 15, and Salzman-Mitchell (2005).
10 See Solodow (1988) 44 for this characteristic transitional device.
11 Compare this transformation with the metamorphosis of Perdix in similar circumstances at 8.236–59 and of Ino and her companions at 4.550.
12 On the elegiac characteristics of Alcyone's speech see Fantham (1979) 330–45 and Walde (2008). Cf. Propertius. 1.6.7–18; 2.20.18, 28b, 39 and Tibullus; 1.2.26, 1.3.36, 1.9.16 and 2.6.3.
13 On Ovid's personifications see Tissol (1997) 64f, and Salzman-Mitchell (2005).
14 Compare the visualization of Sleep or *Somnus* (11.586–649) with that of Envy or *Invidia* (2.760–832), Rumour or *Fama* (9.137; 12.39–63), and Hunger or *Fames* (8.784–822).
15 Recall that the elegiac tradition traced its origins to grave dedications and funeral epitaphs, the traditional etymology of the word 'elegy' assumed to derive from the Greek '*e legein*', 'to cry woe'.
16 For a detailed overview of this story see Fantham (1979).
17 According to tradition, the couple failed to invite the goddess Strife to their wedding but she came nonetheless, bringing the gift of an apple inscribed with the words 'to the fairest'. Juno, Minerva and Venus fight over which of them deserves it, resulting in Greek mythology's most notorious beauty contest. Each goddess attempts to bribe the judge, but Venus wins by offering to give him the most beautiful woman in the world – Helen, the wife of Menelaus, king of Sparta.
18 On the pattern and structure of book 12 see Zumwalt (1977) and Papaioannou (2007).
19 Ellsworth (1980) 23, suggests that: 'At this point there is a major break in Ovid's narrative, since he turns from the chiefly "mythological" period to "historical" times'. See also Fränkel (1945) 101; Otis (1970) 83–6, 278–305, 315f; and Papaioannou (2005) 1.
20 Compare the visualization of Rumour or *Fama* (12.39–63) with that of Sleep or *Somnus* (11.586–649), Envy or *Invidia* (2.760–832), and Hunger or *Fames* (8.784–822).
21 See Hardie (1993).
22 This Cycnus is *not* the same as the characters of the same name we met previously in books 2 and 7 – although all three somewhat confusingly metamorphose into swans.
23 For a discussion of the gendered dynamics that shape the structure of Ovid's 'little *Iliad*' in general and the Caenis/Caeneus story in particular, see Keith (2000) 81–86.
24 On the battle of Lapiths and centaurs as Ovid's 'little *Iliad*', see Musgrove (1998) 223–31 and Papaioannou (2005).
25 For a close reading of the Cyllarus and Hylonome digression see DeBrohun (2004). She suggests (2004) 417 that in this interlude Ovid explores 'both hybridity itself and the relationships and

possible combinations of a number of conceptual opposites: *natura* and *cultus*, human and animal, male and female, love and war, and the contrasting values of lyric-elegiac and epic poetry'.

26 Musgrove (1998) 226, n11.
27 For an excellent survey of the rhetorical aspects of Ajax and Ulysses' speeches, see Hopkinson (2000) 1–22.
28 See Nikolopoulos (2004). On Ajax's misreading of Homer see Papaioannou (2007).
29 On this familiar style of transition between stories see Solodow (1988) 44.
30 Memnon is the main character in Arctinus' epic *Aethiopis*, from which Ovid clearly draws material for this tale. But the linguistic echo of the Latin word *memor* in his name might also have suggested Memnon as a suitable character for inclusion in this sequence of tales concerning commemoration.
31 On Ovid's '*Odyssey*' see Ellsworth (1988).
32 See in particular Hopkinson (2000) 29–34 and Galinsky (1975) 221.
33 Holzberg (2002) 52f and Kennedy (1993), 71–77, who reads the semiotics of hair in elegy as figuring the elegist's control over both his poetry and his girl.
34 See Nagle (1988a) and Mack (1999) on this 'trio of love triangles'.
35 On the epic character of Ovid's Polyphemus, see Farrell (1992) and Segal (1968).
36 On Ovid's literary relationship to his poetic predecessors see Hardie (1993) and Barchiesi (2001).
37 For a detailed overview of Ovid's 'little *Aeneid*' see Papaioannou (2005). On allusion and intertext in this narrative see Hinds (1998).
38 Ovid takes his cue for this inset narrative (echoing the tragic love triangle between Circe-Glaucus-Scylla) from a reference in Virgil's *Aeneid* to a statue of the Latin prince Picus (Latin for 'woodpecker'), ancestor of Latinus, and husband to Turnus' half-sister Canens ('the singing girl'), who Circe, 'possessed by lust, struck . . . with her rod of gold and changed him into a bird, sprinkling colours on his wings' (*Aeneid* 7.189–91).
39 Compare the phoenix-like rising of the heron from Ardea's ashes with the story of Memnon (13.576–622) and the daughters of Orion (13.675–99).
40 On the apotheosis of Aeneas see Myers (1994b) and Tissol (2002). Compare Aeneas' apotheosis here with that of Hercules (9.134–272), Romulus and Hersilia (14.772–851), Julius and Augustus Caesar (15.832–870), and Ovid himself (15.871–9).
41 See Littlefield (1965) and Gentilcore (1995).
42 Myers (1994a) 225. Jones (2001) 375f suggests that the nature of Pomona's transformation 'introduces a different approach to change that Ovid pursues in his final book. Vertumnus' physical changes produce a psychological change in Pomona, inverting the poem's usual process of metamorphosis.'

43 Compare the apotheosis of Romulus and Hersilia with that of Hercules (9.134–272), Aeneas (14.581–608), Julius and Augustus Caesar (15.832–870), and Ovid himself (15.871–9).

44 On Pythagoras' speech see Hardie (1995) and Galinsky (1998).

45 The problems of time encountered after Phaethon's disastrous chariot ride in book 2 appear to have re-emerged in the poem's narratological space-time continuum.

46 See in particular his retelling of Odysseus' encounter with Circe (14.1–434).

47 On the 'logic' of such miraculous transformations in the natural world as providing a precedent for similar metamorphoses to the human body see Buxton (2009) 157–247.

48 See Gildenhard and Zissos (1999). The story of Hippolytus would have been familiar to Ovid's Augustan audience not only from Euripides' tragedy, but also from its telling in Callimachus' *Aetia*.

49 Hardie *et al* (1999) 7.

50 On the Cipus story see Galinsky (1967).

51 As in the stories of Europa (2.833–75) and Achelous (8.882–9.97), Cipus' horns (*cornua*) once more signal the approaching end of a book by indicating the horn book-ends (*cornua*) of the text.

52 See Feeney (1999).

53 On the Augustan politics of Ovid's retelling of Roman history see Tissol (2002).

54 Compare Caesar's apotheosis here with that of Hercules (9.134–272), Aeneas (14.581–608), Romulus and Hersilia (14.772–851), and Ovid himself (15.871–9).

55 See Little (1976), Segal (1969a), Curran (1972) and Barchiesi (1997).

56 On the encomiastic frame of the *Metamorphoses* see Knox (1986) 75f.

57 On the problem of concluding a *carmen perpetuum* see Davis (1980). See Knox (1986) for a reading of the *Metamorphoses* that figures Ovid as a Roman Callimachus.

58 See Hershkowitz (1998) 190. Compare Ovid's own projected apotheosis here with that of Hercules (9.134–272), Aeneas (14.581–608), Romulus and Hersilia (14.772–851), Julius and Augustus Caesar (15.832–870).

CHAPTER 4: RECEPTION AND INFLUENCE

1 Hughes (1997) viii.

2 Brown (1999) 1.

3 Some of the best places to find images from the *Metamorphoses* are online. See, in particular: *Ovid Illustrated: the Reception of Ovid's Metamorphoses in Image:* http://etext.virginia.edu/latin/ovid/about. html.

4 Martindale (1988) 4.

5 See Allen (2002) on Ovid in art.

6 On the history of Ovid in English translation see Martin (1998) and Lyne (2002).
7 Martin (1998) xxvii.
8 Hughes (1997) vii.
9 Hofmann and Lasdun (1994) xiii.
10 On Ovid and the Moderns, see Ziolkowski (2005).
11 Haughton (2007) 170.
12 See Kennedy (2002) 323.
13 On Ovidian themes in cinema see Winkler (2001), and Brown (2005).

BIBLIOGRAPHY

Allen. C. (2002) 'Ovid and Art', in Hardie, P. (ed.), *The Cambridge Companion to Ovid* (Cambridge) 336–67

Anderson, W.S. (1963) 'Multiple Change in the *Metamorphoses*', *Transactions and Proceedings of the American Philological Association* 94: 1–27

— (1982) 'The Orpheus of Virgil and Ovid: *flebile nescio quid*', in Warden, J. (ed.), *Orpheus: The Metamorphosis of a Myth* (Toronto) 25–50

— (1989) 'Lycaon: Ovid's Deceptive Paradigm in *Metamorphoses* 1', *Illinois Classical Studies* 14: 91–101

— (1993) 'Form Changed: Ovid's *Metamorphoses*', in Boyle, A.J. (ed.) *Roman Epic* (London and New York) 108–24

— (1995) 'Aspects of Love in Ovid's *Metamorphoses*', *Classical Journal* 90: 265–9

— (ed.) (1972) *Ovid's Metamorphoses Books 6–10* (Oklahoma)

— (ed.) (1997) *Ovid's Metamorphoses Books 1–5* (Oklahoma)

Barchiesi, A. (1991) 'Discordant Muses', *Proceedings of the Cambridge Philological Society* 37: 1–21

— (1997) *The Poet and the Prince: Ovid and Augustan Discourse* (Berkeley)

— (2001) *Speaking Volumes: Narrative and Intertext in Ovid and Other Latin Poets* (London)

Barkan, L. (1986) *The Gods Made Flesh: Metamorphosis and the Pursuit of Paganism* (Yale)

Barsby, J. (1978) *Ovid* (Oxford)

Bass, R.C. (1977) 'Some Aspects of the Structure of the Phaethon Episode in Ovid's *Metamorphoses*', *Classical Quarterly* 27: 402–8

Bate, J. (1993) *Shakespeare and Ovid* (Oxford)

Binns, J.W. (ed.) (1973) *Ovid* (London)

Bömer, F. (1969–86) *P. Ovidius Naso: Metamorphosen* (Heidelberg)

Boyd, B. (ed.) (2002) *Brill's Companion to Ovid* (Leiden)

Brown, R.D. (1987) 'The Palace of the Sun in Ovid's *Metamorphoses*', in Whitby, M. and Hardie, P. (eds), *Homo Viator: Classical Essays for John Bramble* (Bristol and Oak Park) 211–20

Brown, S.A. (1999) *The Metamorphosis of Ovid: From Chaucer to Ted Hughes* (London)

— (2005) *Ovid: Myth and Metamorphosis* (London)

Buxton, R. (2009) *Forms of Astonishment: Greek Myths of Metamorphosis* (Oxford)

Cahoon, L. (1990) 'Let the Muse Sing On: Poetry, Criticism, Feminism, and the Case of Ovid', *Helios* 17: 197–211

— (1996) 'Calliope's Song: Shifting Narrators in Ovid, *Metamorphoses* 5', *Helios* 23: 43–66

Coleman, R. (1971) 'Structure and Intention in the *Metamorphoses*', *Classical Quarterly* 21: 461–77

Crabbe, A. (1981) 'Structure and Content in Ovid's *Metamorphoses*', *Aufstieg und Niedergang der römischen Welt* 2.31.4: 2274–327

Curran, Leo, C. (1972) 'Transformation and Anti-Augustanism in Ovid's *Metamorphoses*', *Arethusa* 5: 71–91

— (1978) 'Rape and Rape Victims in the *Metamorphoses*', *Arethusa* 11: 213–41

Davis, G. (1980) 'The Problem of Closure in a Carmen Perpetuum: Aspects of Thematic Recapitulation in Ovid *Met.* 15', *Grazer Beitrage* 15: 123–32

Davis, N.G. (1983) *The Death of Procris: 'Amor' and the Hunt in Ovid's Metamorphoses* (Rome)

Davis, P. (2006) *Ovid and Augustus: A Political Reading of Ovid's Erotic Poems* (London)

DeBrohun, J.B. (2004) 'Centaurs in Love and War: Cyllarus and Hylonome in Ovid *Metamorphoses* 12.393–428', *American Journal of Philology* 125: 417–52

Downing, E. (1990) 'Anti-Pygmalion: The *Praeceptor* in *Ars Amatoria, Book 3*', *Helios* 17: 237–49

Due, O.S. (1974) *Changing Forms: Studies in the Metamorphoses of Ovid* (Copenhagen)

Ellsworth, J.D. (1980) 'Ovid's *Iliad* (*Metamorphoses* 12.1–13,622)', *Prudentia* 12:23–9

— (1988) 'Ovid's *Odyssey*: *Metamorphoses* 13.623–14.608', *Mnemosyne* 41: 333–40

Elsner, J. and Sharrock, A. (1991) 'Reviewing Pygmalion', *Ramus* 20:149–82

Faber, R. (1998) 'Daedalus, Icarus, and the Fall of Perdix: Continuity and Allusion in *Metamorphoses* 8.183–259', *Hermes* 126.1: 80–9

Fantham, E. (1979) 'Ovid's Ceyx and Alcyone: The Metamorphosis of a Myth', *Phoenix* 33.4: 330–45

— (2004) *Ovid's Metamorphoses* (Oxford)

Farrell, J. (1992) 'Dialogue of Genres in Ovid's "Lovesong of Polyphemus" (*Metamorphoses* 13.719–897)', *The American Journal of Philology* 113: 235–68

— (1999) 'The Ovidian Corpus: Poetic Body and Poetic Text', in Hardie, P., Barchiesi, A. and Hinds, S. (eds) *Ovidian Transformations: Essays on Ovid's Metamorphoses and its Reception* (Cambridge) 127–41

Feeney, D. C. (1991) *The Gods in Epic* (Oxford)

— (1999) '*Mea Tempora*: Patterning of Time in the *Metamorphoses*', in Hardie, P., Barchiesi, A. and Hinds, S. (eds) *Ovidian Transformations: Essays on Ovid's Metamorphoses and its Reception* (Cambridge) 13–30

— (2004) 'Introduction', *Ovid: Metamorphoses* (London) xiii–xxxiv

Feldherr, A. (2002) 'Metamorphosis in the *Metamorphoses*', in Hardie, P. (ed.) *The Cambridge Companion to Ovid* (Cambridge) 163–79

Feldherr, A. and James, P. (2004) 'Making the Most of Marsyas', *Arethusa* 37: 75–104

Forbes-Irving, P.M.C. (1990) *Metamorphosis in Greek Myths* (Oxford)

Fränkel, H. (1945) *Ovid: A Poet Between Two Worlds* (Berkeley)

Galinsky, C.K. (1967) 'The Cipus Episode in Ovid's *Metamorphoses* (15.565–621)', *Transactions and Proceedings of the American Philological Association* 98: 181–91

— (1975) *Ovid's Metamorphoses: An Introduction to the Basic Aspects* (Berkeley and Los Angeles)

— (1998) 'The Speech of Pythagoras in Ovid *Metamorphoses* 15.75–478', *Papers of the Liverpool Latin Seminar* 10: 313–36

Garth, S. (trans.) (1717) *Ovid's Metamorphoses* (London)

Gentilcore, R. (1995) 'The Landscape of Desire: The Tale of Pomona and Vertumnus in Ovid's *Metamorphoses*', *Phoenix* 49.2: 110–20

Gildenhard, I. and Zissos, A. (1999) 'Problems of Time in *Metamorphoses* 2: 31–47', in Hardie, P., Barchiesi, A. and Hinds, S. (eds) *Ovidian Transformations: Essays on Ovid's Metamorphoses and its Reception* (Cambridge) 31–47

Glenn, E. (1986) *The Metamorphoses: Ovid's Roman Games* (New York)

Golding, A. (trans.) (2006 [originally published 1567]) *Ovid's Metamorphoses* (London)

Gowers, E. (2005) 'Talking Trees: Philemon and Baucis Revisited', *Arethusa* 38: 331–65

Graf, F. (2002) 'Myth in Ovid', in Hardie, P. (ed.) *The Cambridge Companion to Ovid* (Cambridge) 108–21

Griffin, A. (1991) 'Philemon and Baucis in Ovid's *Metamorphoses*', *Greece and Rome* 38.1: 62–74

Hallett, J. (2000) 'Mortal and Immortal: Animal, Vegetable and Mineral: Equality and Change in Ovid's Baucis and Philemon Episode (*Met.* 8. 616–724)', in Dickson, S. and Hallett, J. (eds), *Rome and her Monuments* (Wauconda, IL.) 545–61

Hardie, P. (1990) 'Ovid's Theban History: The First Anti-Aeneid?', *Classical Quarterly* 40: 224–35

— (1993) *The Epic Successors of Virgil* (Cambridge)

— (1995) 'The Speech of Pythagoras in Ovid *Metamorphoses* 15: Empedoclean Epos', *Classical Quarterly* 45: 204–14

— (2002a) *The Cambridge Companion to Ovid* (Cambridge)

— (2002b) *Ovid's Poetics of Illusion* (Cambridge)

Hardie, P., Barchiesi, A. and Hinds, S. (eds) (1999) *Ovidian Transformations: Essays on the Metamorphoses and its Reception.* Cambridge Philological Society Suppl. Vol. 23. (Cambridge)

Haughton, H. (2007) *The Poetry of Derek Mahon* (Oxford)

Heath, J. (1991) 'Diana's Understanding of Ovid's *Metamorphoses*', *Classical Journal* 86: 233–43

— (1994) 'The Failure of Orpheus', *Transactions and Proceedings of the American Philological Association* 124: 163–96

Helzle, M. (1993) 'Ovid's Cosmogony: *Metamorphoses* 1.5–88 and the Traditions of Ancient Poetry', *Papers of the Liverpool Latin Seminar* 7: 123–34

Henderson, A. A. R. (ed.) (1979) *Ovid Metamorphoses III* (Bristol)

Hershkowitz, D. (1998) *Madness in Epic: Reading Insanity from Homer to Statius* (Oxford)

Hill, D. (1965) *Ovid: Metamorphoses 1–4* (Warminster)

— (1992) *Ovid: Metamorphoses 5–8* (Warminster)

— (1999) *Ovid: Metamorphoses 9–11* (Warminster)

— (2000) *Ovid: Metamorphoses 13–15* (Warminster)

Hinds, S. (1987) *The Metamorphoses of Persephone: Ovid and the Self-Conscious Muse* (Cambridge)

— (1993) 'Medea in Ovid: Scenes from the Life of an Intertextual Heroine', *Materiali e Discussioni* 30: 9–47

— (1998) *Allusion and Intertext: Dynamics of Appropriation in Roman Poetry* (Cambridge)

— (2002) 'Landscape with Figures: Aesthetics of place in the *Metamorphoses* and its tradition', in Hardie, P. (ed.) *The Cambridge Companion to Ovid* (Cambridge) 122–49

Hofmann, H. (1985) 'Ovid's *Metamorphoses*: Carmen Perpetuum, Carmen Deductum', *Papers of the Liverpool Latin Seminar* 5: 223–42

Hofmann, M. and Lasdun, J. (eds) (1994) *After Ovid* (London)

Holzberg, N. (1999) review of Boyd, B. *Ovid's Literary Loves,* in *Classical Review* 49: 59–60

— (2002) *Ovid: the Poet and his Work* (Cornell)

Hopkinson, N. (2000) *Ovid: Metamorphoses 13* (Cambridge)

Hornblower, S. and Spawforth, A. (1999) *Oxford Classical Dictionary* (Oxford)

Horsfall, N. (1979) 'Epic and Burlesque in Ovid, *Met.* viii. 260ff.', *The Classical Journal* 74.4: 319–32

Hughes, T. (trans.) (1997) *Tales from Ovid* (London)

Huxley, H.H. (1996) 'Ovid's debt to Virgil', *Vergilius* 42: 83–102

James, P. (1991) 'Pentheus Anguigena: Sins of the Father', *Bulletin of the Institute of Classical Studies* 38: 81–93

Janan, M. (1988) 'The Book of Good Love? Design versus Desire in *Metamorphoses 10*', *Ramus* 17: 110–37

— (2004) 'The Snake Sheds Its Skin: Pentheus (Re)Imagines Thebes', *Classical Philology* 99: 130–46

— (2009) *Reflections in a Serpent's Eye: Thebes in Ovid's Metamorphoses* (Oxford)

Jenkins, T.E (2000) 'Writing in (and of) Ovid's Byblis Episode', *Harvard Studies in Classical Philology* 100: 439–51

Johnson, P. J. (1996) 'Constructions of Venus in Ovid's *Metamorphoses* V', *Arethusa* 29: 125–49

Johnson, P. J. and Malamud, M. (1988) 'Ovid's *Musomachia*', *Pacific Coast Philology* 23: 30–8

Jones, P.J. (2001) 'Aversion Reversed: Ovid's Pomona and Her Roman Models', *Classical World* 94.4: 361–76

Joplin, P. (1984) 'The Voice of the Shuttle is Ours', *Stanford Literary Review* 1: 25–53

Keith, A. M. (1992) *The Play of Fictions: Studies in Ovid's Metamorphoses Book 2* (Ann Arbor)

— (1999) 'Versions of Epic Masculinity in Ovid's *Metamorphoses*', in Hardie, P., Barchiesi, A. and Hinds, S. (eds) *Ovidian Transformations: Essays on the Metamorphoses and its Reception* (Cambridge) 214–39

— (2000) *Engendering Rome: Women in Latin Epic* (Cambridge)

Kennedy, D.F. (1992) 'Augustan and Anti-Augustan: Reflections on Terms of Reference', in Powell, A. (ed.), *Roman Poetry and Propaganda in the Age of Augustus* (Bristol) 26–58

— (1993) *The Arts of Love* (Cambridge)

— (2002) 'Recent Receptions of Ovid', in Hardie, P. (ed.) *The Cambridge Companion to Ovid* (Cambridge) 320–35

Kenney, E.J. (1986) 'Introduction and Notes', in Melville, A.D. (trans.) *Ovid: Metamorphoses* (Oxford)

Kenney, E.J. and Clausen, W. (eds) (1982) *The Cambridge History of Classical Literature vol. II Latin Literature* (Cambridge)

Knox, P.E. (1986) *Ovid's Metamorphoses and the Tradition of Augustan Poetry* (Cambridge)

Konstan, D. (1991) 'The Death of Argus, or What Stories Do: Audience Response in Ancient Fiction and Theory', *Helios* 18: 15–30

Leach, E. W. (1974) 'Ekphrasis and the Theme of Artistic Failure in Ovid's *Metamorphoses*', *Ramus* 3: 102–42

Little, D. (1976) 'Ovid's Eulogy of Augustus: *Metamorphoses* XV 851–70', *Prudentia* 8: 19–35

Littlefield, D.J. (1965) 'Pomona and Vertumnus: A Fruition of History in Ovid's *Metamorphoses*', *Arion* 4.3: 465–73

Lively, G. (1999) 'Reading Resistance in Ovid's *Metamorphoses*', in Hardie, P., Barchiesi, A. and Hinds, S. (eds) *Ovidian Transformations: Essays on the Metamorphoses and its Reception* (Cambridge) 197–213

— (2002) 'Cleopatra's Nose: Naso and the science of Chaos', *Greece and Rome* 49.1: 27–43

— (2003) 'Tiresias/Teresa: A Man-Made-Woman in Ovid's *Metamorphoses* 3.318–38', *Helios* 30.2: 147–62

— (2005) *Ovid: Love Songs* (London)

Ludwig, W. (1965) *Struktur und Einheit der Metamorphosen* (Berlin)

Lyne, R. (2002) 'Ovid in English Translation', in Hardie, P. (ed.) *The Cambridge Companion to Ovid* (Cambridge) 249–63

Mack, S. (1988) *Ovid* (New Haven and London)

— (1995) 'Teaching Ovid's Orpheus to Beginners', *Classical Journal* 90: 279–85

— (1999) 'Acis and Galatea or Metamorphosis of Tradition', *Arion* 6.3: 51–67

Makowski, J. (1996) 'Bisexual Orpheus: Pederasty and Parody in Ovid', *Classical Journal* 92.1: 25–38

Martin, C. (ed.) (1998) *Ovid in English* (London)

Martindale, C. (ed.) (1988) *Ovid Renewed: Ovidian Influences on Literature and Art from the Middle Ages to the Twentieth Century* (Cambridge)

McKim, R. (1985) 'Myth and Philosophy in Ovid's Account of Creation', *Classical Journal* 80: 97–108

Melville, A.D. (trans.) (1986) *Metamorphoses by Ovid* (Oxford)

Miller, F. J. (ed. and trans.) (1984) *Ovid Metamorphoses* Vol. 2, rev. G. P. Goold (Cambridge, MA)

Murray, J. (2004) 'The Metamorphoses of Erysichthon: Callimachus, Apollonius, and Ovid', in Harder, A., Regtuit, R. and Wakker, G. (eds), *Callimachus 11* (Groningen) 207–42

Musgrove, M.W. (1998) 'Nestor's Centauromachy and the Deceptive Voice of Poetic Memory (Ovid *Met.* 12.182–535)', *Classical Philology* 93: 223–31

Myerowitz, M. (1985) *Ovid's Games of Love* (Detroit)

Myers, S. (1994a) '*Ultimus Ardor*: Pomona and Vertumnus in Ovid's *Met.* 14.623–771', *Classical Journal* 89.3: 225–50

— (1994b) *Ovid's Causes: Cosmogony and Aetiology in the Metamorphoses* (Ann Arbor)

— (1999) 'The Metamorphosis of a Poet: Recent Work on Ovid', in *Journal of Roman Studies* 89: 190–204

— (2010) *Ovid: Metamorphoses 14* (Cambridge)

Nagle, B.R. (1980) *The Poetics of Exile: Program and Polemic* (Brussels)

— (1983) 'Byblis and Myrrha: Two Incest Narratives in the *Metamorphoses*', *Classical Journal* 78: 301–15

— (1988a) 'Erotic Pursuit and Narrative Seduction in Ovid's *Metamorphoses*', *Ramus* 17: 32–51

— (1988b) 'Two Miniature Carmina Perpetua in the *Metamorphoses*: Calliope and Orpheus', *Grazer Beitrage* 15:99–125

Newlands, C. (1997) 'The Metamorphosis of Ovid's Medea', in Clauss, J. and Johnston, S. (eds) *Medea* (Princeton) 178–208

Nicoll, W. (1980) 'Cupid, Apollo, and Daphne (Ovid, *Met.* 1.452 ff.)', *Classical Quarterly* 30.1: 174–82

Nikolopoulos, A. (2004) *Ovidius Polytropos: Metanarrative in Ovid's Metamorphoses* (New York)

Nisbet, R. G. M. (1987) 'The Oak and the Axe: Symbolism in Seneca *Hercules Oetaeus* 1818ff', in Whitby, M. and Hardie, P. (eds), *Homo Viator: Classical Essays for John Bramble* (Bristol) 243–51

Otis, B. (1970) *Ovid as an Epic Poet* (Cambridge)

Papaioannou, S. (2005) *Epic Succession and Dissension: Ovid, Metamorphoses 13.623–14.582 and the Reinvention of the Aeneid* (Berlin and New York)

— (2007) *Redesigning Achilles: Recycling the Epic Cycle in the Little Iliad: Ovid, Metamorphoses 12.1–13.622* (Berlin and New York)

Parry, H. (1964) 'Ovid's *Metamorphoses*: Violence in a Pastoral Landscape', *Transactions and Proceedings of the American Philological Association* 95: 268–82

Raeburn, D. (trans.) (2004) *Ovid: Metamorphoses. A New Verse Translation.* With an Introduction by D. Feeney (London)

Raval, S. (2001) 'A Lover's Discourse: Byblis in *Metamorphoses* 9', *Arethusa* 34.3: 285–311

Richlin, A. (1992) 'Reading Ovid's Rapes', in Richlin, A. (ed.) *Pornography and Representation in Greece and Rome* (New York) 158–79

Robinson, M. (1999) 'Salmacis and Hermaphroditus: When Two Become One (Ovid, *Met.* 4.285–388)', *Classical Quarterly* 49.1: 212–23

Rosati, G. (1999) 'Form in Motion: Weaving the Text in the *Metamorphoses*', in Hardie, P., Barchiesi, A. and Hinds, S. (eds) *Ovidian Transformations: Essays on the Metamorphoses and its Reception* (Cambridge) 240–53

Rosner-Siegel, J.A. (1982) 'Amor, Metamorphosis and Magic: Ovid's Medea (*Met.* 7.1–424)', *Classical Journal* 77. 3: 231–43

Salzman-Mitchell, P. (2005) *A Web of Fantasies: Gaze, Image, and Gender in Ovid's Metamorphoses* (Ohio)

Sandys, G. (trans.) (1632) *Ovid's Metamorphosis* (Oxford)

Schlam, C.C. (1984) 'Diana and Actaeon: Metamorphosis of a Myth', *Classical Quarterly* 3: 82–10

Segal, C. (1968) 'Circean Temptations: Homer, Vergil, Ovid', *Transactions and Proceedings of the American Philological Association* 99: 419–42

—— (1969a) 'Myth and Philosophy in the *Metamorphoses*: Ovid's Augustanism and the Augustan Conclusion of Book XV', *American Journal of Philology* 90.3: 257–92

—— (1969b) *Landscape in Ovid's Metamorphoses* (Wiesbaden)

—— (1994) 'Philomela's Web and the Pleasure of the Text: Reader and Violence in the *Metamorphoses* of Ovid,' *Mnemosyne* 130: 257–79

—— (1998) 'Ovid's Metamorphic Bodies: Art, Gender, and Violence in the *Metamorphoses*', *Arion* 5.3: 9–41

Segal, N. (1988) *Narcissus and Echo: Women in the French Récit* (Manchester)

Slavitt, D. (trans.) (1994) *The Metamorphoses of Ovid* (Baltimore)

Solodow, J.B. (1988) *The World of Ovid's Metamorphoses* (Chapel Hill)

Tarrant, R. (1995) 'The Silence of Cephalus: Text and Narrative Technique in Ovid, *Metamorphoses* 7.685ff', *Transactions and Proceedings of the American Philological Association* 125: 99–111

Thomas, R.F. (2001) *Virgil and the Augustan Reception* (Cambridge)

Thibault, J.C. (1964) *The Mystery of Ovid's Exile* (Berkeley)

Tissol, G. (1997) *The Face of Nature: Wit, Narrative, and Cosmic Origins in Ovid's Metamorphoses* (Princeton).

— (2002) 'The House of Fame: Roman History and Augustan Politics in *Metamorphoses* 11–15', in Boyd, B. (ed.) *Brill's Companion to Ovid* (Leiden) 305–35

Walde, C. (2008) 'Narration in a Standstill: Propertius 1.16–18', in Liveley, G. and Salzman-Mitchell, P. (eds) *Latin Elegy and Narratology* (Ohio) 123–41

Watson, P. (1983) 'Puella and Virgo', *Glotta* 61: 119–43

Weiden Boyd, B. (2002) ' "When Ovid Reads Vergil . . .": A Response and Some Observations', *Vergilius* 48: 123–30

Wheeler, S. (1995) '*Imago Mundi*: Another View of the Creation in Ovid's *Metamorphoses*', *American Journal of Philology* 116: 95–121

— (1997) 'Changing Names: The Miracle of Iphis in Ovid *Metamorphoses* 9', *Phoenix* 51.2: 190–202

— (1999) *A Discourse of Wonders: Audience and Performance in Ovid's Metamorphoses* (Philadelphia)

— (2000) *Narrative Dynamics in Ovid's Metamorphoses* (Tübingen)

Williams, G. (1994) *Banished Voices: Readings in Ovid's Exile Poetry* (Cambridge)

Winkler, M. (ed.) (2001) *Classical Myth and Culture in the Cinema* (Oxford)

Wise, V.M. (1977) 'Flight Myths in Ovid's *Metamorphoses*: An Interpretation of Phaethon and Daedalus', *Ramus* 6: 44–59

Ziolkowski, T. (2005) *Ovid and the Moderns* (Cornell)

Zissos, A. (1999) 'Ovid's Rape of Proserpina (*Met.* 5.341–661): Internal Audience and Narrative Distortion', *Phoenix* 53: 97–113

Zumwalt, N. (1977) 'Fama Subversa': Theme and Structure in Ovid *Metamorphoses* 12', *California Studies in Classical Antiquity* 10: 209–22

INDEX